# ESSAY

ON THE

# SACRED LANGUAGE, WRITINGS, AND RELIGION OF THE PARSEES

# ESSAY

ON THE

# SACRED LANGUAGE, WRITINGS, AND RELIGION OF THE PARSEES.

MARTIN HAUG, Dr. PHIL.

GYAN

*Published by*

GYAN

Gyan Publishing House
5, Ansari Road
Daryaganj, New Delhi-110002
Phone: 011-47034999, 9811692060
E-mail: books@gyanbooks.com

*Distribution Network*
gyanbooks.com
India, USA, Canada, UK, Australia, France



ISBN: 978-81-212-8712-8 (PB)
First Published, 1862

2nd Impression 2023

*Printed at:* Gyan Press, Delhi.



**ESSAY ON THE SACRED LANGUAGE, WRITINGS, AND RELIGION OF THE PARSEES**

Author: Martin Haug

# ESSAYS

ON THE

# SACRED LANGUAGE, WRITINGS, AND RELIGION OF THE PARSEES.

BY

MARTIN HAUG, Dr. PHIL.,

Late of the Universities of Tübingen, Göttingen and Bonn; Superintendent of Sanscrit Studies, and Professor of Sanscrit, in the Poona College; Honorary Member of the Bombay Branch Royal Asiatic Society; etc.

---

BOMBAY:

Printed at the "BOMBAY GAZETTE" Press.

1862.

---

# PREFACE.

The four Essays which I here lay before the public, contain the ripest results of my laborious researches into the Sacred Writings and Religion of the Zoroastrians. Their principal aim is to present in a readable form, all the materials for judging impartially of the character of the Scripture and Religion of the Parsees. The Scripture being written in a language very little explored hitherto, I have thought it necessary to supply an outline of its grammar; a principal use of which I trust may be to enable the Parsees to learn their Sacred language, and make researches of their own into their Zend Avesta. The Roman Alphabet has been employed throughout; and my system of transliteration may be learnt from the alphabet of Zend characters with their Roman equivalents, which is added at the end.

My best thanks are due to my subscribers, who have enabled me to bring out the work.

MARTIN HAUG.

*Poona, 2nd February* 1862.

TO

EDWARD I. HOWARD, ESQUIRE, M. A.,

DIRECTOR OF PUBLIC INSTRUCTION BOMBAY PRESIDENCY,

THIS Work is inscribed as a token of gratitude and respect,

BY

THE AUTHOR.

# CONTENTS.

# I.

# HISTORY

OF THE

# RESEARCHES INTO THE SACRED WRITINGS AND RELIGION OF THE PARSEES

FROM THE EARLIEST TIMES DOWN TO THE PRESENT.

---

## 1.—THE REPORTS OF THE GREEKS, ROMANS, ARMENIANS, AND MOHAMMEDANS.

In this chapter I intend to give a brief outline of the gradual acquaintance of the western nations with the Zoroastrian religion, (now professed only by the small Parsee community in India, and by a very insignificant portion which remained in the ancient fatherland in Persia,) and principally to trace the history of the scientific researches attempted in Europe into the original records of this ancient creed, where the true doctrine of the great Zoroaster and his successors, buried for thousands of years, is to be found.

To the whole ancient world Zoroaster's lore was better known by the name of the doctrine of the Magi, which denomination was commonly applied to the priests of India, Persia, and Babylonia.

The earliest mention of them is made in the Prophet Jeremiah (39, 3), who enumerated among the retinue of king Nebuchadnezzar at his entry into Jerusalem, the "Chief of the Magi" (*rab mag* in Hebrew), from which statement we may distinctly gather, that the Magi exercised a great influence at the court of Babylonia 600 years B. C. They were, however, foreigners, and are not to be confounded with the indigenous priests. In the Old

Testament no account of this religion is given; only once (Ezekiel VIII., 16,17) it is hinted at.* The Persians, whose only priests the Magi appear to have been, however, are never spoken of as adherents to idolatry. The Persian kings, chiefly Cyrus, (called *Koresh* in Hebrew, *Kurush* in the cuneiform inscriptions) favored the Jews. In Isaiah this great king is called "the anointed of the Lord (*mashiakh* in Hebrew 45, 1,), the shepherd who carries out the Lord's decrees (44, 28); he is the eagle† called from the orient, the man appointed by the Lord's counsel (46, 11); he is strengthened by the Lord to subdue the heathens (45, 1.)‡ From these high terms, in which king Cyrus, who professed the religion of the Magi, is spoken of, we are entitled to infer that this religion was not so diametrically opposed to the Mosaic as the other ancient religions were; that Cyrus, at all events, was no idolworshipper,—a supposition, we shall find confirmed by Herodotus, and by the sacred books of the Parsees themselves. The Zoroastrian religion exhibits even a very close affinity to, or rather identity with several important doctrines of the Mosaic religion and Christianity, such as the personality and attributes of the devil, and the resurrection of the dead, which are both ascribed to the religion of the Magi, and are really to be found in the present scripture of the Parsees. It is not to be ascertained whether these doctrines were borrowed by the Parsees from the Jews, or by the Jews from the Parsees; very likely neither is the case, and in both these religions they seem to have sprung up independently.

* The religious custom alluded to in Ezekiel, undoubtedly refers to the religion of the Magi. The prophet complains that some of the Jews worship the sun, holding towards their face certain twigs. Exactly the same custom as being observed by the Magi of holding a bundle of twigs in the hands, when engaged in praying, is reported by Strabo (XV., p. 733, edition of Casaubon). It is the so-called Barsom (Bereçma in Zend) used up to this time by the Parsee priests when engaged in worship.

† In *Aeschylus's* celebrated play "the Persians," the eagle is the symbol of the Persian empire (verses 205-10). The eagle was, as Xenophon reports, (Cyropœdia VII., I. 2.) the ensign of the ancient Persians.

‡ The Hebrew word *goyim*, (literary 'people') used in the plural as it is here, denotes the heathenish nations, the idol worshippers, in their strictest opposition to the Israelites.

In the Zend-Avesta we meet only with two words,* which may be traced to the Semitic languages, neither of them referring to religious subjects. In the later books of the Old Testament we find several Persian words, and many names, but they have nothing to do with religion. The most famous of these Persian words in the Old Testament now spread over the whole civilised world, is the word "paradise," which means originally a park, a beautiful garden fenced in.†

The name Magi occurs even in the New Testament. In the Gospel according to St. Matthew (2, 1) the Magi (Greek magoi, translated in the English Bible by "wise men") came from the East to Jerusalem, to worship the new born child Jesus, at Bethlehem. That these Magi were the priests of the Zoroastrian religion, we know from Grecian writers.

The earliest account of the religion of the Magi among the Greeks, is to be found in HERODOTUS, the father of history, (450 B. C.) In his first book (ch. 131-32), we read the following report on the Persian religion :—

"I know that the Persians observe these customs. It is not customary among them to have idols made, temples built, and altars erected ; they *even* upbraid with folly those who do so. I can account for that, only from their not believing that the gods are like men, as the Hellenes do. They are accustomed to bring sacrifices to Zeus on the summits of mountains ; they call the whole *celestial* circle Zeus. They bring sacrifices to the sun, moon, earth, fire, water and winds, these *elements* originally being the only objects of worship; but they accepted from the As-

* These are *tanûra*, an oven ; and *hara*, mountain to be found only in the name *Harô berezaiti*, *i. e.* high mountain considered to be the head of all mountains ; preserved now-a-days in the name *Elborz*. *Tanûra* is evidently the same with the Hebrew *tanûr* (Gen. XV., 17. Isaiah XXXI., 9) an oven ; *hara* is identical with *har* is Hebrew, *i. e.* mountain.

† The original form of the word is *pairi-daêza* (in the Zend-Avesta), i. e. circumvallation ; in Hebrew we find it in the form *pardes* ; in Greek as *paradeisos*. *Pairi* is *peri* in Greek ; *daêza* corresponds *deha* in Sanskrit, i. e. enclosure, generally applied to the body. Of the same root is the English *thick* (very likely identical with S. *digdha* past participle of the root *dih* to besmear, pollute, in a more comprehensive sense "surround.")

syrians and Arabs the worship of Aphrodite, the Queen of Heaven, whom the Assyrians call Mylitta, the Arabs Alitta, the Persians Miṭra.*

"The Persians bring sacrifices to the aforesaid gods in the following manner. They neither erect altars nor kindle fires when they are about to bring a sacrifice; they neither use libations, nor flutes nor wreaths, nor barley; but when any one is willing to bring a sacrifice, he then carries the sacrificial beast to a pure spot, and after having twined round his turban a great many wreaths of myrtle in preference to any other leaf, he invokes the deity. The sacrificer ought not to pray only for his own prosperity; he must also pray for the welfare of all the Persians, and for the king, because he is included among them. When he has cut the animal into pieces, he then boils its flesh, spreads the softest grass he can get, especially preferring clover, and places the pieces of flesh on it. After having made this arrangement, one of the Magi who is present, sings a theogony,† as they call the incantation (which is used); without one of the Magi no sacrifice can be brought. After waiting a short time, the sacrificer takes off the pieces of flesh, and uses them as he likes.‡"

In the 138th Chapter of the same book, the father of history says: "Lying is regarded as the most discreditable thing by them; next to it is the incurring of debt, chiefly for this reason, that the debtor is often compelled to tell lies. If any one of

* Here Herodotus has committed a mistake; not as to the matter, but as to the name. The Persians, in later times, worshipped a great female deity, who might be compared with the Mylitta of the Babylonians (the Astarte of the Old Testament), but she was called ANAHITA (in the Zend-Avesta, and in the cuneiform inscriptions), known to the Arabs and Grecian writers by the name of ANAITIS. She represented the beneficial influence of water. Mitra is the well known sun-god of the Persians and a male deity.

† Herodotus, who shews throughout the whole report, an intimate knowledge of the Persian sacrifices, means by thegony here, those sections of the sacred books which are called *Yashts* or invocations, containing the praises of all the feats achieved by the deity in whose honour the sacrifice is to be brought. See the third chapter.

‡ This custom is still maintained by the Parsees. The flesh (or any other offering) to be offered is first consecrated by the priest, then for a short time left near the fire, and finally taken off by the sacrificer, to be used by him; but it is never thrown into the fire.

the inhabitants of a town is affected with leprosy, or white spots, (another kind of leprosy) he cannot enter the town, nor have any intercourse with the other Persians; they believe him to have that disease in consequence of having sinned in one way or other against the sun.* All foreigners affected with these *diseases* are driven out of the country; for the same reason many expel even white pigeons. They neither make water, nor spit, nor wash their hands in a river; nor will they allow any one else to do so; for they pay a high reverence to rivers."

In another passage (III. 16) Herodotus reports that the Persians believe Fire to be a god; wherefore Cambyses committed a great sin, as he says, in burning the corpse of the King Amasis.

The chief Greek writers on the manners and religion of the Persians were KTESIAS (B. C. 400,) the well known physician to King Artaxerxes II., DEINON (B. C. 350), who is looked upon as a great authority in Persian matters by Cornelius Nepos (in the life of Konon), THEOPOMPOS, of Chios, (B. C. 300) and HERMIPPOS, the philosopher of Smyrna, (B. C. 250). The books of all these writers being lost, save some fragments preserved by later authors, such as PLUTARCH, DIOGENES of LAERTE, and PLINY, we cannot judge how far they were acquainted with the religion of the Magi. The two chief sources whence to derive information on the religion of the Magi, were for the Greeks and Romans. THEOPOMPOS' eighth book of the history of King Philip of Macedonia, which was entitled "on miraculous things," where chiefly the doctrine of the Magi was treated; and HERMIPPOS, who wrote a separate book "on the Magi." We are left without information, whether or not Theopompos borrowed his statements on the lore of the Magi from his intercourse with the Persian priests themselves; but Hermippos, who composed, besides his work on the Zoroastrian doctrine, biographies of lawgivers, the seven sages of Greece, &c., is reported by Pliny (Historia Naturalis XXX., 1) to have made very laborious investigations into all the Zoroastrian books, which were said to

* The name given to sinners against the sun is *mithrô-drukhs*, i. e. one who has belied mithra (sun). Such diseases were believed to be the consequence of lying.

comprise two millions of verses, and to have stated the contents of each book separately. He therefore really seems to have had some knowledge of the sacred language and texts of the Magi, for which reason the loss of his work is greatly to be regretted.

It is not my intention to produce all the reports on the Zoroastrian religion and customs to be met with in the ancient writers, but I shall only point out some of the most important.

According to Diogenes of Laerte (Pro-œmium, chap. 6), EUDOXOS and ARISTOTLE stated, that in the doctrine of the Magi there were two powers opposed to each other, one representing the good god, called ZEUS and ORMASDES (Ahuramazda, Ormuzd), and the other representing the devil, whose name was HADES and AREIMANIOS (Angrô Mainyus, Ahriman.) Of this chief doctrine of the Magi THEOPOMPOS had given a further illustration. According to Plutarch (De Iside et Osiride) and Diogenes of Laerte (Pro-œmium, chap. 9) he reported that Oromasdes ruled for three thousand years alone, and Areimanios for three thousand more. After this period of six thousand years had elapsed, they began to wage war against each other, one attempting to destroy the other ; bnt finally, (he says) Areimanios is to perish, mankind is to enjoy a blessed state of life ; men will neither be any more in need of food, nor will they cast shadows ; the dead are to rise again, men will be immortal, and everything is to exist in consequence of their prayers.

A brief, but full account of Zoroaster's doctrine is to be found in Plutarch's book " on Isis and Osiris" (chap. 46-47,) which being in detail, seems to have been borrowed from a writer who was actually acquainted with the original texts. The philosopher Hermippos, above mentioned, being the only scholar of antiquity who can be supposed with sufficient reason to have had a real knowledge of the sacred language of the Zend-Avesta, we may regard him as the author of Plutarch's statements. These are as follows :—

" Oromasdes sprang out of the purest light ; among all things perceived by the senses that element most resembles him ; Areimanios sprang out of darkness, and is therefore of the same nature with it. Oromasdes, who resides as far beyond the sun, as the sun is far from the earth, created six gods (the six *Ameshaçpentas*, now Amshashpand, the archangels) ; the God of benevolence *(vohumanô*, i. e. "good-mind," now called *Bahman)* the god of truth, *Ashavahista ; Ardibehesht) ;* the god of order *(Khshathra vairya ; Shahravar) ;* the god of wisdom *Armaiti ; Isfendermat*) ; and the god of wealth and delight in beauty *(Haurvatat* and *Ameretât*, *Khordâd* and *Ameredâd)*. But to counterbalance him, Areimanios created an equal number of gods counteracting those of Oromasdes Then Oromasdes decorated heaven with stars, and placed the star Sirius *(Tistrya, Tashtar)* at their head as a guardian. Afterwards he created twenty-four other gods,* and set them in an egg; but Areimanios forthwith created an equal number of gods who opened the egg ; in consequence of this, evil is always mingled with good. Thus the good god and the demon are engaged in a constant war. Of plants and animals some belong to the good, some to the evil spirit ; to the good one belong dogs, birds ; and crabs ; to the evil one, water-rats. At the end, the time is to come when Areimanios will perish, and disappear in consequence of disease and famine, caused by himself. Then the earth will become even, and equal, and there will be only one state, and one language, and one and the same manner of living to the happy men who then speak only one language.

STRABO the geographer (B. C. 60) has given in the 15th book of his celebrated geography an account of the religion and customs of the Magi, of which I shall translate some passages. "To whatever deity the Persians may bring a sacrifice," says he, "they first invoke fire, which is fed at their sacred places with dried barkless pieces of wood, and is never to be extinguished ;

* This statement seems at the first glance to be very strange. But one may easily explain it from the Zend texts. This writer had evidently in view the 30 genii presiding over the particular days of the month ; he was informed, or he gathered it from his own reading of the texts, that there are two distinct classes of divine being to be worshipped, six forming the higher order, twenty-four the lower ; the Supreme being, the creator Ahuramazda, was not comprised in these. In the Parsee Calendar (Sirozah, 30 days) Ormazd is included in the number.

they put fat over it, and pour oil into it; if any body happens to throw or blow into it any thing dirty, or dead, he is to die; the fire is to be kindled by blowing.

In another passage (XI. p. 512) he enumerates as Persian deities *Anaitis Omanes*, and *Anadates* or *Anandates*.*

PAUSANIUS, the celebrated Grecian traveller (180 A.D.) has the following report on the fireworship of the Magi V. 27, 3). In the temples of the Persians there is a room where ashes of another colour than those being burnt on the altar, are to be found.† To this room he first repairs, puts dry wood upon the altar, puts on the tiara, and then sings the invocation of the god, reading it from a book, in a language utterly unintelligible to the Greeks. The wood is to be ignited on the ashes, without fire, and to flame up into a bright blaze.

I shall pass over DIO CHRYSOSTOMOS (130 A.D.) who has left to us, in his sermons, some remarks on the theological ideas of the Magi, chiefly on their comparing the universe with a chariot in continual motion, which is drawn by four horses; but I shall give a translation of an important passage of the historian AGATHIAS (500 A.D.) respecting Zoroaster. He says (II, 24): "The present Persians almost entirely neglect their former customs, and have even changed them, and observe some strange and spurious usages, professing the doctrines of Zoroaster, the son of Ormasdes.‡ The time when this Zoroaster or Zarades (he is called by these two names) flourished and gave his laws, is not to be ascertained. The Persians now-a-days simply say, that he lived at the time of Hystaspes; but it is very doubtful, and doubt cannot be resolved whether this Hys-

* *Anaites Anâhitâ*, a goddess, representing the celestial waters. Omanes is Vohumanô-Bahman; Anandates is Ameretat, genius of the trees.

† The two kinds of ashes mentioned here are those of the Dâd-gâh (Dâityô-gâtus) or common hearth of the temple (or any house) and of the Atesh-gâh or place for the sacred fire, which is fed with the greatest care. By tiara (a turban) the Penom (paitidâna) is meant, a cloth, used to cover the lips to prevent the sacred fire from being polluted. Pausanius well describes here the divine service as performed before the sacred fire. The observance is still maintained.

‡ Plato (Alcibiades I., p. 121) says the same, calling Zoroaster a son of Ormazdes *i. e.*, Ahuramazda, Ormazd.

taspes was the father of Darius or another Hystaspes. At whatever time he may have lived, he was at all events their prophet, and the master of the Magic rites. He after having changed the ancient form of worship, introduced manifold and strange doctrines. For they (the Persians) formerly worshipped Zeus and Kronos, and all other gods celebrated by the Greeks, only under other names, as for example they call Zeus, *Bel*, Heracles, *Sandes*, Aphrodite, *Anaitis*,* and the others otherwise as is reported by BEROSOS the Babylonian, and ATHENOKLES and SIMAKOS, who wrote on the most ancient history of the Assyrians and Medians."

Before I conclude my notice of these Grecian records, and proceed to those of the Armenians and Mohammedans, I shall notice some passages of later Grecian writers, who lived after Christ at the time of the Sassanids, on the supposed primitive principle of Zoroastrian theology, of which I shall treat fully in the last chapter of this book.

The first Grecian writer who alludes to it, is DAMASCIUS. In his book "on primitive principles" (125th pag. 384 ed. Kopp) he says, "The Magi and the whole Arian nation† consider, as Eudemos writes, some Space, and others Time as the universal cause, out of which the good god as well as the evil spirit were separated, or as others assert, light and darkness, before these *two spirits arose*."

On the same matter THEODOROS of MOPSUESTIA writes as follows, according to the fragment preserved by the polyhistor Photios (Biblioth 81). In the first book of his work (on the doctrines of the Magi), says Photios,‡ he propounds the nefarious doctrine of the Persians which Zarastrades introduced, viz. that on

* In this report true and false statements are mixed together. It is true that the religion of the Parsees anterior to Zoroaster was much nearer to that of the Greeks than after his time: but it is not true that the Persians at that time worshipped BEL, who was the chief god of the Babylonians, and entirely unknown to the Zend Avesta.

† By this name the Medians are to be understood. According to Herodotus their original name was "Arioi."

‡ He was a Christian.

Zarouam* whom he makes the ruler of the whole universe, and calls him Destiny; and who when bringing sacrifices in order to generate Hormisdas, produced both Hormisdas and Satan.

This opinion on the primitive principle of the Zoroastrian theology, seems to have been current among the Christians at the time of the Sassanids, as we may learn more fully from Armenian writers of the 5th century, from Eznik, who wrote a book against heretical opinions, and from Elisæus, who compiled a history of Vartan, and the wars waged by the Armenians against the Persians. I shall give a translation of Eznik's report. He says in his refutation of heresies (in the second book) containing a "refutation of the false doctrine of the Persians:—"

"Before any thing, heaven or earth, or creatures of any kind whatever, therein were existing, *Zeruan* existed, whose name means fortune or glory.† He brought sacrifices for a thousand years, in the hope of obtaining a son, Ormizt by name, who was to create heaven, earth, and every thing therein. After having spent a thousand years in sacrificing, he began to deliberate. Are these sacrifices of mine to produce any effect, and will a son, Ormizt by name, be born to me? While he was thus deliberating, Ormizt and Arhmen were conceived in the womb of their mother, Ormizt as the fruit of his sacrifices, Arhmen as that of his doubts. When Zeruan was aware of this event, he said, two sons are in the womb; he who will come first to me, is to be made king. Ormizt, having perceived his father's thoughts, revealed them to Arhmen, saying, Zeruan, our father intends to make him king who shall be born first. Having heard these words, Arhmen perforated the womb, and appeared before his father. But Zeruan, when he saw him, did not know who he was, and asked him, who art thou? He told him:—'I am thy son.' Zeruan answered him, my son is well scented and shining, but thou art dark, and ill-scented. While they were thus talking, Ormizt, shining and well scented, appeared before Zeruan, who, seeing him, perceived him at once

* He means *Zarvan akarana*, i.e. boundless time.

† This interpretation is wrong. The word *zarvan* means simply "time" in Zendavesta, preserved in the modern Persian *zamân*.

to be his son Ormizt on account of whom he was sacrificing. He took the rod,* which he had used in sacrificing, and gave it to Ormizt, saying: Hitherto this has been used by myself in bringing sacrifices for thy sake; henceforth thou mayst sacrifice for my sake. When Zeruan handed over his rod to Ormizt, and blessed him, Arhmen approached him saying: Hast thou not vowed to make that one of thy two sons King who should first come to thee? Zeruan, in order to avoid breaking his vow, replied to Arhmen: Oh thou liar and evil doer! the empire is to be ceded to thee for nine thousand years; but I place Ormizt over thee as chief, and after nine thousand years, he will reign and do what he like. Then Ormizt and Arhmen began the work of creation; every thing produced by Ormizt was good and right, and every thing wrought by Arhmen was bad and perverse."

From both these Armenian writers, EZNIK and ELISAEUS, we further learn, that the Zoroastrians at their times (5th century A. D.) were split into two parties, inimically opposed to each other; the one is called MOG (Magi, Maghava,) the other ZENDIK.†

I shall now pass over to MOHAMMEDAN writers, who lived after the conquest of Persia by the Mohammedans (640 A. D.); but I can notice of course only some interesting passages.

M'ASUDI, the celebrated Arabian historian and traveller (950 A. D.), has preserved to us the following notice of the sacred books of the Parsees.‡ The first book, made by ZERADUSHT, was Avesta. The Persians, not being able to understand it, Zeradusht made a commentary, which they called ZEND; further he made a commentary to this commentary, and called it PAZEND. After Zeradusht's death the Persians made a commentary of the

* This is the so called Barsom (Bereçma, a bundle of twigs) used by the Parsee priests always, when engaged in worship.

† The Magi were chiefly spread in the West, in Media and Persia; the Zendiks in the East, in Bactria. The former seem to have acknowledged only the AVESTA or original texts of the sacred writings; the latter followed the traditional explanation, called ZEND.

‡ S. Chwolsohn in the Zeitschrift der Deutsch Morgenländischen Gesellschaft, Vol. VI., p. 408-9.

commentary, and an explanation of all the books just mentioned, and called it YAZDAH.*

In another passage, he has the following remark on the origin of the word ZENDIK, i. e. heretic in Persian :—the ZEND being only a commentary on what was formerly revealed from heaven (viz. the AVESTA), the Persians called any one, who put forward religious opinions opposed to the Avesta, a ZENDIK, because he held his own interpretations (Zend) against that of the "Avesta."

On Zoroaster's age he remarks that according to the Magi he lived 280 years before Alexander the Great (about 516 years B. C.)†

Shahrastani, a celebrated Mohammedan writer, (who died at Bagdad 1153 A. D.) has given in his highly valuable work "on religious sects & creeds" *(kitâb el-milel we na'hal)* an account of the religion of the Magi, of which he had a better opinion than many other Mohammedan writers. Whilst DIMISHQI (died 1327 A. D.), EBN FOZLAN and others‡ identify the Magi with idolators and pagans, Shahrastani brings them under the same head with JEWS, CHRISTIANS, and MUSALMANS, or those, the creed of whom is founded on revealed books; and makes them diametrically opposed to those who follow their own imagination and inventions as many philosophers did, the Brahmans and Sabeans (starworshippers). From his reports we further learn that the Magi were split into several sects, which very likely arose at the time of the Sassanids, such as the MAZDAKYAHS, who believed in the transmigration of souls like the Brahmans and Buddhists (a doctrine which is altogether strange to the Zend-Avesta); the KAYOMARTHIYAH, who believed in a revelation made by God to the first man, called GAYOMART by the Parsees, corresponding to ADAM of the Bible; the ZERVANITS who believed in ZARVAN AKARANA, i. e. the boundless time as the supreme deity, which doctrines

* He understands by it those pieces, which are called *Yashts*, and are undoubtedly the latest productions in *Zend-Avesta.*

† S. Chwolsohn, Die Sabier II, p. 690.

‡ S. Chwolsohn I, p. 281.

being altogether strange to the ancient books, were derived from other creeds.

Before taking final leave of these Mohammedan writers, I must notice a peculiar circumstance which deserves attention. In several Mohammedan writings, chiefly in vernacular Persian dictionaries, we find ZOROASTER, or as he is called there ZARADUSHT, identified with ABRAHAM, the patriarch. The Magi are said to have called their religion *Kesh-i-Ibrahim*, i. e. creed of Abraham, whom they considered as their prophet and the reformer of their religion. They traced their religious books to Abraham, who was believed to have brought them from heaven. Of all this, however, no single word is true. The Magi or Parsee priests invented it for the purpose of escaping the persecutions of the Mohammedans, and that they might be tolerated to a certain extent; for only those creeds were tolerated by the Mohammedans, the followers of which were able to convince them of their possession of sacred books, connected in any way with the Jewish religion, the prophets of which had been acknowledged by Mohammed.

---

## 2.—THE EUROPEAN RESEARCHES.

The nations of modern Europe come into contact with the adherents of the Zoroastrian religion in the western part of India, where they had settled when they left their fatherland Persia, to escape the persecutions of the Mohammedans. Already in the 17th century, manuscripts of the sacred books of the Parsees were brought to England as a mere article of curiosity, but were a sealed book to every one. The first, who attempted to give a complete description of the doctrines of the Magi, was the celebrated Oxford Scholar, HYDE. In his very learned work, "Historia religionis veterum Persarum corumque Magorum," the first edition of which was published in the year 1700, he displays a vast deal of information, derived from all the sources which were accessible to him, on the Parsee religion from Grecian and Roman, as well as from Arabian and Persian writers, and tries his utmost to throw light on the religion of the Magi, so famous in antiquity; but being utterly unable to read the original texts of the Zend-Avesta, though he himself was in possession of several manuscripts of them, he could not succeed in furnishing his readers with a real insight into that ancient creed. His work acted, however, as a stimulus to others to take more interest in the matter.

The first scholar, who made the European nations acquainted with the contents of the sacred books of the Parsees, was the celebrated Frenchman ANQUETIL DU PERRON. His ardour and zeal are almost unparallelled in the history of scholarship. He happened once to see a fac simile of some pages written in Zend characters, which were circulated as a mere curiosity. Actuated by the liveliest desire of earning the glory of first opening the Zend-Avesta to Europeans, he suddenly resolved upon setting out for Western India in order to purchase manuscripts of all the sacred books of the Zoroastrian religion, and to obtain a thorough knowledge of their contents, and of the religious customs of the Parsees from the priests. Being himself unable to afford the means required for carrying out his plan, he entered himself as a sailor in a ship of the French Indian Company, bound for Bombay in the year 1754, where he safely arrived after a very protracted and dangerous voyage. All the hardships he had to suffer during his passage would have been endured in vain, and he would have ultimately failed in obtaining what he was aiming at, if the French Government had not granted him support. The Parsee priests being full of distrust towards him, were not willing to sell him valuable manuscripts, and far less to teach him the language of their sacred books.* Finally the only means of obtain-

* Since the Parsees and their priests have come more into contact with the Europeans, this distrust has subsided to a certain extent. I myself have conversed often with Dustoors on their sacred books and their religion; they showed themselves very kind towards me, and always ready to give me any explanation of rites and ceremonies for which I might ask.

ing the object wished for was money. He bribed one of the most learned Dustoors, Dustoor Dârâb, at Surat, to procure him manuscripts, and to instruct him in the Zend and Pehlevi languages. But to ascertain whether he was not deceived by the Dustoor, he opened an intercourse with some other priests (Kaus and Manjerj,) and was very much satisfied at finding that the manuscripts he purchased first, were genuine. When he thought himself proficient enough in Zend and Pehlevi, he set about making a French translation of the whole ZEND-AVESTA. He commenced that work in March 1759, and was engaged in it up to the time of his departure. He left for Europe in 1761, after six years' stay in different places of Western India. He had purchased about 180 manuscripts in different oriental languages, among the number of which were copies of the sacred books of the Parsees. When, after a long and painful passage he arrived in Europe, he did not proceed at once to his fatherland, France, but went first to England to ascertain, whether or not the Zend manuscripts to be found there agreed with those in his own possession. Finding that they did not differ, he returned quite satisfied to France. All his manuscripts, together with the dictations of the Dustoors, were deposited at the Imperial library at Paris, where they may be still inspected, and used by the student. Ten years after his departure from India he published, (in 1771), as the fruit of his indefatigable zeal and industry, the following highly important work in French, *Zend-Avesta, the work of Zoroaster, containing the theological, physical, and moral ideas of this lawgiver, the ceremonies of the divine service which he established, and several important traits respecting the ancient history of the Persians, translated into French from the Zend Original, with notes and several treatises for illustrating the matters contained in it. By Anquetil du Perron. 2 vols. 4to.*

This groundwork for the Zend studies in Europe created an immense sensation when it was published. A new world of ideas seemed to have been disclosed to the European scholars; the veil which covered the mysteries of the famous founder of the doctrines of the Magi seemed to be lifted. But the philosophers found themselves soon greatly disappointed. KANT, the great German philosopher, said, after a careful perusal of the whole work, that throughout the whole Zend-Avesta not the slightest trace of philosophical ideas could be discovered.

The chief question, however, was the authenticity of these books. Some contested, others advocated it. In England, the opinion prevailed, that the books were forged, and Anquetil imposed upon by the priests. The celebrated oriental scholar SIR WILLIAM JONES, published in 1771 a letter in French, addressed to Anquetil du Perron, (W. Jones' works vol. x., pp. 403—99) where he tried to prove that the works translated by that scholar could not be considered as the composition of the celebrated Zoroaster. The chief reason alleged by him was, that their contents grossly contradicted common sense and all sound reasoning; the authority of these books as the chief source of information on the doctrines of Zoroaster was thus denied, and they were represented as the fictions of priestcraft brought forward as the works of Zoroaster. RICHARDSON, the celebrated Persian lexicographer, tried to prove the spuriousness of the Parsee books translated by Anquetil mainly from philological reasons. He held the opinion (in the preface to his Persian Dictionary) that the two languages *Zend* and *Pehlevi*, from which the learned Frenchman had translated them, were merely invented, never having been living in the provinces of the Persian Empire. His opinion was founded upon four reasons; (1) there is too great a number of Arabic words in both of them, which is a strong proof against their genuineness; (2) the harsh combinations of consonants are contrary to the genius of the Persian language; (3) there is no connection between them and modern Persian; (4) the contents of the books besides are so childish that they cannot be ascribed to the ancient Persians. All these reasons are easily to be refuted from the present state of the researches into the Zend Avesta; but it would be a mere wasting of space and time to enter into a real discussion about the authenticity of Zend and Pehlevi. In Zend and Pehlevi there are no Arabic words whatever; Zend is quite a pure Arian dialect, the elder sister of Sanskrit, as will be seen easily from the outline of a grammar of that language which I intend to give in the second chapter; in Pehlevi there are many Chaldee, but no Arabic words, as we shall see afterwards, as well as its close connection with modern Persian.

In France the authenticity was not doubted, and the great merits of Anquetil at once acknowledged. In Germany the opinions of the scholars were at an issue. Some, as MEINERS and TYCHSEN, acceded to the proofs alleged against the genuineness of these books; but another renowned German scholar, KLEUKER, not only espoused the authenticity of Anquetil's work, but translated the whole of it into German, and added several appendices, containing the passages of the ancient writers on the religion of the Magi. In advocating the authenticity of Anquetil's Zend-Avesta, he relied chiefly on the accordance of the reports of the classical writers with those contained in these books. That this is actually the case, we shall see at the end of this work.

For a long time the correctness of Anquetil's translation was not doubted by any one, for he had learned the languages from the most clever Parsee priests themselves, who were supposed to possess necessarily a thorough and profound knowledge of their sacred books. In Germany the work was thenceforth the standard authority for all researches into the ancient Persian religion, and the divines used it even for the interpretation of the Old Testament. In England it was laid aside as spurious, and not deserving any attention. The most comprehensive and best description of the Persian religion, chiefly according to the work of Anquetil, was compiled by RHODE, "The holy tradition of the Zend people." (1820).

Inquiries into the real nature of the Zend and Pehlevi languages were not made, until more than fifty years after Anquetil's work had appeared. The first, who attempted to broach this difficult subject, was the great Danish scholar RASK, who himself had been in this Presidency (Bombay) and had purchased many valuable Zend and Pehlevi manuscripts for the library at Copenhagen. He wrote in 1826 a pamphlet "On the age and genuineness of the Zend language." In this little book he proved the close affinity of the language of the Zend-Avesta to the Sanskrit. This proof was sufficient to remove any doubts whatever entertained on the genuineness of the Zend language. If this language was a true and genuine sister to the Sanskrit, then of course it could not be a mere invention of priests, who besides would have been utterly unable to invent such a well organised language as the Zend really is. Although Anquetil had deposited all the rough copies of his work together with the dictations of his Parsee teachers (they go by the name "les brouillons d' Anquetil") at the Imperial library at Paris for the purpose of subjecting his translation to public examination, for a long time no examiner was to be found. As he possessed neither a grammar nor a dictionary of the Zend languages (because they did not exist), there were in fact no means of subjecting his work to a rigid examination. First, the grammatical structure of this ancient language and the etymology of the words were to be discovered. But how could that be arrived at? The only means serving this purpose were the Sanskrit, with which highly finished language the Europeans have become acquainted since the end of the last century. Anquetil himself was thinking of acquiring a knowledge of this language from the Brahmans and translating the Vedas, but he did not succeed. The study of Sanskrit spread rapidly from England to France and Germany; everywhere the high importance of this classical language was at once acknowledged. The scholars discovered soon its close affinity to Greek and Latin, and as soon as attention was directed towards the Zend-Avesta, the closest possible relation of its language to the Sanskrit could not but strike the enquirer, even at a glance. As I have already mentioned, Rask first proved the close affinity, but he gave only some hints which were apt to lead men of high talents to discoveries; on that account Rask himself cannot be considered as one of the founders of Zend philology. This honour was reserved to a Frenchman also.

The first, who laid the foundation of a real Zend philology, was EUGENE BURNOUF, professor of Sanskrit at the College de France at Paris, one of the most gifted and talented scholars of the whole world, a man of whom, as their countryman, Frenchmen have just reason to be proud. Being himself exceedingly well versed in the so-called classical Sanskrit (not in that of the Vedas)—of his mastery over which language he left to us more than sufficient specimens in his translation of the *Bhâgavata Purâna* and his classical works on Buddhism,—he applied his sound and critical knowledge of it to the discovery of the rudiments of Zend grammar and etymology ; and his laborious researches were crowned with success. He first discovered then the great incorrectness of Anquetil's translation, being the necessary result of his total want of acquaintance with any thing like the grammar of the Zend language. In making his researches he availed himself of NERIOSENGH'S Sanskrit translation of the greater part of the prayer-book *Yasna*, but criticised it by applying comparative philology, chiefly Sanskrit. Most of his researches he laid down in his excellent work entitled " Commentary on the Yasna" (1833-35), in which, starting from Neriosingh's Sanskrit translation, he gave the translation, with too copious an explanation, of only the *first* chapter out of the seventy-two, which make up the present Yasna or prayerbook. In several numbers of the " Journal Asiatique (1844-46)" he published a revised text, translation and explanation of the 9th chapter of Yasna, containing the praise of *Homa* (corresponding to the Soma of the Brahmans). He published besides, lithographed, the fairest copy of a *Vendidsâde* comprising the *Vendidâd*, *Yasna*, and *Visparad*, without the Pehlevi translation) which he found among the manuscripts brought by Anquetil. This was the first edition of Zend texts which appeared in Europe (1829-43). After that publication he left the Zend studies, and engaged himself chiefly in re-searches into Buddhism. In 1852 a premature death put an end to his important discoveries in several branches of the Oriental antiquities.

Before I proceed to trace the further course of the Zend studies chiefly in Germany, I intend to review briefly the merits of the two Frenchmen who have just claims to be regarded as the founders of our investigations into the Zend-Avesta.

Anquetil du Perron furnished Europe with all the materials for these researches, and by his translation introduced the literary world to the chief contents of the sacred books of the Zoroastrians. His work, although utterly incorrect and inaccurate, nevertheless gives a notion of the whole of the Zoroastrian ideas. One could learn from his books the different names of the divine beings, of the evil spirits, ceremonies, observances, doctrines and the contents in general. The reader could see for instance that in the first chapter of the *Vendidâd*, the names of sixteen countries were enumerated, which being originally good, were spoiled by the bad creations of the devil; that in its second chapter, the story of Yima (Jemshid) was treated, that the *Yasna* contains prayers of different kinds, addressed to different objects of worship &c. But it is in the easier parts only that he could gain even an approximate knowledge of the contents; in the more difficult ones, as the Gâthas, he could not attain thus much, because there nearly all was translated by Anquetil du Perron according to his own fancy and imagination. Anquetil being utterly unable to distinguish cases, tenses, moods, personal terminations &c., was liable to the gravest errors and mistakes, which gave rise to wrong conception not only of subordinate points, but of such as were of the highest importance to those interested in the Zoroastrian religion.

To enable the reader to judge of Anquetil's way of translating, I shall give his translation of one of the most celebrated passages of the Vendidad (19, 9 edition of Westergaard) which was supposed to prove *Zarvan akarana*, i. e. the boundless time, to be the primitive being, the creator of the good and the bad spirits.

"Ahriman,* master of the bad law! the being absorbed in glory has given (created) thee, the boundless Time has given thee, it has given also, with magnificence, the Amshashpands, &c." According to this translation Ormuzd and Ahriman are not the two

* The verse concludes an old song, describing the devil's attacks made upon Zarathrusta, and the conversation carried on between them. In the third chapter of this work the reader will find a translation of the whole.

primitive spirits, but they themselves were created by a Supreme being called *Zaruan akarana*, i. e. the boundless time. This doctrine being altogether strange to the Zend-Avesta, as we shall see afterwards, was merely interpreted into this passage by Anquetil according to the teaching of his masters, the Dustoors, in consequence of his grammatical ignorance. He translates the words "*Zruni akaranê*" as nominative case, whilst a very superficial knowledge of Zend and Sanskrit grammars suffices to recognise both the forms as so called locatives ; they are therefore to be translated only "in the boundless time," the subject of the sentence being *çpentô mainyus*, i. e. the white spirit (a name of Ormuzd) ; were it the nominative case, and the subject of the sentence, then we should have to expect "Zarva akaranem." The right translation which I anticipate from the third chapter, in order to compare it with that of Anquetil, is as follows :

"Oh evil-knowing Angrômainyus (Ahriman)! The white spirit made (these weapons required to defeat the influences of the bad spirit) in the boundless time,* the immortal holy Saints assisted him in making *them*."

Although we may distinctly gather from this specimen, that Anquetil is nowhere to be relied upon, lacking always accuracy, yet we must thankfully acknowledge, how much we owe to him, as the founder of all researches subsequently made into the Zend-Avesta. Whilst the translation itself is utterly inaccurate and erroneous, his descriptions of ceremonies and rites are quite correct, as I myself can assure the reader from my intercourse with Parsee priests. He was a trustworthy man in every respect, and wrote only what he was taught by the Parsee Dustoors.†

* That means only, at a time unknown, at a time immemorial, or in the beginning.

† The European reader will not be a little astonished to learn, that Anquetil's work was regarded afterwards as a kind of authority by the Dustoors themselves. So for instance the late Highpriest of the Parsees at Bombay, Eduljee Darabjee Rustomjee, who passed for the most learned Priest of his time in India, quotes in his Guzaratee work "Mujizât-i-Zartosht" (the miracles of Zoroaster) p. 10 Anquetil as an authority in order to countenance his strange and quite erroneous explanation of the word "*çtehr-paêçanhem*" (decorated with stars) to mean "*Sadarah*" the shirt worn by the Parsees, an interpretation which contradicts the tradition as well as the contexts of the passages, and was consequently not acknowledged by other Dustoors.

These High-priests of the Parsee community, who are the only preservers of the religious traditions, and their interpreters, derive all information on their religion not from the original Zend texts themselves, but from the Pehlevi translation made of them at the time of the Sassanids. Considering that even this translation is not quite correct, and besides, that it is not understood by the Dustoors in a critical and philological way, how can Anquetil be expected to have furnished us with an accurate translation? In many instances Anquetil misunderstood the Dustoors, also; so that his translation was tinged with errors of three kinds, viz. those of the Pehlevi translations, those of the Dustoors, and those of his own misunderstandings. His work, therefore, cannot stand the test, and from a critical point of view it cannot be styled even a translation; it is only a summary report, in an extended form, of the contents of the Zend-Avesta. But he cannot be blamed for that; at his time it was quite impossible for the most learned and sagacious scholars to do more than he really did. From the Dustoors he learned the approximate meanings of the words, and starting from this very rudimentary knowledge, he then simply guessed the sense of each sentence.

Burnouf, who first investigated, in a scientific way, into the language of the Zend-Avesta, would never have succeeded in laying a foundation of Zend philology without Anquetil's labours. Anquetil had left ample materials for researches to be instituted in future, and had furnished the scholars with a summary of the contents of the Zend-Avesta. Burnouf, in making his researches, availed himself chiefly of a Sanskrit translation of the Yasna, or prayer-book of the Parsees, and found on a closer inquiry, that this work was more reliable than Anquetil's translation. The Pehlevi translation, upon which that into Sanskrit is founded, would have better answered his purposes; but as he did not take the trouble required to study this quite peculiar language, it was of no use to him. Neriosengh's Sanskrit translation was then, as to grammatical forms and etymologies rectified by Burnouf, through comparative philology, chiefly Sanskrit. But these aids did not prevent him from committing many errors. On the one side he relied too much on Neriosengh's imperfect work, on the other, he applied too often to Sanskrit etymologies. It is true, he had made extensive preparations, before he commenced his researches, for he compiled for his private use a dictionary of the Zend words with quotations from the Zend-Avesta, where each particular word occurs. In making his laborious inquiries into the meaning of any particular word, he quoted parallels, the broad ground on which the whole of modern philology, so highly developed, rests. But there being at his disposal no printed editions of the Zend-Avesta, based on different manuscripts, and pointing out the various readings, he could not peruse the whole of it so carefully, as would have been required to guard him against many mistakes, which he was otherwise unable to avoid; he, therefore, was often obliged to forego and overlook the important passages which would have guided him, in many instances, in fixing the exact meaning.

In his etymological proofs he was not always fortunate.* He lacked, to a certain extent, the skill required for making sound etymologies (which is really a very difficult task), and, besides, his acquaintance with the most ancient forms and words of the Sanskrit, as they are to be met with in the Vedas only, was too superficial. The Iranian languages, such as Persian, (the application of which requires even much greater skill and knowledge than that of the Sanskrit), were but little attended to by him. Whilst Burnouf often failed in his etymologies, he was

* I cannot enter here into details; I shall only point out some etymological mistakes. *Âkhtûirya*, (Ys. 9,14 Vend 10, 11) he says, is derived from the Vedic root *anj*, to which he ascribes the meaning "to sing," attributing to that word the sense of "made for being sung." That is utterly wrong. The root *anj*, to which he traces the word in question, never means in the Vedas "to sing" as he asserts, but "to smear, anoint;" (it is identical with the Latin *unguo*, to smear). The context of the passage, where the word in question occurs, besides, requires another meaning. Had he cast a slight glance only at Vend 10, 8, 7, he would have recognised the word to be a numeral, meaning "four times" (literally "till the fourth time) and being composed of the preposition *â* (up, to, till, as far as) and *khtûirya* (*quatuor* in Latin, *keturi* in Litthuanian, four). To the word *karafan* (he writes the crude form wrongly *karafna*, guessing it from the very frequent genitive of the plural, *karafnãm*) he ascribes the meaning *deaf*, while it means according to the Vedic language the "performers of sacrifices," as we shall see afterwards.

almost always successful in determining the grammatical terminations, their affinity to those of the Sanskrit being too close not to be recognised at once by a good Sanskrit scholar. But notwithstanding some undeniable defects in his researches, he was the first, who gave not a mere paraphrase or an approximate statement of the contents, but a real translation of two chapters of the Yasna (1st and 9th). That was a great step taken towards a sound philological interpretation of the whole Zend-Avesta. But the great scholar seems to have become in the course of his studies weary of spending many years in the explanation of a few chapters only, and did not pursue further his inquiries. After having simply pointed out the way, and paved it partially, he left it to others to follow his tracks. His results refer chiefly to grammatical points and the meanings of words, but very little to the contents of all the sacred books of the Zoroastrian religion, its origin, and development. About these matters his knowledge went only a little beyond that of Anquetil. He had no idea of the importance of the Gâthas; he neither knew that their language differs from the usual Zend language of the other books, nor that they are metrical compositions, their metres agreeing with those of the Vedic songs: so that he was unable to trace even the slightest features of a history of the Zoroastrian religion and its sacred writings. The task was, however, at his time too difficult to be carried out. He, however, discharged his duties as the founder of the first outlines of Zend philology with an accuracy, faithfulness, conscientiousness and sagacity, which endear him to every sincere reader, and make his premature death to be deeply regretted. He was really a master in scholarship and scientific investigations, and every page he wrote, even where he erred, bears witness to the truth of this statement.

Whilst the honour of having first opened the venerable documents of the Zoroastrian doctrines to the civilized world, belongs to France, Germany and Denmark have to claim the merit of having further advanced this entirely new branch of philological and antiquarian studies.

The first German scholar who made up his mind to take up the study of the Zend-Avesta, was JUSTUS OLSHAUSEN, Professor of oriental languages at Kiel (now one of the Directors in the Office of the Minister of Public Instruction in Prussia). He intended to publish an edition of the Zend-Avesta, according to the manuscripts extant in Europe, chiefly at Paris and Copenhagen, and to furnish the learned public with a grammar and dictionary. He commenced his edition by publishing the first four chapters of the Vendidad, or the code of the Parsees, in the year 1829; but after this first number had appeared, he stopped his edition, and left this extremely difficult, and in many respects thankless branch of studies.

This fragment, published by Olshausen, and the edition of a copy of a Vendidad-sâdah, belonging to the Imperial library at Paris, by Burnouf, were the only means available for German scholars who had a desire to decipher the language and teaching of the great Zoroaster. The utter insufficiency of these, in order to make any progress in these studies, was felt by all oriental scholars in Germany. They were, therefore, driven to content themselves with the results arrived at by Burnouf.

The first who made an extensive and useful application of them, now and then adding some remarks of his own, was FRANCIS BOPP, the celebrated compiler of the first comparative grammar of some of the chief languages of the Arian stock. He tried to give an outline of Zend grammar, chiefly according to the results arrived at by Burnouf, but no where made real discoveries of much importance in the Zend language as that famous Frenchman did. His sketch of Zend grammar, scattered throughout his comparative grammar, although imperfect and imcomplete as a first outline, was, and is up to this time, a valuable assistance to that larger number of oriental scholars who are desirous of acquiring some knowledge of Zend without taking the immense trouble of investigating into the original texts themselves.

The first step to be taken by German scholars towards an advancement in the unravelling of the mysteries of the Zend-Avesta, was to put themselves in possession of larger and better materials for their researches. There being no Zend manuscrip of importance in any German Library, the students were obliged to go to Paris, Copenhagen, London and Oxford, the only places where Zend manuscripts of value are to be found in Europe. Among the German States the honour of having provided scholars with the necessary means to stay at these places in order to collect more ample materials, belongs to BAVARIA.

The Bavarian government granted considerable sums for these purposes to two scholars of its country, to JOSEPH MÜLLER, now Professor of Oriental languages at Munich, and FREDERIC SPIEGEL, now Professor of Oriental languages at the Bavarian University Erlangen. Joseph Müller went to Paris to copy out the most important Zend and Pehlevi manuscripts. He seems to have been very busy during his stay at Paris; he himself, however, made but little use of the materials collected by him. He published two small treatises only, one "on the Pehlevi language" (in the French Asiatic Journal 1838), treating of the alphabet solely, and one "on the commencement of the Bundehesh" (in the Transactions of the Bavarian Academy of Sciences). Both are valuable, but chiefly based on Anquetil's papers, which the author thankfully acknowledged. Müller, very likely deterred by the enormous difficulties like many others, then left this branch of studies, and handed most of his materials over to his younger and more energetic countryman, FREDERIC SPIEGEL.

This scholar intended to give to the learned world the first critical edition of all writings in the Zend language, and commonly called the Zend-Avesta, to be based on a careful comparison of all manuscripts then extant in Europe. The materials left to him by Joseph Müller and Olshausen, not being sufficient to achieve this task, he went, munificently supported by the Bavarian government, to Copenhagen, Paris, London and Oxford, and copied out all those manuscripts, which he required for his purpose. His intention was not only to publish all the original texts together with the ancient Pehlevi translation, but to prepare a German translation of them with notes, and to issue both at the same time. But before he was so far advanced as to be able to publish a part of his large work, an edition of the *Vendidad Sâdah* (comprising the proper *Vendidád*, *Yasna* and *Visparat*,) in Roman characters, with an index and glossary, appeared in 1850 at Leipsic.

The author of this really very useful work, which made the original texts of the Zend-Avesta known to the learned public at large, was HERMANN BROCKHANS, Professor of Sanskrit at the University of Leipsic. He, not being in possession of such extensive materials as Spiegel, contented himself with a transcription of Burnouf's edition in Zend characters into those of the Roman alphabet, and pointed out in foot-notes the various readings of Framjee Aspendiarjee's edition published at Bombay in the years 1842-43 in Guzarathi characters. To facilitate to the students these researches, he added an index, indicating in alphabetical order, the passage where each particular word occurs. In a glossary (distinct from the index), he collected the explanations of the Zend words as far as they had been given by Burnouf, Bopp, Speigel, &c. It was a rudimentary Zend dictionary, but of course very incomplete, the author confining himself only to those words which were already explained by other scholars. Now and then he corrected errors.

This useful book contributed largely towards encouraging the Zend studies in Germany. Burnouf's edition and commentary on the first chapter of the Yasna were too costly and comprehensive to become generally used among the students of German universities. The work of Brockhaus, then, formed the manual for those Sanskrit students who had a desire of making themselves acquainted with the sacred language of the Zend-Avesta. The German Sanskrit Professors began to teach now and then Zend, but their knowledge of this language being very limited, they could not succeed in training young men for this branch of studies in the same way as they did successfully in Sanskrit. The subject is actually so extremely difficult, that every one who is desirous of acquiring a real knowledge of it, is compelled to lay aside for many years nearly all other studies, and devote his time solely to Zend. The language could not be learnt like Sanskrit, Arabic, Persian, Hebrew, Chaldee, Syriac, Aethiopic

Turkish, Chinese, etc. (all which languages are taught in German Universities, but of course not always at the same place) from grammars and dictionaries ; in fact, the Zend language before it could be learnt, had first to be discovered. But even to begin this task, a very comprehensive and accurate knowledge of several oriental languages, as the starting point for further inquiries, was indispensable.

In the mean time, the importance of the Zend language for antiquarian and philological researches became more generally known, chiefly in consequence of the attempts made to read the cuneiform inscriptions to be found in Persia. The first language of these inscriptions (which exhibit in Persepolis and the rock of Bisutûn three languages) is an Arian one, and decidedly the mother of the modern Persian. Its very close affinity to the Zend language, struck every one at the first glance ; thence the great importance of this language for deciphering these inscriptions was at once acknowledged. That circumstance removed chiefly in England many doubts which were entertained, nearly up to the present time, on the genuineness of the Zend language. The first work, written in English, which shews an acquaintance with the original Zend texts, is Revd. Dr. Wilson's book on the Parsee religion, published at Bombay in 1843.

Whilst Spiegel was preparing his critical edition of the Zend-Avesta, WESTERGAARD, Professor at Copenhagen, announced another one also, prepared from the same materials which were at the former's disposal. This great Danish scholar had the first claims to the publication of an edition of the Zend texts, on account of the great trouble he had taken to collect additional materials for such a work. Not satisfied with the materials extant in Europe, he left for India and Persia in order to search after new ones. During his stay in India and Persia (1841-43) he unfortunately did not succeed in obtaining new manuscripts of high value. There are, however, as I am told by Dustoors, some very old copies of the Zend books extant in Guzerat, but it is very difficult to purchase them. In Persia, no books, hitherto unknown, could be discovered by Westergaard, and even of those known to the Parsees of India, he found only very few copies. We must therefore consider Western India, chiefly Guzerat, as the only place where some books, hitherto unknown, may be discovered. In the advertisement of his edition of the Zend-Avesta, Westergaard announced the addition of a complete Dictionary, with a grammar of both the Zend dialects, an English translation of the whole, and an account of Iranian antiquities according to the Zend-Avesta.

The first fruit of Westergaard's Iranian studies was, however, not the edition of the Zend-Avesta, but that of the *Bundehesh*, *i. e.* on the origins of the creatures, now extant only in Pehlevi, the Zend original being lost. It is a compendious description of the whole Parsee religion, but not acknowledged by the Dustoors as a canonical book, like those styled Zend-Avesta. Its contents agreeing so exceedingly well with the reports of Theopompos and Hermippos, quoted above, we are driven to assign to the original or its sources a date not later than the 4th century before the Christian era. Westergaard's edition (Copenhagen, 1851) exhibits, however, only a lithographed version of one very old codex of the Bundehesh, extant in the library of Copenhagen. He added neither translation nor notes ; the only addition he made, was the transcript of two inscriptions of the Sassanids, found at Hajiâbâd, which were copied out by him during his stay in Persia. I undertook to review this edition, and the substance of my review was a short sketch of the Pehlevi grammar (1854.)

Before Spiegel issued the first number of his edition of the Zend texts, he published " a grammar of the Pârsi language" (Leipsic, 1851). He means by Parsi language that one which is now called by the Dustoor Pâzend. It differs very little from the modern Persian, except in the want of Arabic words, and is identical with the Persian, as written by the great Persian poet Firdûsi (1000 A. D.) We, therefore, are fully entitled to call it a somewhat obsolete form of the modern Persian. Spiegel added some specimens of religious literature, extant in Pârsî, with a German translation. I reviewed the book (1853), and was able to point out at once that want of really scientific research and sound philological training, which I afterwards discovered to be the characteristic of all his publications on the Zend-Avesta. His philology and method of inquiry are out of date; philological subjects were thus treated fifty years ago. The truth of this remark will be seen from the remaining portion of this first chapter.

A short time after this grammar, the first number of his edition of the Zend-Avesta, comprising the Zend text of about 10 chapters of the Vendidâd, appeared. It was beautifully printed with new type at the Imperial printing office at Vienna (1851,) and is really a master-piece of typography. This number, containing the mere text, without various readings or the Pehlevi translation, did not suffice to enable the reader to form a judgment of the way in which the text was made up. The publication of the larger remaining portion of the Vendidâd, together with the Pehlevi translation of the whole was, although printed, delayed till 1853. In the same year the first number of Westergaard's edition, printed at Copenhagen, appeared. It comprised the text of the Yasna only, chiefly based on a very old codex (copied about 500 years ago, the oldest of all Zend manuscripts now extant in Europe) with foot notes indicating some of the more important various readings of other codices. The edition, although not so beautifully printed as that of Spiegel, was very cleverly made, and made a much better impression upon the student than that of his rival. In this first number one could see that he had recognized the five Gâthas as metrical pieces (I had seen that before the publication). These first numbers of Spiegel's and Westergaard's editions, together with Spiegel's translation of the whole Vendidâd, were reviewed (1852-53) by one of the most distinguished and sagacious Sanskrit scholars of Europe, THEODOR BENFEY, Professor of Sanskrit at the University of Göttingen, in Hanover. He showed that the method adopted by Spiegel of giving a critical revision of the Zend texts, and a translation and explanation of them, was utterly wrong, pointing out that the student, pursuing Spiegel's way, never could arrive at a real insight into the sense of the Zend-Avesta. Spiegel, neither sufficiently trained in Sanskrit, nor knowing how to apply well the results of comparative philology to the interpretation of the Zend-Avesta, relied, in his translation, mainly on the Pehlevi translation, which was inaccessible to all other German scholars except himself. He supposed, that this ancient translation, made about 1300 or 1400 years ago by the most learned Parsee priests in Persia, was the only true basis on which a sound Zend philology could be founded. The correctness of this translation is to be tested by the comparison of the Iranian dialects, such as Pehlevi, Parsee, and modern Persian ; and then, in the last instance, Sanskrit and some other languages may be applied too. References to parallel passages are, according to his opinion, useful, but by all means subordinate to the traditional explanations of the priests. To judge impartially of his work, first a knowledge of the Pehlevi language was to be obtained. Benfey could not enter into a discussion on the correctness or incorrectness of the Pehlevi translation, because it was inaccessible to him ; but he showed Spiegel, that by the application of Sanskrit, the forms of which language are so very near to Zend, and by comparative philology, one might arrive at a much better understanding of the Zend-Avesta than by his method. From his translation, which teems with passages unintelligible to the reader, almost all oriental scholars in Germany, as well as other educated men, who took an interest in the studies, were driven to the conclusion that the Pehlevi translation is either totally incorrect or misunderstood by Spiegel. The book, therefore, met with but little success in Germany ; it was too far below what had been already achieved by Burnouf in the translation of the Zend-Avesta, and appeared nothing but a somewhat improved Anquetil. Spiegel, however, pretended boldly to be the first translator of the Vendidâd, asserting that Anquetil had not understood thoroughly the Pehlevi translation, and that he could not regard this Frenchman even as his predecessor. But on a closer inquiry we find, that Spiegel started from the rough copies of the dictations which Anquetil had received from the Dustoors, and deposited at the Imperial library at Paris ; without those rough copies (where the Pehlevi is written in Roman characters and explained in Persian) Spiegel would have been utterly unable to translate a single line with reference to the Pehlevi translation. Anquetil, therefore, is his predecessor, and to him he owes nearly all ; Spiegel therefore is by no means the first translator of the "Avesta." If one understands by a translation an approximate statement of contents, or an unintelligible rendering of passages misconceived, then Anquetil's as well as Spiegel's works may be styled translations ; but if one feels, that this name should be given only to an accurate rendering of words in such a manner as to prove quite intelligible to the reader, then the title "translation" is to be awarded to the works of neither. Burnouf's rendering of the two chapters of the Yasna can alone stand the test, and the most severe critic is compelled to allow it to be a real translation. But none of Burnouf's qualities will be discovered in Spiegel's works.

Burnouf took the great trouble of collecting the parallel passages, where the particular forms and words occur, sought their correspondents in the Sanskrit, and rectified in this way Neriosengh's Sanskrit translation, which guided him as to the general sense. Spiegel, believing the Pehlevi translation to be in most cases infallible, only now and then requiring the elucidation of an ambiguity, or a trifling amendment to be arrived at, from a comparison of the other Iranian languages, could of course entirely dispense with such time-wasting and painstaking preparations in collecting parallels as Burnouf, Westergaard, and I myself had found it necessary to make. As the "first translator" of the Avesta, according to his principles, did not require such tedious preparations, we may expect him to have spent a great deal of his time, before he published his translation of the Vendidâd, in making a glossary of the Pehlevi translation, and in a careful study of this dark language, hitherto strange to almost all the European scholars. But when I commenced the study of Pehlevi, with no other means than such as were in the hands of all other scholars (Westergaard's Bundehesh and Spiegel's edition of the Pehlevi translation of the Vendidâd), I was not a little astonished at finding that nowhere throughout the whole was a real study of the Pehlevi translation and the Pehlevi language to be perceived.* It was evident that almost all he had picked up of Pehlevi was due to Anquetil's rough copies, and that this Frenchman had a much better knowledge of Pehlevi than "the first translator of the Avesta." Notwithstanding, Spiegel is not ashamed of pretending to be the first translator of the Avesta according to the Pehlevi translation, and endeavours to deprive Anquetil of this honour,

* I shall give here as a sample, of his way of translating, his interpretation of the very commencement of the Vendidâd ; and to enable the reader to judge for himself on Spiegel's way of using the Pehlevi translation, I shall add an English translation of this version also. First I shall write the original Zend text, with an interlinear version of my own.

*Mraot Ahurô Mazdâo çpitamâi Zarathustrâi : azem dadhâm*<br>
spoke the living wise to Spitama Zarathustra I made<br>
*çpitama Zarathustra açô râmô-dâitim, nôit kudat shâitîm ;*<br>
Spitama Zarathustra place of an agreeable situation not anywhere habitable hitherto<br>
*yêdhi zi azem nôit daidhyâm çpitama Zarathustra açô*<br>
if then I not would have made Spitama Zarathustra place<br>
*râmô-dâitîm nôit kudat shâitîm, viçpô aṇhus açtvâo*<br>
of an agreeable condition not anywhere habitable all life existing<br>
*Airyanem vaêjô frâshnvât*<br>
after Iran the pure would have been poured forth.

This passage is rendered in the Pehlevi translation, together with explanatory notes interspersed (which I shall include in brackets) as follows :

• Hormuzd said to Sapetman Zerdosht : I made, Sapetman Zerdosht, a beautiful situated place that which had not been made *hitherto* comfortable [the men of this place who were born and brought up there thought that *place* to be excellent, which had been made by myself better and more comfortable.] Because if I had not made a place beautifully situated, Sapetman Zerdosht, which had not been made comfortable (previously), the whole iving creation would have gone to Iran vej. [Had this happened (had people been drawn after Iran vej, the paradise) then the world would have been unable to go on ; for it could not have continued in its proper course from zone to zone ; some are of opinion, it would have fallen a prey to the devils]. Spiegel, who professedly adheres strictly to the Pehlevi translation, if not compelled by very palpable reasons to deviate from it, (and in this passage no such reasons are to be found) translates as follows :—

"Ahura Mazda said to the holy Zarathustra : I created, holy Zarathustra, a place, a creation of pleasantness where nowhere was created a possibility (for drawing near). For if, holy Zarathustra, I had not created a place, a creation of pleasantness, where nowhere was created a possibility, the whole world endowed with bodies, would have gone to Airyana vaêjô." The notes of the Pehlevi translation, as given by myself, are completely omitted by Spiegel, which is almost always the case, if the notes were not intelligible to him at the first glance. Spiegel now deviates here in two essential points from the Pehlevi translation : first he translates, "çpitama," the usual surname of Zoroaster in the Zend-Avesta, by "holy," whilst all the Dustoors for obtaining which he had risked so much. Spiegel's translation of the Vendidâd is, to say it in short, the produce of a study of Anquetil's papers and misunderstandings of the Pehlevi translation, and the original Zend text, now and then trimmed up with some of the results of comparative philology, but nowhere deserving the name "translation." The first translation of the Vendidâd, according to the Pehlevi translation, as well as to the principles of comparative philology, is still to be made. Spiegel's translation is, on an average, not a bit more reliable than Anquetil's, giving neither the traditional explanation, nor the results of real philological researches.

Before Spiegel published the second volume of his edition of

consider it to be a proper name of one of Zoroaster's ancestors; Spiegel followed simply Burnouf's explanation of the word, which I did also, but afterwards I discovered the mistake. Spiegel as the strict follower of the tradition, ought here not to have deviated from it, before having ascertained, from strict investigation that it actually meant "holy," (which it never does.) The second deviation is Spiegel's translation of the words *nôit kudat shâitîm*. In the Pehlevi text there is written:—*râ âk jahabunt jakavvimunit âçânish*, which means literally, "not which made happened comfort." Spiegel introduces "nowhere" and then the word "possibility," strange to the Zend as well as to the Pehlevi text and its glosses. He misunderstood two words entirely: *kudat* and *shâitîm*; *kudat* is an adverb, meaning "anywhere," and joined to the negative *nôit* "nowhere." But Spiegel makes it two words as the Pehlevi translation does: *ku dat*; the first he takes as an adverb, meaning, combined with the negative *nôit*, "nowhere," and *dat* is, according to him, a past participle of the root *dâ*, to make, create. The Pehlevi translation takes *ku* simply as a relative particle, but not in the meaning "anywhere," and to *dat* it gives the same meaning that he does. Only to the whole word *kudat*, can the meaning "anywhere" be reasonably given, but by no means to the first part, as Spiegel may learn from the Persian grammar. To take *dat*, being here a pronominal enclitic (like *chit* in Sanskrit, *kvachit* "anywhere,") as a past participle, is a gross and unpardonable grammatical blunder, showing an utter ignorance of the very first principles of grammar. The past participle of the root *dâ*, to make, is in Zend always *dâta* (corresponding to the Latin *datus*, given) but never *dat*; *âçânish*, by which *shâitîm* is translated, never means in Persian "possibility," but ease, comfort. He had very likely in view the Sanskrit *çakti*, power, strength, which meaning is altogether strange to *shâiti*, a derivation of the root *kshâ*, *kshi*, "to live, reside." Whatever derivation he might have thought of, at all events the rendering of the Pehlevi translation "comfort" is far preferable to that ventured upon by its professedly strict follower. The correct philological rendering of the whole passage is as follows:

"I made Spitama Zarathustra! into a delicious spot what was (hitherto) nowhere habitable. For had not I, Spitama Zarathustra, converted into a delicious spot, what was (hitherto) nowhere habitable; all earthly life would have been poured forth after Airyana Vaêjô" (the paradise; the whole earth then would be now a desert), the Zend-Avesta, (1858, containing the Yasna and Visparad, with the Pehlevi translation), Westergaard succeeded in editing all the Zend texts which are known as yet; and to him we owe therefore the first complete edition of the Zend-Avesta. The work is entitled *Zend-Avesta, or the religious books of the Zoroastrians, edited and translated, with a Dictionary, Grammar &c.* By N. L. *Westergaard.* Vol. I: The Zend texts Copenhagen 1852-54: of the two remaining volumes nothing has appeared yet. Westergaard knows too well the enormous difficulties with which the study of the Zend-Avesta is beset, to come forward with a hasty translation, grammar, and dictionary; he knows that none but he who spends many years in mere preparatory studies, is able to give any thing like a translation of even a few of the fragments of the Zend-Avesta. As a first edition of all the Zend texts, Westergaard's work deserves much praise; he follows, in most cases, the best manuscripts; but if he finds their readings entirely incorrect, he amends them according to sound philological principles. Compound words, as far as he could discover them, are always marked. From a careful perusal of his work, one may gather that Westergaard understood already a good deal of the texts (except perhaps the most ancient and difficult pieces, the Gâthas) and had extensive collections of words, forms, various readings &c., at his disposal. In every respect, except typography, Westergaard's edition is by far preferable to that of Spiegel.

I may pass over some small treatises by Spiegel, published occasionally in the journal of the German Oriental Society and the Transactions of the Bavarian Academy, as having contributed but very little towards the elucidation of the Zend-Avesta,* and

* The best essay written by Spiegel is his explanation of the 19th Fargard of the Vendidâd. Here he was less hasty than in his other publications. His "Grammar of the Huzvâresh (Pehlevi) language" (Vienna 1856) contains valuable materials for a well trained philologist, who will undertake to compile a Pehlevi grammar, from which the student might learn thus much as to be able to understand to a certain extent the Pehlevi translations of Zend-Avesta, and the linguist gain a fair insight into the nature of that dark language; but on account of the author's want of critical judgment (as I pointed that out in a review, published in 1857 in the notices on literary subjects of the University, Göttingen) every reader, expecting to attain by means of Spiegel's work, to either of these scopes, will find himself soon wholly disappointed.

shall now speak of my own researches made into the sacred writings of the Parsees.

I commenced the studying of the Zend language in the autumn of 1852, shortly after the publication of the first number of Westergaard's edition of the Zend-Avesta, containing the Yasna. I was already acquainted with the results arrived at by Burnouf, which knowledge I chiefly owed to Brockhans' valuable compilation above noticed. But I was quite convinced, at the very outset of my studies, that from all that had been hitherto written on the Zend language and the Zend-Avesta, one could obtain nothing but a smattering of this subject. Actuated by mere love of these ancient records, and cherishing the hope of making some discoveries in this terra incognita, I set about the task of instituting inquiries of my own into these sacred texts. I was not possessed of any other aids but those which were accessible to all other scholars, while Spiegel and Westergaard had all the manuscripts or copies thereof, and the Pehlevi and Sanskrit translations, at their disposal. Westergaard's edition of the Yasna enabled me to commence this study, but I soon was aware of the unusually great difficulties which every step in this branch of philological studies was to encounter. I first directed my attention towards the metrical portions of the Yasna, called the five Gâthas or songs, the explanation of which never had been attempted before by any oriental scholar. It is true, Spiegel observed first, that their language is different, from the usual Zend language to be found in the Vendidâd, the Yashts, Visparat and the later portions of the Yasna; but he rested satisfied with pointing out some of the most striking differences, such as the constant length of the vowels at the end of a word &c., and never undertook to translate these songs. I first tried to make out the meaning of a few lines by means of Anquetil's translation, but I soon convinced myself of his utter insufficiency even as a guide for ascertaining the general sense only. In the Vendidâd and the other books, Anquetil may guide one in this respect; but not in the Gâthas. The chief reason is the peculiarity of this portion as to language and ideas; they contain no descriptions of ceremonies and observances, as the Vendidâd, nor any enumeration of the glorious feats of angels, as the Yashts, but philosophical and abstract thoughts, and they differ widely from all other pieces contained in the Zend-Avesta. As they have been unintelligible to the Parsee priests for several thousand years, we cannot expect Anquetil to have given even a faint approximate statement of their general contents. Having no other aids save Anquetil's work, which proved in this case to be no aid at all (his rough copies were not accessible to me), I was left to my own resources. First I took the great trouble of collecting all the parallels throughout the Zend-Avesta, and arranging them alphabetically; the index of Brockhaus to Vendidad, Yasna, and Visparat, aided me considerably; but to the Yashts, which forming about one-half of all the Zend texts extant, were for the first time published in Westergaard's edition, I was obliged to make an index of my own. Being convinced, like Burnouf, that the language of the Vedas stands among all Arian dialects nearest to the Zend language, I betook myself to the study of the sacred writings of the Brahmans, chiefly to that section, which is called *Rigveda Samhitá*, being a collection of a little more than 1,000 very ancient hymns. Only the eighth part of this large work being published at the time, when I made up my mind to investigate into the Zoroastrian writings, I found it necessary to copy out from a manuscript, kindly lent me by my friend, Professor Benfey, at Göttingen, the remaining seven parts. After that was done, an alphabetical index, at least to some portions of this extensive collection of sacred songs, was to be made also. In this tedious work I was supported by a friend, Gottlob Wilhelm Hermann (a young clergyman in my native country Würtemberg), who possesses a remarkable knowledge of Sanskrit. Not contenting myself with these aids, I commenced the study of the Armenian (which is affiliated to the Iranian languages), and also that of the Pehlevi language (with modern Persian I was already acquainted). The study of Pehlevi, which language is a mixture of Persian and Chaldee, was much facilitated to me in consequence of my being acquainted to a certain extent with all

Semitic tongues, which knowledge I chiefly owe to my great teacher, Professor EWALD, at Göttingen. After having been prepared in this way, I commenced my philological operations in the following manner: First I turned up all the other passages, where the word or form to be investigated into, occurred, in order to ascertain its approximate meaning. But the parallels, referred to, being often as obscure as the passage, upon which they were to throw some light, I was often obliged first to make out their meaning also by a reference to other parallels. Having thus arrived, in most cases after many troubles only, at the approximate meaning of the word in question, I ventured upon confirming or modifying the results obtained in this way by means of a sound etymology. First I applied to those words and forms of the Zend language itself, which I had reason to suppose to be cognate to the word in question; then I consulted the Vedas, chiefly the hymns of the Rigveda. There being neither index nor glossary, I had to take here the same trouble as I did in the Zend-Avesta, in order to ascertain from the parallels the meaning of the Vedic word I referred to. I could not asquiesce always in the results I had gained in this way, but I searched after the Zend words to be explained in modern Persian and Armenian, and now and then in Latin and Greek also. Modern Persian, chiefly in its older shape, commonly styled Parsee, was of the highest value for such etymological researches. But the appeal to this genuine niece of the sacred language of the Zend-Avesta is on an average rendered more difficult, and subjected to more errors than that to the Vedic Sanskrit, which is the elder sister to the Zend. In the modern Persian a good many of the Zend words are preserved; but they have undergone such great changes as to make them indiscernible to a somewhat inexperienced etymologist. Such corruptions of the ancient words being, however, reducible to certain rules, these, only partially known as yet, were first to be discovered. I shall illustrate these remarks on the corruption of ancient words in the modern Persian by some examples: e. g. the Zend *zaredaya*, i. e. heart, has become *dil* in modern Persian; *çareda*, i. e. year, is *sál*; *kerenaoiti*, i. e. he amazon.in

**Tax Invoice/Bill of Supply/Cash Memo**
(Triplicate for Supplier)

**Sold By :**
Facsimile Publishers
C2/12 Pragati Market, Ashok Vihar Phase 2
NEW DELHI, DELHI, 110052
IN

**Billing Address :**
Vikalp Kumar
47 Veerappa Nagar, Alwarthirunagar
CHENNAI, TAMIL NADU, 600087
IN
**State/UT Code:** 33

**PAN No:** AAACG4699N
**GST Registration No:** NotApplicable

**Shipping Address :**
Vikalp Kumar
Vikalp Kumar
47 Veerappa Nagar, Alwarthirunagar
CHENNAI, TAMIL NADU, 600087
IN
**State/UT Code:** 33
**Place of supply:** TAMIL NADU
**Place of delivery:** TAMIL NADU

**Order Number:** 171-2575264-3281949
**Order Date:** 06.10.2024

**Invoice Number :** IN-2225
**Invoice Details :** DL-132759261-2425
**Invoice Date :** 06.10.2024

| Sl. No | Description | Unit Price | Qty | Net Amount | Tax Rate | Tax Type | Tax Amount | Total Amount |
|---|---|---|---|---|---|---|---|---|
| 1 | Essays on Kasmiri Grammar [Hardcover] ( 9384337263 + PB1111018702928 )<br>HSN:49011010 | ₹545.00 | 1 | ₹545.00 | 0% | IGST | ₹0.00 | ₹545.00 |
| | | | | | 0% | IGST | ₹0.00 | |
| | | | | | 0% | None | ₹0.00 | |
| | Shipping Charges | ₹154.00 | | ₹154.00 | 0% | IGST | ₹0.00 | ₹154.00 |
| | | | | | 0% | IGST | ₹0.00 | |
| | | | | | 0% | None | ₹0.00 | |
| TOTAL: | | | | | | | ₹0.00 | ₹699.00 |

**Amount in Words:**
**Six Hundred Ninety-nine only**

**For Facsimile Publishers:**

**Authorized Signatory**

Whether tax is payable under reverse charge - No

makes is *kunad* ; *âtars* i. e. fire, is *atesh* *&c.* In the Sanskrit as the elder sister, the corresponding words are much easier to be recognised. So *zaredaya* is *hrdaya*, *çaredha* *çarad* (in the Vedas), *kerenaoiti* *krnoti* (vedic form, in the classical Sanskrit changed into *karoti*), *âtar-s* is *athar* (preserved only in the derivative *atharvan*, i. e. fire-man, priest), &c. Of the ancient grammatical forms such as the terminations of cases, tenses &c., nothing is remaining in the modern Persian, but all are extant in the Vedic Sanskrit. From these remarks every one can draw the conclusion that Sanskrit is, for the deciphering of the Zend language, of much greater use than the modern Persian.

The first fruit of my laborious researches was an attempt to explain the 44th chapter of the Yasna (forming a part of the second Gâtha) which appeared in the journal of the German Oriental Society (1853-54). It was on account of the immense difficulties of the subject and the then insufficiency of my preparations, that it was impossible for me, even in the majority of my interpretations, to be sure of being right. But being convinced from this faint attempt, that the Gâthas contained the undoubted teaching of Zarathustra himself, as he imparted it to his disciples, I thought it worth the trouble to pursue these studies for six years more. The last and ripest results of these laborious studies, I published in a work entitled, *The five Gâthas, i. e. collections of songs and sayings of Zarathustra, his disciples and successors. Edited, translated* and *explained* (2 Vols., Leipsic, 1858-60). It contains a revised text according to philological principles, transcribed into Roman characters, a literal Latin, and a more free German translation, and a complete critical and philological commentary with introductions to the several chapters (17) and a general introduction to the whole at the end. The basis of the whole work is the commentary, which gives in full length the results of my comparing the parallels of the Zend Avesta and the Veda, and the etymological researches in Zend and the cognate languages together with a partial review of the traditional explanations, as far as they were accessible to me in a bad transcript of Neriosenghs Sanscrit trauslation of the Gâthas. Some portions of the work, but much revised, will be submitted to the reader in the third chapter of this book.

About half a year after the publication of the first part of my work, "the first translator of the Avesta" published a translation of the whole Yasna, together with Visparat, including the Gâthas also. He complained very much of my encroachment on his monopoly, and pretended boldly, (although he had devoted but little time, as he confessed himself in the preface, whereas I had spent six years on this difficult portion) to offer here to the public the first translation of the Gâthas. But he found himself soon disappointed in his expectation; for nobody acknowledged his pretensions. It would be mere wasting of time and paper to expatiate here on his work; written exactly in the same style as his Vendidâd, it is made without any philological preparations, simply according to Neriosengh's Sanskrit translation; no study of the subject is perceptible. The work, therefore, is completely useless as far as the Gâthas are concerned, in the explanation of which, still, after the publication of my work, much remains to be done. In the introduction he repeats chiefly Anquetil's reports on the forms of worship among the Parsees.

Before I conclude this introductory chapter, I have to mention some other publications relative to the Zend-Avesta. LASSEN, the well known Sanskrit scholar, published an edition of the Zend text of the five first chapters of Vendidâd (Bonn 1851), but adding neither translation nor explanatory notes.

WINDISHMANN, a Roman Catholic clergyman of a high position at Munich, published two valuable essays, one "on (the deity) Anaitis," worshipped by the ancient Persians, and mentioned in the Yashts; the other is a translation of the Mihir Yasht, with notes (Leipsic, 1857.)

MAX DUNCKER, the author of a History of Antiquity which is highly valued in Germany, treated, in the second volume of his work, of the ancient Persian religion, its sacred books and prophets.

* In several translations of Grecian reports, as given above, I was compelled to follow him, the original texts of the authors not always being accessible to me in this place.

Although he himself is a mere historian by profession (no oriental scholar), he succeeded in drawing up a fine and correct general picture of the ancient Iranian life according to the reports of the Greeks and the modern researches into the Zend-Avesta.

This much I had to notice on the general course of the researches into the sacred writings of the Parsees, undertaken in Europe solely out of interest in the remote and glorious past of Persians and Bactrians. Slowly a whole world, buried for thousands of years in documents written in a now unintelligible tongue, begins to be unfolded; but many years and many labourers will be required to make this new field for antiquarian and philological researches yield much ripe fruit. The Dustoors, who are first concerned, and other younger talented and well-to-do members of the rich Parsee community, ought to consider it their duty to equip themselves with all the implements (knowledge of Sanskrit, Persian, Chaldee, Hebrew, &c.), now required for a successful investigation into the Zend and Pehlevi languages, in order to learn the foundations on which their religion rests. For the benefit of the Parsee youth chiefly this work is intended. May it be a useful guide to them in their studies!

# II.

# OUTLINE

OF A

# GRAMMAR OF THE ZEND LANGUAGE.

---

## 1—THE IRANIAN LANGUAGES.

The languages of Persia, commonly called Iranian, form a separate family of the great Arian stock of languages, which comprises, besides the Iranian idioms, the Sanskrit (with its daughters), Greek, Latin, Teutonic (with English), Slavonian, Letto-Litthuanian and Celtic dialects. The Iranian idioms themselves are to be brought under two heads:

1. Iranian languages in the strictest sense.
2. Affiliated tongues.

The first division comprises the ancient, middle age, and modern languages of Iran, *i. e.* of Persia, Media, and Bactria, or chiefly of those countries which are styled in the Zend-Avesta, the "Arian countries" (*airyâo dañhâvô*). We may class them as follows :—

(*a.*) The East-Iranian or Bactrian branch, extant only in the two dialects, in which the scanty fragments of the Parsee scripture are written ; the more ancient of them may be called the "Gâtha dialect," because the largest and most important pieces preserved in this peculiar idiom, are the so called Gâthas or songs; the younger, in which most of the books, which now make up the Zend-Avesta, are written, may be called "ancient Bactrian" or the "classical Zend language," which was for many centuries the spoken and written language of Bactria. The chief differences of the two dialects will be pointed out in the grammatical sketch to be given in this chapter, and the question as to their relationship to each other, will be briefly discussed at the end. The Bactrian languages seem to have been dying out in the third century B. C., no daughters of them having been left.

(*b.*) The West-Iranian languages or those of Media and Persia. They are known to us during the three periods, antiquity, middle ages, and modern times, but only in one dialect, viz., that which at every period served as the written language throughout the Iranian provinces of the Persian Empire. There are several dialects mentioned by lexicographers, but we know but very little of them.* Of the ANCIENT PERSIAN a few documents are now extant in the cuneiform inscriptions of the Kings of the Achæmenian dynasty, to be found in the ruins of Persepolis, on the rock of Behistun, near Hamadan, and some other places of Persia. This language stands nearest to the two Bactrian dialects of the Zend-Avesta, but shows, however, some peculiarities; for instance, instead of *z* we find *d* used, e. g. *adam I,* in Zend *azem*; *dasta* hand, Zend *zaçta*. It is undoubtedly the mother of the modern Persian. The differences between both are nevertheless great, and to read and interpret the cuneiform inscriptions written in the ancient Persian, Sanskrit and Zend, although they be only sisters, have proved to

* In Sayid Hossein Shâh Hakîkat's Persian grammar, entitled *Tochfat ul ajam*, there are seven Iranian languages enumerated, which are classed under two heads, viz., (*a*) obsolete or dead, and (*b*) such tongues as are used. Of the ancient he knows 4: *Soghdhi* (the language of the ancient Sogdiana, *çughdha* in the Zend-Avesta); *Zâuli* (instead of Zâbuli, the dialect of Zabulistan); *Siksi* (spoken in Sejestan, called *Sakastene* by the Greeks); and *Hirwi* (*Harôyu* in the Zend-Avesta, the modern Herat). As languages in use, he mentions *Parsee*, which, he says, was spoken in Istakhar (Persepolis), the ancient capital of Persia; then *Deri* or Court language, according to this author, spoken at Balkh, Bokhara, Merw and in Badakshan; and *Pehlevi* or *Pehlevâni*, the language of the so called *Pehlev*, comprising the districts of Rai (*Ragha* in the Zend-Avesta), Ispahan and Dinur. *Deri* he calls the language of Firdausi, but the trifling deviations he alleges to prove the difference of *Deri* from *Parsee* (for instance they say in Deri *ashkam* belly for *shakam*, and *abâ* instead of *bâ* with), refer only to slight changes in spelling, and are utterly insufficient to induce a philologist to make Deri an idiom different from Parsee.

be more useful than its daughter, the modern Persian. The chief reason is the loss of nearly all the grammatical inflexions in nouns, verbs, genders, &c., in the modern Persian, while in the Persian, as written and spoken at the time of the Achæmenids (500—300 B. C.), we find still a great many inflexions agreeing with those of the Sanskrit, Zend, and of the other ancient Arian tongues. At what time the Persian lost almost all its terminations, and came into the condition of its present grammatical poverty, which makes it appear rather like the Chinese than the Arian sister tongues (whose grammar is so highly developed), we cannot ascertain. But there is every reason to suppose, that this dissolution and absorption of the terminations on account of their having become for the greater part utterly unintelligible, began before the Christian era, because in the later inscriptions of the Achæmenids (400 B. C.), we find already the grammatical forms confounded, which confusion we discover in many portions of the Zend-Avesta also. No inscription of the successors of the Achæmenids, the Arsacids, in the vernacular Persian being extant, we cannot trace the successive dissolution of the ancient Iranian. Among the Persian inscriptions still extant, those which stand, as to their time, next to those of the Achæmenids, belong to the Sassanids, who ascended the throne of Iran in A. D. 235. From them, although very rare, except on coins, we may learn that the general grammatical structure of Persian, at the Sassanian times, as regards the want of grammatical terminations, was almost in the same state as we find it now. But besides the loss of the terminations, another considerable change is to be observed, viz. the intermixture of a foreign (Semitic) language. The coins of the Sassanids (from A. D. 235—640) show many Semitic words, but with Arian terminations. To make that clear, I shall give the reader a short specimen of this style.

In the inscription of King Shapur I. (who reigned from A. D. 238 to 269), found at HAJIÂBÂD, copied by Westergaard, and added to his edition of the Bundehesh (without any explanation), we find the following titles:—

*Mazdayasn bagi Shahpuhri malkán malká Irán v Anirán minô*

*chatri min yazdán barj mazdayasn bagi Artashatr malkán malká Irán minó chatri min yazdán nafi bagi Babagán malká, i. e.*, the Ormuzd worshipper, the ruler Shapur, the emperor of Irân and Not-Irân (Turan), of divine origin through God, the son of the Ormuzd-worshipper, the ruler Ardeshir, emperor of Irân, of divine origin through God, grandson of the ruler Babagan, the king.

*Mazdayasn* is in the old language *Masdayaçna*, the terminating *a* being lost; *bagi* is the ancient *baga* (literally, god) applied to kings, like the Grecian *theos*, god,* and the Sanscrit *deva;* the final *i* is the so called *Idhâfat*, or the relative particle which joins one noun to the other or an adjective to the substantive, which use is extremely frequent in the modern Persian. *Shahpuhr-i*, the proper name of the king; in ancient Persian it would sound *Khshathra puthra*. The final *i* is of the same nature as that in *bagi*; it connects the name of the King with his titles. *Malkân Malká* corresponds to the ancient Persian *khshayathiya khshayathiyânam*, King of Kings, and the modern Persian *Shahanshâh*; it is of Semitic (Chaldee) origin (compare *malká*, the king, in Chaldee, and *malkó* in Syriac), but with the Iranian plural termination *án*, which was originally used for the genitive plural only, but afterwards applied to all cases of the plural indiscriminately. *Irán* and *Anirán* are in the ancient language *Airyana* and *Anairyana*; *v* (*u*) is a corruption of *uta*, and *minó chitra* would be *mainyu-chitra*, having a heavenly origin; *min* is a Semitic particle meaning "from" instead of ancient Persian *hacha* and modern Persian *az*; *yazdân*, mod. Pers. *yazdán*, god, which corresponds to the ancient *yazatanãm*, the genitive plural of *yazata*, i. e. a being deserving worship.† *Barj* is the Chaldee *bar*, son (*ben* in Hebrew and Arabic); the *j* at the end is another pronunciation of the relative *i* above mentioned. *Naf-i*, is the Zend *napâ*, S. *naptâ*, Lat. *nepos*

* One might take this terminating *i* as an adjectival termination, but on the coins we often find the simple *bag*.

† The plural is here used as a term of respect; compare the Hebrew *elohím*, a plural, and the Aethiopic *amlák*, a plural too, but both applied to god.

grandson (preserved, but with a somewhat changed meaning in *nephew*).

Besides coins and a few inscriptions, books also are extant from the Sassanian times. It is hard, and in many instances impossible, to ascertain the accurate date when they were written; thus much is only certain, that they exhibit that form of the Persian tongue which was current in Persia during the Sassanian rule (235—640 A. D.), and for the period immediately subsequent to its overthrow. This Pehlevi literature, as far as it is preserved, is of a merely religious character, being closely connected with the restoration of the Zoroastrian religion by the Sassanids. The most important remnant of it is a translation of the chief parts of the Zend-Avesta (Yasna, Visparad and Vendidâd), and some minor pieces. Other religious books, without a Zend original, are extant, such as the *Bundehesh*, *Shikandgumâni*, *Dinkart*, *Atash Bahrâm*, etc., and by searching in the libraries of ancient priestly families, one might discover several Pehlevi books, utterly unknown hitherto.

As to the nature of the Pehlevi language to be found in all these books, and the relationship in which it stands to that on the coins and inscriptions, I shall quote here some of my remarks made about this subject in my German pamphlet "On the Pehlevi language and the Bundehesh" (Göttingen 1854).

The Pehlevi of the books differs from that to be met with on coins and inscriptions, but these differences are not so great as to justify the supposition, maintained by Westergaard, that both are utterly distinct languages, the former a pure Iranian, the latter a Semitic idiom. The main character of both is the same, viz. a mixture of Semitic and Iranian elements, the Semitic part being always identical with Chaldee forms and words, and the Iranian with Persian. The difference consists only in the larger or smaller intermixture of either. The inscriptions at Hajiâbâd, mentioned above, exhibit one and the same text in two very nearly related, yet not identical idioms. The first, marked (A) at the end of Westergaard's Bundehesh, the commencement of which inscription we have explained above, shows the same idiom which we find on the coins; it is full of Semitic words, but the structure is Iranian, not Semitic; thus we have for instance the Persian plural termination in *ân*, the Persian way of expressing the genitive case by means of the suffix *i* (to be traced to the relative pronoun *yat*). In the other idiom marked (B), the Semitic element prevails even in the structure; it thus stands nearer to the Semitic than to the Iranian character, though it is nowhere to be recognised as a really Semitic language. We find in it, for instance, the Chaldee plural in *în*, e. g. *malkîn*, kings, and instead of the Iranian *bag*, divine, the Semitic *alâhâ*, divine. In comparing these two idioms with the Pehlevi of the books, we find some differences, but they are not of any great importance. On the contrary, we meet many of those strange looking forms and words, which made Pehlevi appear in the eyes of several scholars as a fabricated language, on the inscriptions (where certainly no fabricated language could be made use of by the kings) as well as in the books, *e. g.* the particles, *aik* which, what, *amat* when, *val*, (*var* in the books, *l* there being often not distinguished from *r*), *apan*, *avan* to, towards, *panij* before, etc., all being of Semitic origin. The non-irânian element is called *Huzvâresh* by the Parsee priests. If they read Pehlevi, they generally read the corresponding Persian instead of these foreign words,* being, however, ready, if called

* They read, for instance, *kah* which, instead of *aik; khâstan* to wish, want, instead of *bunshunastan; nishistân* to get, instead of *jatibuntan*, etc. This circumstance has very likely given rise to Westergaard's strange opinion, that the foreign words of the Pehlevi books are mere ideographic signs, invented to conceal the meaning of the sacred books from laymen. But the priests, if asked, whether or not the foreign word, styled by Westergaard an ideograph, has a peculiar pronunciation, answer in the affirmative, and pronounce then the signs, character by character, saying at the same time "that is Huzvâresh." This name, therefore, is to be confined to the Semitic element in the Pehlevi only, and not applied to the Pehlevi language in general. To facilitate the reading of these Semitic words, styled *Huzooresh* (this is in all probability the right pronunciation and not *Huzvâresh*), we find often an Iranian termination added to a Semitic word, e. g. *abi-dar* father, *ami-dar*, mother, where *dar* at the end indicates that *abi* and *ami* is to be pronounced as *pâdar*, *mâdar*, the Persian substitutes for the Semitic *ab* father, *am* mother; *yahavvunand* (read by the priests *janoonand*) they are, where *yahavvun* is the 3rd person plural of the second tense (its meaning being that of the present and future) of the Chaldaic verb *havâ* to be, and the termination of the 3rd plural, present tense, of the Persian *hastand*, they are.

upon, to pronounce them according to the characters in which they are written; but their pronunciation of these Semitic words, whose roots and forms are unintelligible to them, is in many cases evidently wrong. The chief reason of this is the great ambiguity of the Pehlevi writing, where not only the short vowels are omitted (as is usual in all Semitic alphabets, except the Aethiopic), but one and the same character is capable of three or four different meanings; so, for instance, *o*, *u*, *v*, *n* are expressed by one character, for initial *j*, *h*, *s* there is one sign indiscriminately used, etc. The correct form and pronunciation is to be ascertained from the Chaldee only, a good knowledge of which tongue is indispensable in order to understand Pehlevi.

Now the question arises, do these three idioms of the Pehlevi language, which we can discover, represent dialects of three different districts in Iran, or do they belong to different periods, or are they mere products of peculiarities existing in different styles? The two idioms, found in the Hajiabad inscriptions, which are written in two distinct kinds of characters, one of which (B) resembles very much the Hebrew writing, exhibit certainly two dialects of one and the same language, as spoken in two neighbouring provinces. The book Pehlevi (called *Zend-Pehlevi*, *i. e.* Pehlevi of the commentary) differs from the Pehlevi on the coins only as far as the style is concerned; it was very likely that kind of language, which was used in the schools by scholars only, and not by the people. At the time when Pehlevi ceased to be a living language, and the restoration of the pure Iranian words was begun, the scholars, not daring to change the writings, descended from the Sassanian times, accustomed themselves to substitute in reading the Persian equivalents for the foreign Huzooresh words. This circumstance gave at length rise to a new form of writing commentaries on religious subjects, consisting in the use of the more distinct and clear Zend characters, where each sign has but one phonetical value, and in exterminating all the foreign Huzooresh words, to be replaced by pure Persian ones. This new form was called *Pâzend*, serving, as is the case up to the present day, to facilitate the reading and understanding of the ancient

Pehlevi books only. Thus Pâzend has two meanings like Zend, it means explanation of the Zend commentary, this explanation being written in the pure Iranian, it is applied also to the language used for that purpose.

The Iranian part of the Pehlevi differing but little from modern Persian, we dare say, that the Persian language, as written 1600 years ago, was, in grammatical respects, almost in the same state as we find it at present. It needed only the Chaldee words to be exterminated and pure Iranian ones re-established throughout in their room, in order to arrive at that state of the modern Persian which is presented to us in the Shâhnâmeh by FIRDAUSI. Soon after the conversion of the Persians to the Mohammedan faith, a great many Arabic words were incorporated with the Persian tongue, forming now an inseparable part of the language, such as the Norman words in modern English. That mixture of Persian with Chaldee was called *Pehlevi* (the Semitic part went by the name *Huzooresh*, the purified Persian by that of *Parsee* or Pâzend). As to the time, the period of *Pehlevi*, extends from A. D. 200 (if not earlier) to 700; that of *Parsee* from 700 to 1100; and that of *modern Persian*, the language of *Jámi*, *Nizámi*, and *Háfiz*, from 1100 up to the present. The only changes in the Persian for 1600 years have been in the words; many words used in the Parsee books and Firdausi are now obsolete, and unintelligible to an unlearned Persian. Although there are translations of many parts of the grand Shâhnamah, yet up to the present day Firdausi's language is not yet properly investigated into, the explanation of many things in the poem requiring more than an ordinarily good oriental scholarship.

The second chief division of the Iranian tongues comprises the *affiliated languages*, that is to say such as share in the chief peculiarities of this family, but differ from it in many essential points. To this division we must refer the *Ossetic*, spoken by some small tribes in the Caucasus, but completely differing from the other so called Caucasian languages; also the *Armenian* and the *Afghanic* (*Pushtoo*).

## 2—THE ZEND LANGUAGE.

The general character of the Zend language in both its dialects is that of a highly developed idiom. It is rich in inflexions, in the verbs and in the nouns. In the former, where three numbers and eight cases can be distinguished, it agrees almost completely with the Vedic Sanscrit, and in the latter, it exhibits a greater variety of forms, than the classical Sanscrit. Besides, we find a multitude of compound words of various kinds, and the sentences are joined together in an easy way which is apt to contribute largely towards a quick understanding of the general sense of passages. It is a genuine sister of Sanskrit, Greek, Latin, and Gothic; but we find her no longer in the prime of life; she is presented to us rather in her declining age. The forms are not always kept strictly distinct from each other, as is the case in Sanskrit, Greek, and Latin; but are now and then confounded, much less, however, in the verbs than in the nouns, where the dissolution first began; the crude form, *i. e.* the original uninflected state of the word, is often used instead of the originally inflected forms. So, for instance, we find *daêva* (the Indian gods) which is the very crude form, employed as the instrumental singular, which ought to be *daêvêna*, or at least *daêvâ*, and as nominative plural, which ought to be *daêvâoṇhô*, or at least *daêvâ*. The long vowels of the feminine in the nominative, *â* and *î*, are out of course, so that from the termination alone the gender is not so easily to be recognised as in Sanskrit; so we have *daêna*, creed, belief, instead of *daênâ*; moreover the forms of the dative and instrumental, chiefly in the plural, are often confounded. These deviations from the original forms, and the confusion of terminations are by far more frequent in the classical Zend, than in the Gâtha dialect, where the grammar in most cases is quite correct.

The chief reason of the grammatical defects of the present texts of the Zend-Avesta lies, I think, in the want of grammatical studies among the ancient Persians and Bactrians. Had the study of grammar, as a separate science, flourished among the ancient Mobeds and Dustoors, as was the case with Sanskrit among the ancient Brahmans, and had Iran produced men like

Pânini, Kâtyâyana, and Patanjali, who became the lawgivers of the classical Sanskrit language, we should have less ground to complain of the bad condition of the texts, and found less difficulties in explaining them, than we have now to encounter. There is every reason to believe, that the grammar of the Bactrian language was never fixed in any way by rules; thus the corruptions and abbreviations of forms, which gradually crept from the popular and colloquial into the written language, became unavoidable. In Sanskrit the grammarians built, by means of the numerous rules, under which every regular or irregular form of that language was brought, a strong bulwark against the importation of forms from the popular and vulgar language, which was marked by them as *Prâkrit*. Grammar became a separate branch of study; manuscripts were then either copied out or written in the strictest accordance with rules of grammar, but always with respect to phonetical peculiarities, especially in Vedic books, if they had any real foundation. To these grammatical studies of the Brahmans, which belong to an age gone by long ago, we chiefly owe the wonderfully correct and accurate grammatical state of the texts of the Vedas and other revered books of antiquity. In Iran almost all knowledge of the exact meaning of the terminations died out at the same time that the ancient Iranian languages underwent the change from inflected to uninflected ones. Books were extant and learnt by heart for religious purposes, as is still done by the Parsee priests. But when the language of the Zoroastrian books had become dead, there were no means for the priests, who cared more for a merely mechanical recital of the sacred texts, than for a real insight into their meaning, to prevent the corruptions of the texts. Ignorant of any thing like grammar, they copied them out merely mechanically like the monks in Europe in the middle ages, or wrote them down from memory, of course full of blunders and mistakes. For this reason, we find the copies, now in use by Mobeds and Dustoors, in the most deplorable condition as regards grammar; the terminations are often written as separate words, and vowels inserted according to the wrong pronunciation of the writer, where they ought to be omitted.

The best text, comparatively speaking, is to be found in the oldest copies only, while in Vedic manuscripts (if written for religious purposes) there is not the slightest difference, whether they are many centuries old, or executed at the present day. Westergaard has taken great trouble to give a correct text, chiefly according to the oldest manuscripts, which were accessible to him. His edition is in most cases far preferable to the manuscripts of the priests of modern times. The Dustoors, therefore, should consider it their bounden duty to agree on an accurate text according to the oldest manuscripts, which they could procure very easily. In this task they will be aided much by Westergaard's valuable edition, and the grammatical researches of other European scholars. Why will they remain behind the Brahmans and the Jews, who have preserved their sacred writings so well, and facilitated modern researches to so great an extent ? The era for a sound philological explanation of the time-hallowed fragments of the ancient Zoroastrian writings has now come, and the Dustoors as the spiritual guides of the Parsee community, should take a chief part in it. The darkness in which a good deal of this creed is enshrouded, must be dispelled. But the only way of attaining such a desirable result is a sound and critical knowledge of the language.

---

## 3—SOUNDS, VOWELS, AND CONSONANTS.

### (A) Vowels.

*a, â, ã ; i, î; u, û ; e, ĕ, ê (aê) ; o, ô ;—ai, âi ; au, ao ; âu, âo ; ĕu, êi (aêi) ; ou, oi, ôi ; ui, ûi.**

For so many vowels (12 simple, and many diphthongs) separate characters, or combinations thereof, are used in the Zend manu-

* The long vowels are marked by the circumflex. The vowels to be pronounced in the continental manner ; *ã* is a long *â* with a slight tinge of a nasal sound to be pronounced like *â* in the French *âme* soul ; *ôi* is equal to *ĕ*.

scripts; which fact shows clearly, that in ancient times each of them had its own pronunciation, but at present the priests pronounce several of them, such as *a* and *e*, and *o* and *u*, without any distinction. Therefore the original pronunciation of them can be only guessed by us rather than really ascertained.

Of the vowels given in the above list, I shall point out only such ones as are peculiar to Zend. Whilst the short and long *a*, *i*, *u*, *e*, *o*, &c., are easily understood by any one, *ã*, always occurring before *m* or *n*, is a long *á*, with a slight tinge of a nasal sound; it is chiefly used in the genitive plural termination *anãm*, *ãm*=S. *ánám.*—Of the *e* sounds, *e* and *ĕ* are to be noticed. Whilst the Sanskrit has only one *e*, which is always long, having originated from a fusion of *a* and *i*, the Zend has a short *e* besides, which has either no correspondent in Sanskrit, or which corresponds to the short *a*. This *e* is often in Zend a mere vehicle for facilitating the pronunciation. Quite peculiar is *ĕ*, which is a long vowel, and prevalent chiefly in the Gâtha dialect, where it often replaces the final *ó* of the usual Zend; for instance, *kĕ*, who?=*kó*; *yĕ*, who,=*yó*; *vachĕ*, word,=*vachô* &c. The writers confound it often with *í*, which circumstance seems to hint at its close affinity to that sound.

The frequent use of *a* before *é* and *ó* is very likely not a peculiarity of pronunciation, but of writing. The Zend texts are handed down to us not in their original characters, but in a later form* of writing, which arose very likely, shortly after the commencement of the Christian era, when Syriac literature began to spread in Persia. For the Zend characters are written from right to left, like all the Semitic alphabets (except the Himyaritic in South Arabia and the Aethiopic); while the Sanskrit, and the ancient Bactrian alphabets, such as are to be found on coins, and in the cuneiform inscriptions exhibiting the ancient Persian tongue, are written from left to right. The form of the Zend characters besides, bears a great resemblance to some Syriac alphabets. Now to revert to *aé* and *ao*

* As the Old Testament has been preserved in the Chaldee characters though originally written in the Samaritan.

at the beginning of words, it is a peculiarity of the Semitic languages to introduce every initial vowel by prefixing an *Elif* (a soft aspirate sound, generally rendered by *a*, but not exactly corresponding to it). This peculiarity has crept into the writings of the Zend texts, so that a word hardly ever commences with *é* but with *aé*. In the middle of words, *aê* may be a peculiar diphthong; for instance, in *viçpaêshãm* (genitive plural of *viçpa* all), etc.

In the Gâtha dialect, we observe this peculiarity that if words terminate in vowels, they terminate always in long, never in short ones. This lengthening of the vowels at the end extends even to the shortest of all, the short *e*, which, according to its origin, is not even to be considered as a full vowel (it is similar to the *shvá* in the Hebrew). So we find *rázarē* instead of *rázare*, rule, way, (Yas. 32, 12). The reason of this peculiar circumstance lies certainly not in the nature of the Gâtha dialect, but in the liturgical application of the pieces written therein. They are, as we shall see afterwards, the most important and holiest prayers used in the Zoroastrian divine service, and were originally sung (see p. 4. 8). The way of singing them was very likely analogous to that in which the Brahmans, the nearest relations of the Parsees, used to sing the verses of the *Sâmaveda* at the time of solemn sacrifices only, and which is preserved up to this day on such occasions. From hearing a Sâmaveda priest sing some verses of this Veda, one can ascertain, that he lengthens the terminating vowels of a word, even if they are short. In Sanskrit, where the grammar was fixed by rules, the texts were not changed according to the mode of singing them, while in Zend, where nothing regarding the grammar and pronunciation was settled, these peculiarities produced by singing the Gâthas and some other pieces, crept into the manuscripts, which were often written from memory only, as is now often the case.

On the changes of one vowel into another, I shall make but few remarks. There are in Zend two vowels, *i* and *u*, and one semivowel *y*, which change an original *a* preceding or following, into *ai*, *é* or *ó*, a circumstance, which we observe in the Teutonic languages also.* So instead of *barati*, he bears, we find *baraiti* (*ai* instead of *a*, influenced by the terminating *i*), *yêzi* or *yêidhi*, "if," instead of *yadi*, as it is in Sanskrit, *verezyêiti*, instead of *verezyati*, he works. Now and then the *y* which has produced the change of *a* into *ê*, disappears, e. g. *naçê* (Vend. 8, 21) imper. flee! perish! instead of *naçya* which is the regular form. In the Gâtha language we perceive, besides this change of *a* into *ai* or *ê*, that of *a* into *ô*, for instance, *verezyôtû*, instead of *verezyatû*, he may work; *vatôyôtû* for *vatayatu*, he may tell, announce (Yas. 35, 6).

---

## (B) Consonants.

Gutturals.—*k*, *kh*, *q*, *g*, *gh*, *h*.
Palatals.—*ch*, *j*.
Dentals.—*t*, *th*, *d*, *dh*.
Labials.—*p*, *f*, *b*.
Semivowels.—*y*, *r*, *v*, *w*.
Sibilants.—*ç*, *sh*, *s*, *z*, *zh*.
Nasals.—*m*, *n*, *ṅ*, *ṇ*, *ñ*.

I shall now make some remarks on the sounds which are peculiar to the Zend language. Of all gutturals *q* (corresponding to the Latin *qu*) is one of this sort; in modern Persian, *kho* corresponds with it, e. g. *khvâb*, sleep, in Zend *qafna* (S. *svapna*, Latin *somnus*, Greek *hypnos*). In the Gâtha dialect this sound is more frequent than in the usual Zend, e. g. *qyēm*, I may be, instead of *hyām*, Lat. *sim*; *çpeñtaqyâ* (gen. sing. of *çpeñta*, holy) instead of *çpeñtahê*.

The palatal sounds, *ch* and *j*, as well as the soft sibilants, *z* and *zh*, which are in many respects near to the palatals, are always changed into a harsh guttural sound *kh*, before *t*, *th* (confounded now and then with *dh*, e. g. *ukhdhem*, "what is spoken, a word, instead of *ukhthem*), and *s*: e. g. *berekhdha* "high, elevated,"

* Compare staff, pl. staves, *a* being pronounced in the plural like *ê* of the continental languages.

instead of *berezta*; *aokhta*, he spoke, instead of *avachta*, from *vach* to speak, *vâkh-s* nom. sg. speech, acc. sg. *vâchem*; *drukh-s* nom. sing., *drujem*, acc. sg., the palatal reappearing always immediately before vowels.

Among the dental class, *th* is of a peculiar nature, and not to be identified with *th* of the Sanskrit, which is simply an aspirate *t*; it is rather near to the English *th*. In most cases it is only a change of the simple *t* on account of its being followed by *r*, *w*, and sometimes *y*; e.g. *thri* S. *tri*, three, *thwâ* S. *tvâ*, thee; *ithyêjô* ruin (from the S. root *tyaj* to leave). A very instructive example occurs in *âtar-s*, fire; the gen. sg. is *âthrô*, the acc. *âtarem*, *t* being changed into *th* before *r*, and retained before the vowel. Now and then it corresponds with S. *th*; e. g. *atha*, then, after, S. *atha*. If a word terminates in *t*, we find generally a separate sign used for it; but it appears to be rather a calligraphic peculiarity than to imply a separate dental sound; for that reason I left distinguishing this final *t* (in certain words as *tbaêsh* S. *dvish* to hate, *tkaêsha* religion S. *dîkshâ*, it is used at the beginning also instead of the common *t*). *Dh*, the soft aspirate of the dental class, is not more strictly distinguished from the simple *d*, which fact causes now and then a confusion, rendering it, for instance, difficult to distinguish *dâ*, to give, from *dhâ*, to make, create.

Of the labial class *f* is not to be identified with S. *bh*; it is an aspiration of *p*, as *th* is of *t*, on account of its being followed by *r*, or *s* and *sh*; e. g. *fra* S. *pra*, Greek and Latin *pro*, for; *âfs*, water, (nom. sg. of *ap* water); *kerefs*, body, Lat. *corpus* (nom. sing. of *kerefs*); *fshu*, rich, monied. Among the semi-vowels we miss *l*, which in the ancient language seems not to have existed at all; in the Pehlevi and modern Persian we find it, but it is always traceable to an original *r*. In Sanskrit *l* is later than *r*, but it is already known to the Vedic dialect.

In sibilants, the Zend is peculiarly rich, even richer than Sanskrit. The *ç* (to be pronounced as *ss* like the French *ç*) is uniformly put for *t*, if another *t* follows; in Sanskrit one says *vitta* having possessed (from the root *vid* to possess, get), but in

Zend it is always changed into *viçta*,* (compare in Greek *oistha* =Zend *vôiçta*, thou knowest, from *oida*=S. *veda* I know). In the Gâtha dialect we find it often at the end of words instead of *t*, e. g. *çtavaç* instead of *çtavat*, praising. *Z* and *zh* are two soft sibilants, lacking the Sanskrit. Into these soft sounds the dental *d* is changed, if it meets another *d*, e. g. *dazdi*, give, instead of *dad-dhi*. In the Gâtha language, we sometimes find the peculiarity of changing *çt* into *zd* or *zhd*, when a soft sound, *b* or *g*, is in the following syllable, e. g. *azdēbis*, the instr. plur. of *açti*, existence, body (afterwards from ignorance used as a nominative), *vazhdrēng* acc. pl. of *vaçtra*, field.

Of the nasal sounds *ṇ* is used before *h*, e. g. *aṇhus* life, and inserted between *a* and *u* in certain forms, e. g. *merechaṇuha*, kill; *ń* is used before *h* and appears to be stronger, like *ng*. They have, however, nothing to do with the etymology, and are a mere produce of pronunciation; *ñ*, generally used before the dentals, seems to be a half nasal sound, like the Sanskrit Anusvâra.

---

## 4—ROOTS.

The last elements of an aggregate of sounds, which remain, after all the suffixes and terminations have been taken off, are denoted by the name of "root." For instance, to find out the root of *verezyêiti* "he works," first the termination of the 3rd pers. sg. present tense *ti*, and then *yêi* (*ya*), being the characteristic of the present tense and those words, that are derived from it, are to be taken off; the remaining part *verez* then is the root, to which the idea of "working" is attached. Most nouns being traceable to verbs, we shall confine ourselves to the enumeration of some verbal roots. Original roots are of course monosyllabic, consisting now and then of a single vowel only, or being a com-

* It is the first part of the name *Viçtâçpa* the orignal form of the Grecian *Hystaspes* meaning "possessing horses."

bination of a vowel with a simple or double consonant, or of two consonants with a vowel between them, e. g. *i* to go (in *aêiti* he goes S. *eti*, Latin *it*, he goes); *dâ* S. *dâ* to give; *vâ* to blow (*vâoñti*, they blow, *vâta* wind; *gâ* to go (in *gata*, gone); *çru* to hear; *mere* to die; *kere* to make; *mar* to speak, recite, (*framarâitê*, he announces); *char* to walk; *tach* to flow; *vakhsh* to grow; *vach* to speak; *mrû* to say (in *mraot*, he told); *bar* to bring; *as* to be (in *ahmi* I am, *âoṇhat* he was); *bû* to exist &c. From the simple roots others were derived by means of some additional sounds, which, of course, can change the meaning; so *dath* to place, is a derivation of *dhâ*, *dâ* to make, *mereñch* to kill, one of *mere* to die. Now and then we find a verbal root joined to a noun, in order to modify the meaning, e. g. *yaozhdâ*, *yaozh-dath* to purify, make clean. As to their practical use, the reader will soon become aware, that the roots are mere fictions of philology, abstract grammatical notions, but in order to obtain a thorough knowledge of a language, they are nevertheless very useful. They show the common origin of words, which, in the course of time have become different both in forms and sense. So *naçus* a corpse, (*nekys* in the Greek) and *naçaitê*, *nashaitê* he perishes, goes away, are of the same root: *naç*, S. *naç* to perish; *drukhs*, destruction, lie, *aiwidruzhaiti*, he belies, *aiwi-drukhtô*, a liar, are traceable to *druzh* S. *druh* to destroy; *frathwereçem*, I created and *thwôresta* creator, are derivations of *thwereç thwareç*, *thwôres* (only different pronunciation of the same root)=S. *tvaksh* to fabricate, make, create (literally "to cut"); *açti* existence, *ahmi* I am and *açtvâo* existing, come likewise from the root *as* to be.

---

## 5—CRUDE FORMS.

From the root, in which the notions of verbs and nouns are likewise contained, both are then distinguished by means of suffixes, or if they are left, at least by the terminations or inflexions. These new forms, produced in order to distinguish verbal and nominal notions, are called the crude forms ; to these then the inflexions only need being added to make the word complete. I shall illustrate this by some examples. To form from the root *naç* to perish, a noun meaning "what has perished," a dead body, the suffix *u* is required ; *naçu*, therefore, is the nominal crude form to which then the terminations may be added, as *naçu-s* nom. sg. *naçúm*, acc. sg. &c. Sometimes the inflexion is added without the previous formation of a proper crude form, e. g. *drukh-s*, lie, from the root *drush* (the soft *sh* is changed into the harsh *kh* on account of *s* being a harsh sound, see pag 55).

To make up the verbal crude forms, different modifications of the root, which produce a slight change of meaning, must take place. In order to impart, for instance, to the crude form of *çru*, to hear, the causal idea "to make hear, recite," it must be changed into *çrâvay*, or to the root *mereñch*, to kill, the desiderative idea "to wish to kill," it must be altered into *mimerekhsh*. Even the tenses often require a crude form, to which the terminations may be added. In order to form the present tense "he hears," or "he does" from the respective roots *çru* to hear and *kere* (*kar*) to make, the syllable *nu* (used also in Sanskrit and Greek, in certain verbs which conveys the meaning "now,") is to be added. Thus the crude forms of the present tense, *çurunu* (euphonically instead of *çrunu*) and *kerenu* are obtained, to which the termination of the third pers. sg. *ti* is to be joined. In this way, the word *çurunaoiti* (modern Persian *shunad*) "he hears" and *kerenaoiti*,* (modern Persian *kunad*) "he makes," are then formed; the literal meaning of both is hear-now-he, and do-now-he.

---

## 6—MODIFICATIONS OF THE VERBAL ROOTS.

There are three chief modifications of the verbal roots, irres-

* The original *u* of *nu* is changed into *o* before *ti*, in strict accordance with the rules of Sanskrit grammar, where in certain classes of verbs in the singular of the present tenses, active voice, the change of *u* into *ô*, and of *i* into *ê*, always takes place. This change is called *Guna* in Sanskrit grammar.

pective of tense or mood, to be observed viz. Causal, Desiderative, and Intensive forms.

1. CAUSAL FORMS, expressing the idea "to make, to get made," are very frequent in the Zend-Avesta. They are formed exactly in the same manner as in Sanskrit, by lengthening the vowel of the róot and adding the syllable *aya*. Examples: *kârayêiti* S. *kâragati*, he gets made (from the root *kere*, *kar*, to make); *tâpayêiti*, he makes hot (from the root *tap*, to be hot; to burn, Latin *tepere*); *jâmayêiti* (Yt. 17, 21). he makes go out, expels (from the root *jam* to go); *vî-shâvayat* (Vend. 2, 11). he made go asunder, (from *shu* to run, to go); *çrâvayêiti* he makes hear, recites (from *çru* to hear); *ava-çtayat*, he fixed, established, Vend. 2, 34. (from *çtâ* to stand); *khraoçyêiti* (an abbreviation of *khraoçayêiti*), he makes cry, i. e. scares, frightens Vend. 15, 5. (from *khruç* to cry, Persian *khurushîdan*); *dârayêhi*,* thou keepest (from *dar*, *dere*, to hold, modern Persian *dâshtan*).

Closely connected with the proper causal verbs, are the so called DENOMINATIVES, that is to say, verbs which are formed from nouns. Examples: *raêthwayêiti*, he pollutes, literally: touches with *raêthwem*, a fluid (now and then it means the fluid of light); *vyâkhmanyêiti*, Yt. 8, 15. he takes into consideration, derived from *vyâkhman* consideration; *pereçanyêiti*, "he puts the question," from *pereçana*, questioning. There is another way of forming DENOMINATIVES besides the causal suffix *aya*; that is the verbal root *dâ* to make, added to a noun. Examples: *paxdayêiti* Vend. 15, 5. he treads (the dog) with the foot, literally: he makes, applies his foot (*pad*, Latin *pes* foot); *yavô-dayât*, it might grow corn (lit. make corn); *çudhus-dayât*, it might be thrashed (lit. make thrashing); *pistrô-dayât*, it might be ground (lit. make grinding); *guñdô-dayât*, flour might be made (lit. it might make flour) Vend. 3, 32.

2. DESIDERATIVE forms, expressing the wish of obtaining any

* Yas 11, 8: *yô mãm aiwis-hutem dârayêhi* who keepest me, (Homa) without having squeezed my juice. *aiwis-hutem* consists of *hutem*, the past participle of *hu*, to squeeze, to prepare the Homa juice, and the negative *a* joined to *vis*, liquid, juice; *v* is changed into *w* on account of *a* having become *ai* in consequence of the *i* in *vi*

thing, are made up exactly in the same manner as in Sanskrit, viz. by reduplication of the first syllable and addition of *s* to the crude form before the terminations. Examples: *mimarekshâitê*, Vend. 15, 14. he endeavours to kill (from the root *mereñch* to kill); *çuruçrushemnô*,* Yt. 14, 21. desirous of hearing (from *çru*, to hear); *zishnâoṇhemnâo*,† Yt. 13, 49. wishing to know (from *zan* to know, in Sanskrit it sounds *jijnâsamânâh*, wishing to know). In the Gâtha dialect, these forms are on an average more frequent, than in the usual Zend, where they are gradually dying out. Examples from the Gâthas: *dîdereghzhô*, Yas. 44, 15. thou wishest to recite (from *dereñj* to recite prayers), *chikhshnushô*, thou wast desirous of worshipping Yas. 45, 9. (from *khshnu*, to satisfy one, to worship); *mimaghzhô*‡ Yas. 45, 10. thou wast desirous of magnifying (from the root *maz*, *magh*, to be great).

3. INTENSIVE FORMS serve the purpose of enhancing the strength of the verbal notion to make it more emphatic. The original way of forming them is to repeat the whole root, and then to join the terminations to it, thus put twice. Afterwards, as it is usual in Sanskrit, they lengthened only the vowel of the first part, and left out the consonants, which followed it; for instance, the Sanskrit *dêdîpyamâna*, very brightly shining, is an abbreviation of the original, *dîp-dipyamâna*. In Zend the original intensive forms prevail, while the abbreviations are rare. Examples: *nizhdare-dairyât*, Vend. 18, 38. he would tear out with great force (from *dar* to tear; Pers. *darîdân*); *fra-vâza-vazaiti*, Vend. 3,31. he furthers, promotes very much (from *vaz* to carry); *hareke-hare-chayât*, Vend. 5, 60. he would pour abundantly (from *harech* to emit, pour); *naênizhaiti*, Yt. 8, 43. he uproots (from *nizh*, to sweep away, clean, S. *nij*). In the Gâthas we find chiefly the abbreviated form of the Intensives. Examples: *râreshyantî*,

* *Vayãm vâchim çuruçrushemnô*, desirous of hearing the voice of birds.

† It ought to be *zizndoṇhemnâo*, the present participle, middle voice, nom. pl.; but the soft *z* is incompatible with *n*, therefore it is changed into the harsher *sh*; *h* in *hemnô* corresponds with *s* which is after *â* and before *e* generally made *h*.

‡ All these forms in *shô*, *zhô* are second persons sg. imperfect tense of the desiderative form.

Yas. 47, 4. they hurt repeatedly or very much (from *rash*, *resh* to hurt); *vôividâitê*, Yas. 30, 8. it is possessed, held completely (from *vid* to possess, get); *fravôividê*, Yas. 44, 11. I am well known (from *vid* to know).

---

## 7.—VOICES IN THE VERB.

There are three voices to be distinguished in Zend, as well as in Sanskrit and Greek: viz., the active, the middle or reflexive, and the passive. The first and third being well known and generally applied in the modern languages, only the second voice requires some remarks. I have called it the middle or reflexive voice ; it corresponds with the so called Âtmanêpadam in Sanskrit, the middle in Greek, and the deponent in Latin. According to its nature, it occupies the place between the active and passive voices, participating in the nature of both. Originally the middle voice served to express passive as well as reflexive notions, and it was only in the course of time that they established a proper passive form by the addition of *ya* to the root, but without changing the terminations. The original passive meaning of the reflexive voice is, however, now and then, chiefly in the participial forms, preserved. Examples: *hachaitê*, Yt. 8, 60 ; 10, 117 ; 14, 44. means "he is followed, accompanied, provided (*baêshaza* with medicaments), while the corresponding active form *hachaiti*, Yt. 10, 66. means "he follows," requiring an accusative (*yim hachaiti* whom he follows); in the same manner the pres. participle *hachimnô*, conveys merely the passive meaning "followed, provided"; *vazemnô*, Yt. 14. driven, drawn (by horses in a carriage); *baremnô*, borne (in a Palkee) Vend. 8, 73. In all these examples the passive meaning of the middle is evident, the formal passive voice would require the forms: *vaz-yamnô*, *bairyamnô*.

Closely connected with the passive is the reflexive notion, which prevails now in the forms of the middle voice. Thus in the very common middle voice form *yazamaidê*, we worship, the idea "for ourselves, our benefit," is implied. Other examples are: *viçanuha* Yt. 10, 32. (in an address made to the angel *Mithra*) come yourself to my offerings *i. e.* in person;* (*hîs*) *hãm-baraṇuha*, take these things together, receive them for thy own use! *ni* (*hîs*) *daçva*, deposit them for thy use (in thy heavenly abode)! These three forms, just quoted, are imperatives 2nd pers. sg. of the middle voice, and convey evidently a reflexive sense. The active imperative *bara* Yt. 5, 63. means simply "bring," but the corresponding middle form, *baranuha*, means, "bring for yourself" *i. e.* take. *Pereçem, apereçem*, impf. 1st pers. sg. act. means, I asked, put a question; but the corresponding form of the middle voice *apereçê* Vend. 2, 2. is, I conversed; the pres. partic. of the middle voice, *pereçmana* Yas. 30, 6. conversing, deliberating.

Often the meaning of this peculiar voice coincides with that of the active. So *mainyêiñtê*, they believe. To express intransitive or neutral notions this voice is of course more fit than the active; we find it, therefore, often applied for such purposes. Examples: *raodhahê* thou growest (from *rudh* to grow); *çaêtê* Vend. 18, 5. he lies down (from *çi* to lie down); *âçtê* he sits (from *âs* to sit).

---

## 8.—MOODS.

In the Zend language there are four chief moods, which can be used in all the three voices above mentioned, and are distinguished from each other by different characteristics. These four moods are as follows: INDICATIVE, SUBJUNCTIVE, POTENTIAL, and IMPERATIVE.

The INDICATIVE does not require any further remarks. Example: *barâmi* I bring; *mraomi* I say; *barat* he brought, &c.

* The Izad or angel was expected to come himself down from his celestial abode to his devotee, when worshipping him in the proper way.

## 9.—THE SUBJUNCTIVE.

There are two kinds of this mood to be found in the Zend-Avesta, one with long, and the other with short terminations, which both being lost to the classical Sanskrit, are extant in the ancient language of the Vedas also. The characteristic feature of these subjunctive moods is the constant insertion of *á* between the root and the termination, e. g. *van-â-iti, van-â-t* from *van* to destroy.

The FIRST SUBJUNCTIVE takes after its characteristic *â* before the terminations of the present tense indicative *mi, hi, ti* (see below) &c. e.g. *vaênâiti* Yt. 13, 84. he may look (from *vaên,* to see, Pers. *bîn-am,* I see). As to its meaning, we find it applied in various ways, it is commonly to be translated by "might, would or should." It can depend on particles such as *yat, yatha* that, in order that, or it can stand without them. Examples: *yaçe-thwâ* (*Anâhitãm*) *nôit aiwi-druzhâoñti* Yt. 5, 90. that they may not disturb thee (from *druzh* to destroy); *ava hô mairyâitê,* Vend. 7, 37. (and if) he should then die (from the root *mar* to die); *thwãm kainînô jaidhyâoñti,* Yt. 5, 87. the girls shall invoke thee (Anâhita); *niçrinavâhi,* Yt. 5, 87. thou shalt, mayest grant; *bavâhi* thou shalt be; *ava-jaçâi,* instead of *ava-jaçâhi,* Vend. 19, 18. thou shalt go; we find it in general sentences too, e. g. *tâo khshapanô yâo jvâhi,* Vend. 18, 27. for how many nights thou mightst still be living (from *jiv* to live).

Very frequently this first subjunctive mood serves to express the FUTURE TENSE, the original forms of which are dying out in Zend. The idea of the future, and that of the subjunctive are related to each other, both implying a state of uncertainty; in Latin the forms of both are very near also. Examples: *katha khâo tachâoñti* Yt. 8, 5. how will the wells flow (from the root *tach* to flow)? *viçpa drukhs nâshâitê* Yt. 2, 11. every evil doer will perish, or is to perish (from the root. *nâsh* to perish, go off); *jaçâiti tê avaṇhaêcha,* Yt. 1, 9. he will come to thy support (from *jaç* to come); *hô âoṇhâiti,* Yt. 13, 18. he will be (from *as* to be.)

The SECOND SUBJUNCTIVE has after its characteristic *â* only the shortened terminations of the imperfect, 3rd pers. sg. *ât*, 3rd pl. *ãn*, &c. This form is chiefly used in the sense of an Imperative, but in the third pers. sg. only, as *çtavât*, may he praise, let, him praise (from *çtu* to praise); *vanât* Yt. 19, 95. may he destroy let him destroy; *janât*, Yt. 3, 14. may he slay, let him slay. It can change places with the first Subjunctive and be used in conditional sentences conveying the sense of "should, would;" examples: *yat kereñtât*, Vend. 7, 37. if he should cut (from the root *kerent*, in the medical sense "to operate"); *viçpem â ahmât yat bavât* (a common phrase), all for the purpose that it should be, might be. Now and then it is applied to the future tense also, e. g. *kadha nô avi uzyarât*, Yt. 8, 5. when will he come to us? (from the root *ar* to go)

---

## 10.—POTENTIAL.

Of this mood we find two kinds, which, as to their formation, correspond exactly to the Potential (called *Ling*), and Precative (called *Ling Âçishi*) of the Sanskrit grammar. The chief characteristic of both is the addition of an *i* to the crude form of the present tense. In the first form, the proper Potential, this *i* only is required; but in the second, the Precative, *â* is to be added to it; thus we obtain, as the characteristic of this second form, the syllable *yâ* which is to be inserted between the root, or the crude form of the present tense, and the terminations.

The First Potential is of very frequent use, chiefly in the second and third persons sg. and pl.; it is easily recognised by the terminations *ôis* (2nd pers. sg. active voice),—*isa*, *aêsa* (2nd pers. sg. middle voice),—*ôit* (3rd pers. sg. act. voice),—*aêta*,—*îta* (3rd pers. sg. middle voice),—*aêta* (2nd pers. pl. act. voice),—*yadhwem* (2nd pers. pl. middle voice),—*ayen*, *yen* (3rd pers. pl. act. voice),—*yañta* (3rd pers. pl. middle voice). The first persons are but of rare occurrence; instead of them they use the first pers. imperative. We find, however, the following terminations: *aêm* (first pers. sg. act. v.),—*aêma*, (first pers. pl. act. v). e. g.

*jaçaêma*, we may come,—*ôimaidhê* (first pers. pl. middle v)., *búidhyôimaidhê*, Ys. 9, 21. we might awaken (from *budh* to awaken). Now and then we meet a dual form, ending in *aêtem*, *ayatem* (3rd pers. dual act. v).

The application of this first Potential is manifold. In the 2nd pers. it is very frequently used as a polite form of the imperative, when any thing is to be commanded or asked for. Ex. *frabarôis* thou shalt bring (from *bar* to bring); *hiñchôis* thou shalt sprinkle (from *hiñch* to sprinkle) ; *dreñjayôis* thou shalt recite (from *dreñj* to recite); *nipâyôis* thou shalt protect (from *pâ* to protect); *zbayaêsa* thou shalt invoke (from *zbê* to invoke); *fradaidhîsa* Yt. 3, 1. thou shalt keep (from *dhâ* to put); *âhisa* Yt. 10, 32. thou shalt sit (from *âh*, *âs* to sit); *çchiñdayadhwem* Yt. 1, 28. thou shalt cleave for yourselves (from the root *çchiñd* to cleave, Latin *scindo*) ; *vârayadhwem* you shall cover (from *var* to cover); *darezayadhwem* you shall chain (from *darez* to chain, fetter, bind) ; *upazôit* one shall strike, beat (from *zan* to strike, slay); *ava-barôit* he may bring hither ; *barayen* they shall bring. *chikayen* Vend. 15, 12. they shall atone (from *chi*, *ki* to atone, be punished ; it is instead of *chikayen*); *vâdhayaêta* Vend. 4, 44. he may give him in marriage (from *vâdh* to marry, carry home); *framaraêta* he may teach ; *içaêta* he may have, obtain for himself, (from *iç* to have, possess); *nishidhaêta* he may sit down (from *shadh* to sit); *âmayañta* Vend. 7, 37. they may learn ; *hañdarezayañta* they shall chain (from the root *darez* to fasten, make tight).

To express the idea of habitude, the Potential is used as the proper mood e. g. Vend. 4, 47. *yatha maghavô fravâkhshôit*, as the Magian priest is in the habit of reciting (from *vach* to speak) ; Vend. 3, 42. *yatha vâtô framarezôit* as the wind is in the habit of sweeping away (from *marez* to sweep); Yas. 12, 6. *Zarathustrô daêvâis vyâmrvitâ*, Zoroaster was in the habit of speaking against the Daêvas (from *mrû* to speak); *apereçayatem* Yas. 12, 6. these two used to converse.

The SECOND POTENTIAL, which we may style the Potential proper, is used as a PRECATIVE or with the negative *mâ* as a PROHI-

BITIVE and as a CONDITIONAL. The 2nd and 3rd persons prevail in this mood; in conditional sentences the first person is to be found also. The terminations are: 1st sg. *yãm*, 1st pl. *yama*; 2nd pers. sg. act. voice *yâo*, pl. *yata*; 3rd pers. sg. act. v. *yât*, pl. *yân*. Of the first and second persons in the middle voice I could discover no distinct traces; but the 3rd pers. pl. of this voice —*yâres*, is occasionally to be met with.

As to its meaning, it coincides often with the first Potential, but on account of its being a combination of the characteristics of both the Potential and the Subjunctive, it is more emphatical, and solemn than the simple Potential. Its proper place, therefore, is in praying, in imparting blessings, giving an exhortation or a command, or pronouncing curses; joined to the negative particle *mâ*, it is the strictest form of prohibiting a thing. Ex.: *çurunuyâo nô Mithra yaçnahê* Yt. 10, 32. mayst thou hear our prayers, Mithra!; *vaêibya nô ahubya nipayâo* Yt. 10, 93. mayst thou (Mithra) protect us in the two lives (the bodily and spiritual)! *bareçma fraçtarenuyâo* Yt. 12, 3. thou shalt spread the Barsom (from the root *çtar*, *çtere* to spread); *dayâo* Yt. 10,94. thou mayst give (from *dâ* to give); *buyâo* Ys. 62, 2. thou shalt be (from *bû* to be); *buyata*, Yt. 13, 147. you may or shall be; *mâ buyata* Vend. 18, 17. you must not be, do not be; *dâyata* Nyây. 3, 11. you may give (from *dâ*). Examples of the third person: *jamyât* Yt. 1, 33; 10, 5. he shall come (the angel who is invoked); *buyãn* Yt 16, 3. they shall be; *fratereçãn*, they shall fly; *fradvarãn* they shall run away, Yt. 11, 6. (from *tereç* to fear, and *dvar* to run). The vowel *â* is now and then shortened, e. g. *chikayat* Vend. 7, 38. instead of *chikayât*, he may atone. While the 3rd person sg. active voice of this form is rarely applied to express a command, or a wish (for which the 2nd Subjunctive is more usual), the 3rd pers. pl. middle voice, ending in *yâres*, seems to be more common in that sense. Ex.: *daithyâres* Vend. 8, 22. they shall put for themselves (from *dath* to put); *buyâres* Nyây. 3, 11. they shall be (from *bû* to be); *aiwi-çachyâres* Yt. 8, 56. (if they) should or might perform; *hyâre* Vend 17, 9. (these nails) shall be thy lances (from *as* to be).

It is frequently employed in conditional sentences, chiefly in the antecedent clause, introduced by the particle *yêzi* if. Ex. *yêidhi azem nôit daidhyãm* (potential of the perfect tense) Vend 1, 1. if I would not have created (perfect tense of *dhá*) ; *yêzi nôit uzvarezyát* Vend. 4, 25. if he should not atone for (from *varez* to do, to make ; *uz-varez* to do away with a thing, especially a sin by punishment) ; *ahmát hacha irishyát* Vend. 13, 38. and (if) he should be hurt (from *irish* to be hurt, wounded). In the consequent clause of conditional sentences, we find this mood also, see for instance Yt. 8, 11. where the star Tistrya, who brings the rains to mankind from a fabulous sea, says as follows : if men had invoked me with prayers, I had then gone forth (*shushuyãm* from *shu* to go ; it is a perfect form), I would have come (*jaghmyãm* from *gam* to come, perf. tense).

Now and then this precative and conditional mood is used in a strictly potential sense, expressing the faculty or ability to do a thing. Thus we read Vend. 6, 29. as much (*chvat*) as they can grasp (*hañgeurvayãn* : from *gerew* to take) with their hands.

---

## 11.—IMPERATIVE.

This mood, very frequently used, has various forms, which, although they agree with those of Sanskrit, have preserved some peculiarities. The most peculiar feature in these Imperative formations of the Zend and Sanskrit, is the first pers. used in sg. and pl. active and middle voices, a formation unknown to the other Arian tongues, where its want is supplied by conjunctive forms. We have just become aware of the unfrequent use of the first persons of the subjunctive and potential moods in the Zend. The reason is their having been absorbed, for the greater part, by these peculiar Imperative forms, which are very emphatical, expressing through the length of their forms very palpably the idea of intention and volition or duty : I will, I intend, I am resolved, &c. They are made up as follows :

1st pers. sg. act. voice *á*, *âni*, *a* ; middle voice, *ái*, *ânê* ; 1st pers. pl. act. voice *âma*, middle v., *âmaidê*. Ex. *avanayêni* Yt. 19,44. I will carry away (from *ní* to carry) ; *ava-barâni*, I will bring ; *janâni*, I will slay (from *jan* to slay) ; *varedhayêni* Vend 2. I will make grow (or, protect); *barâma*, let us bring ; *kva nidathâma* Vend 6,44. where must we lay down (a dead body) ? We find it often used after relative particles, as *yat*, *yatha*, e. g. *dazdi nô yat bavâma* Yt. 5,58. give us that we may be ; *yatha nijanâma* that we shall certainly slay. The middle form in *ânê* is quite peculiar to Zend, and wanting in Sanskrit. Ex. *víçâni* Vend. 2. I will go myself (from the root *viç* to go, enter, now and then to be taken in the general sense " to be") ; *fravarânê*, I will profess myself (the Zoroastrian religion ; from *var* to choose).

The plural of the middle voice *âmaidê* is rare ; we find it in the Gâtha dialect only ; see Yas. 58,3 : *nemanhê víçâmaidê* let us go for ourselves to prayer ; *nemanhê âvaêdayâmaidê*, let us devote ourselves to prayer (from *vid*, to know, the causal is *vaêday* ; with the preposition *á* it means " consecrate").

In the Gâthas the forms in *âni* are comparatively rare ; those in *á* and *ái* prevail. The form in *á*, being the ancient termination of the first pers. sing. imperative, is solely confined to these ancient prayers. Ex. : *pereçâ* Yas. 44, 1. 2, 3. I will ask ; *yâçâ* Yas. 28, 2. I will pray ; *zbayâ* Yas. 33, 5. I will worship ; *fravakhshyâ* Yas. 45, 1. I will promulgate (from *vach*, to speak, *vakhshya* being here the crude form of the future tense). Before the enclitic *cha* "and" this *á* is shortened to *a* e. g. *vaochacha* Yas. 45, 3. and I will tell.

Besides this Gâtha form in *á* we find one terminating in *ái* in both dialects, conveying the same sense, e. g. *khshnaoshâi* Ys. 46,1. I must worship (from *khshnu* to worship, *khshnaosh* is an Aorist form) ; *mĕñghâi* Ys. 43,4. I will have thought i. e. my wish was to think (from *man* to think, but in the crude form of the Aorist *mĕñg*, *mĕnh* S. *mans*), *mĕvâi* instead of *manyâi* Ys. 45,3. I will think ; *zbayâi* I will invoke ; *jaçâi* I will come, &c. in the usual Zend.

The 2nd pers. imperative active voice sg., terminates either in *a*, that is to say, in the crude form of the present tense; or, if there be another termination, as *nu*, added, or, if the crude form be identical with the root, in *di*, *dhi*. Ex.: *bara* bring! (here it ends in *bara*, which is the crude form of the present tense: *barâmi* I bring); *ava-jaça* come, hither (*jaçâmi* I come); *uçe-hista*, rise! (*ucehistâmi* I rise); *kerenûidhi*, make! (*kerenaomi* I make, from *kere* to make); *çtûidhi*, praise! (*çtaomi*, I praise, from the root *çtu* to praise); *mrûidhi* speak! (*mraomi*, I speak, from *mru*; now and then we find *mru* alone, e. g. *fra-mru* recite); *jaidhi* slay! Ys. 9, 30. (from *jan* to slay); *para-âidhi*, go to! Vend. 22,7. (from *i* to go); *dazdi** give! (from *dâ*) which is in the Gâthas always *daidî* give!; *gaidi*, go! (the Gâtha form, from *gâ* to go). The plural, active voice, terminates always in *ta*, e. g. *çtuta* praise ye! *pâta* protect ye! (from the root *pâ*, to protect); *uçehistata* rise ye! (from *çtâ* to stand, with *uç* to rise); *dâta* give ye!

The second pers. sg. middle voice terminates in *çva* and *aṇuha* which both correspond to the Sanskrit termination *sva*; e. g. *ni-daçva* put, place! Yt. 10, 32. (from *dath* to put); *çnayaṇuha* take a bath! Vend. 18, 19.; *jijishaṇuha*, send for, seek! Vend. 15, 13.; *nizbayaṇuha* invoke! Vend. 19, 13, 14.

To the Gâtha dialect the form in *aṇuha* is not known; there the original *shva*, *hva* is found, e. g. *kereshva* make! Ys. 40.; *gûshahvâ* hear, listen! Ys. 49, 6. (from *gush* to hear). The plural is *dûm*, e. g. *gûshôdûm* listen ye! Ys. 45,1. *thrâzdûm* save ye! Ys. 34, 7. (from *thrât* to protect, save).

The 3rd perss. imperative are of very frequent use, expressing the idea: let him do this or that! he may do! Now and then they are used in the meaning of a future tense, e. g. *jaṇheñtu* they are to come, they will come Vend. 2, 2. (from *jam* to come, *jaṇh* is the crude form of an Aorist). The terminations are as follows:—

Sg. act.—*tu*, pl. *ñtu*; sg. middle voice *tãm*; pl. *ñtãm*. Ex.: *vaṇhatu* he may put on clothes Vend 3, 19. (from *vaṇh* S. *vas* to put on clothes); *qaratu* he may eat! let him eat! (from *qar* to eat); *çraotu* he may hear; *mraotu* he may tell (from *çru*, to hear

* *Dazdi* in the Gâthas is the 3rd pers. sg. active voice, see Ys. 46, 8; 51,6.

and *mru* to tell); *açtu* he may be; let him be! *ayañtu* they may go, let them go (from *i* to go); *âfrineñtu* they may praise (from *frî* to love, be kind); *heñtu* they may be! (from *as* to be). The forms of the middle occur in the Gâtha dialect only,* as *nidyâtãm* Ys. 48,7. let him (*Aêshemô*, one of the bad spirits) be put down! (from *dâ* to put, with *ni* to put down);† *khsheñtãm*, instead of *khshayañtãm*, Ys. 48,5. they may have or possess (from *khshi* to have, possess). Besides we once find in the Gâthas Ys. 48,5. the 3rd pers. dual, middle voice, *verezyâtãm*, in the phrase *gavôi*‡ *verezyâtãm tãm*, two cows (a team) may till her (*Armaiti*, the soil).

In an old formula preserved in Vend 8,38. we find an imperative form terminating in *tât*, which agrees entirely with the ancient Vedic forms in *tât*.§ This formula is *nizhbereta nôit ainizhbereta nizhberetât*,|| let them bring out every thing to be brought out, which was not yet brought out!

## 12.—TENSES.

In the Zend language we find as many tenses as in the Sanskrit, although less than in the Greek, which is, as to tenses, the richest language of the Arian stock. We can distinguish one formation for the present, four for the past, and two for the future, which differ, as regards their crude forms, and partially in respect to their terminations.

* *Jaçeñtãm* Yt. 1, 25. is very likely such a form too, and to be translated, "they may, or shall come."

† Here the form is, properly speaking, passive, but that does not matter anything as to terminations; the passive and middle voice terminations in the present tense, imperative active, are one and the same.

‡ See Aitareya Brâhmana II, 6. (pag. 30 of my edition) *vapâm utkhidatât*, they may tear out the peritoneum!

§ *Gavôi* is a dual like *zaçtê*, the two hands, *ôi* being only another orthography of *ê*.

|| *Nizhbereta* is the past participle of the root *bere*, *bar* to bring, but in the meaning of a verbal adjective (as is frequently the case in the Greek) expressed in English by the termination "able;" *ainizhbereta* is the 3rd pers. sing. impert. middle voice with the augment *a* (a sign of the past). The relative pronoun is omitted.

The terminations are chiefly of two kinds, longer and shorter ones. The chief difference of the latter class from the former is the absence of the terminating vowel or consonant, or, under circumstances, of a whole syllable, which form part of the former kind, e. g. *mi* (1st sg. act. v.) becomes *m*; *añti* is made *ân*, *en*, &c.

The longer forms are used in the present tense, the first subjunctive and the first future tenses, the shorter in the two potentials, the second subjunctive, the imperfect, aorist, and pluperfect, and to a certain extent, with some modifications, in the perfect tense. The imperative has its peculiar terminations, as we have seen. I shall give here the terminations of both the present tense and the imperfect.

| PRESENT TENSE. | | | IMPERFECT. | | |
|---|---|---|---|---|---|
| | Active voice | Middle | | Act. | Middle |
| Sg. 1 | *mi* | *é* | Sg. 1 | *m* | *é*[1] |
| „ 2 | *hi* | *hé* | „ 2 | *s*, *ô* | *e*, *he*[2] |
| „ 3 | *ti* | *té* | „ 3 | *t* | *ta* |
| Dual 1 | *vahi* | | Dual 1 | *âva*[3] | none |
| „ 2 | not more extant | | „ 2 | none | none |
| „ 3 | *tô*, *thô*[6] | *ôithê*[4] | „ 3 | *tem* | *ôithê*[4] |
| Plural 1 | *mahi*, | *maidê* | Plural 1 | *ma* | *madi* (*maidi*[5]) |
| „ 2 | *tha*, | *dûm* G., *dhwem* | „ 2 | *ta* | *dhwem* |
| „ 3 | *ñti* | *ñté* | „ 3 | *en*, *ãn* | *añta* |

[1] *Aguzê* Yt. 17,58. I concealed myself (from the root *guz* S. *guh* to hide).

[2] *Apereçe* or *apereçê* Vend 2,1. thou hadst a conversation; it is very likely a contraction of *apereççe (he)*.

[3] *Bavâva* Vend 5,25. "as far as we two were above the earth" (*âcha pairicha* literally: up to and towards the earth).

[4] *içôithê* Vend 8,10. you two keep; *aç-zayôithê* Ys. 9,10. they two were born (imperf).

[5] *Vairîmaidî* Ys. 35,3. we chose, believed, *mainimaidî* we thought.

[6] *Yûidhyathô* Yt. 8,22. they two fight.

## 13.—CHARACTERISTICS OF THE CRUDE FORMS OF THE PRESENT TENSE.

The crude form, out of which the proper present tense is formed, extends not only to the Indicative, Subjunctive, and Potential moods, of which in most cases no other tense is extant, but to the Imperative and the Imperfect (the first past tense) also. According to the nature of this crude form, the verbs are brought in Sanskrit under ten heads, all of which are to be found in the Zend too. I shall enumerate here the different crude forms of the present tense according to the order introduced by the Sanskrit grammarians.

Class I inserts *a* between the root and termination, and changes *i* or *u* of the root into their respectives gunas *ê* and *ô* (see page 59 note.) Ex. *vaz-â-mi** I carry; *bar-ai-ti* he brings; *baodh-ai-tê* Yt. 17,6. he awakens; *bañd-â-mi* I bind, tie; *gerez-ai-ti*, he cries, weeps; *fratereç-ai-ti* he flees away.

Class II adds the termination immediately to the root; the vowel of the root, if *i* or *u*, is respectively made *ê* and *ô* before the terminations of the sg. active voice (the 2nd person is now and then excepted), and in some persons of the Imperative, 3rd sing. act. and 2nd pl. act. Ex: *çtaomi*, I praise, *çtaoiti*, he praises; *çtavãn*, they praised (from *çtu* to praise); *nipâ-hi* thou protectest, *nipâiti*, he protects (from *pâ* to protect); *mrao-mi* I speak, *mraos* thou spokest, *mrvañti* they speak (from *mrû* to speak); *aêiti* he goes (from *i* to go); *jaiñti*, he slays (from *jan*), *ghneñtê* Yt. 10, 133. they are slain (from *jan*); *jvaiñti* Vend. 2, 41. they live (from *jiv* to live).

Class III reduplicates the root; the terminations are then added immediately. Ex. *dadhãmi* I put, *dadhahi* thou putst, *dadhaiti* he puts; *dadhemahi* we put, *daçta*† you put, *dadaiñti* they put (from the root *dâ*, *dhâ* to put, confounded with *dâ* to give, both being entirely identical in their conjugation); *zazâiti* he pro-

* The inserted *a* is made *â* before the terminations of the first persons of all three numbers; in the other persons it is short.

† A contraction of *dadatha*; *dazda* in the most sacred prayer *yathâ ahû vairyô* is a Gâtha form of the 2nd pers. plur. act, of the root *dâ*.

duces, generates (from *zan* to produce), *zîzananti* Yt. 13, 15. they produce (the intensive of the same root); *zaozaomî* Ys. 43,10. (Sanskrit *juhomi*) I invoke, from the root *zu*.

Class IV adds the syllable *ya* to the root. Ex. *verezyêiti* instead of *verez-ya-ti*, he works, tills the soil (from *verez*), *mainyêiñtê* they believe (from *man* to think, to believe).

Class V marks the present by the addition of *nu* to the root; the same change of the vowel of the root takes place as in the 2nd class. Ex. *kerenaoiti* he makes (from *kere*); *çurunaoiti* he hears, *haonaoiti* Yt. 2,11.* he hears, (only dialectically differing from the first); *hunaoiti*, he prepares the Homa (from *hu*); *frapinaoiti* he pours out, propagates (from *pi*); *ashnaoiti* he hits, reaches (from *ash*).

Class VI is identical with the first, save the change of the vowel of the root, *i* or *u*, into *ê* or *ô*. Ex. *tuçen*, they coughed (*tuç*), *qîçen* they whined (*qiç*).

Class VII incorporates the syllable *na*, which marks the present tense, to the root itself, as in the Sanskrit; see, for instance, *runadhmi* I hinder, from *rudh*, *na* being inserted between *r* and *dh*. Of this class I know only one example in the Zend, viz. *chinahmi*, Ys. 12, 1. *chinaçti* Ys. 19., being to be traced to the root *chith*, *chiç* to perceive, get aware; the first form means: I ascribe, I acknowledge; the second: he ascribes, attributes (as a consequence of his having perceived).

Class VIII is almost identical with the 5th; it adds only *u* to the root, instead of *nu*, but the roots end mostly in *n*. Ex.: *fraçtanvanti* Yt. 10,20. they are stretching themselves (from the root *tan* to stretch).

Class IX adds *nâ* to the root. Ex. *gerewnâiti* he seizes, *gerewnãn* they seized (from the root *gerew*, to seize, take).

Class X adds *aya* to the root, and is the proper causal and denominative form (see page 60). Ex. *nipayêmi* I protect (from *pâ* to protect).

* This small piece, being an old spell, shows several peculiarities, which belong very likely to the popular, and not to the written language.

## 14.—PARADIGMS OF THE PRESENT TENSES OF SOME VERY COMMON VERBS.

(*bû*, to exist, *mrû* to speak; *aç* to be; *verez* to work; *kere*, *kar*, to make, &c.)

| Active voice. | Middle voice. |
|---|---|
| 1st Sing. *barâ-mi*, I bring.<br>,, *mrao-mi*, I speak.<br>,, *ah-mi*, I am.<br>,, *verezyâ-mi*, I work (Yt. 15, 44).<br>,, *kerenao-mi*, I make. | 1st Sing. *buyê*.<br>,, *mruyê*, I speak myself.<br>,, *içê*,* I have, or possess. (Ys. 50, 1).<br>,, *âzby-a*, I invoke. (Ys. 15, 1).<br>,, *tanav-a*, I cast (him) down. (Ys. 19,7). |
| 2nd Sing. *hista-hi*, thou standest.<br>,, *barâ-hi* (subjunct.)<br>,, *ahi*, thou art.<br>,, *verezyê-hi*, thou workest.<br>,, *kerenû-ishi*, thou makest.<br>,, *huna-hi*, thou art getting with child. Vend. 18, 30.<br>Gâtha forms. { ,, *dôi-shi*, thou seest.<br>,, *vashî*(instead of *vaç-shi*), thou wilt.<br>,, *haf-shî*, thou holdest. Ys. 43, 4. } | 2nd Sing. *raodha-hê*, thou growest. |
| 3rd Sing. *bava-iti*, he exists<br>,, *aç-ti*, he is.<br>,, *verezyê-iti*, he works.<br>,, *kerenao-iti*, he makes<br>,, *mrao-iti*, he says. | *baraitê*, he brings<br>*mrûtê*, he speaks.<br>*mainyêtê*, he thinks.<br>*verenvaitê*, he teaches. Ys. 31, 17. |

* It is very likely the middle voice form of *aç* "to be," *a* having been changed in to *i*, on account of the heavier terminations of the middle voice.

| | | |
|---|---|---|
| | 1st Pl. *barâ-mahi* we bring.<br>„ *mahi*, we are. Ys. 35, 2. | 1st Pl. *barâ-maidhê*.<br>„ (3) *içâ-maidê*, we possess, have. Ys. 35, 7.<br>„ (2) *mrû-maidê*.<br>„ *dade-maidê* G. form.<br>„ *vare-maidê*, we choose. |
| Gâtha forms. | „ *vrezyâ-mahi*, we work. Ys. 35, 7.<br>„ *nemagyâ-mahi*, we bring praise.<br>„ *uç-mahi*, we wish. | |
| | 2nd Pl. *çta*, you are. | 2nd Pl. *thwarôzh-dûm*, you cut, prepare. Ys. 29, 1.<br>„ *fravôiz-dûm*, you teach, instruct. Ys. 33, 8. |
| Gâtha forms. | „ *isha-tha*, you come.<br>„ *çûsha-tha*, you perform. | |
| | *taurvaya-ta*, you defeat. Ys. 13, 38. | |
| | 3rd Pl. *bavai-ñti*, they exist.<br>„ *heñti*, they are.<br>„ *verezi-ñti*, (instead of *verezyêiñti*), they work, do. Vend. 15, 5.<br>„ *kerenavañti*, they make.<br>„ *jvai-ñti*, they live. | 3rd Pl. *mainyêiñtê*, they believe.<br>„ *verenv-aiñtê*, they cover. Vend 18, 32.<br>„ *fradhentê*, they thrive.<br>„ *viçeñtê*, they come, appear.<br>„ *pereçeñtê*, they converse. |
| | 1st Dual *uç-vahî*, we two wish. Ys. 46, 16.<br>3rd „ *jaça-tô*, they two come.<br>„ *çtô*, they two are. | 3rd Pl. *iç-ôithê*, they two keep. |

## 15.—PAST TENSES.

### Imperfect, Perfect, First and Second Aorists.

The past tenses of the Zend are as various as those of its ancient sister tongues. We can distinguish three ways of forming them, viz.: (*a*) augmentation, (*b*) reduplication, (*c*) composition with the past tense of the auxiliary verb, *aç*, to be.

(A.) Augmentation consists in prefixing a short *a*, either to the verbal root, or to the crude form of the present tense; in both cases, the terminations which are to be added, are shortened. This augment early became unintelligible, and was often left out; hence it does not regularly appear in the Zend. Both forms are in fact imperfects, and to be found in the Sanskrit and Greek also, where the grammarians made a distinction. The Greeks called the first formation SECOND AORIST (indefinite tense), the second IMPERFECT. As to the meaning of both formations almost no difference is to be discovered; the shorter form, which is to be regarded as the older, was, on account of its being too in distinct, in most cases superseded by the longer, the proper imperfect.

We find more frequent use made of the shortest (second Aorist) form in the more ancient Gâtha dialect, than in the usual Zend, where it is very rare; the augment there is always left out. Ex. 1st sg. *dãm** Ys. 48, 7. I gave, entrusted; 2nd sg. *dâo* Ys. 43, 1. thou gavest; 3rd sg. *dât* Ys. 31, 18. he gave (the same form is to be found in the Yashts 9,26.); *ni-dâma* Ys. 45, 8. we put down; *dâta* Ys. 29, 10. you gave; *dã*, *dãn* Ys. 45, 5. 47, 1. they gave; *dâitê*, Ys. 31, 11. middle v., he gives himself; *pât* Ys. 32,13. he protected (from *pâ* to protect); *gât* Ys. 46,6. he went (from *gâ* to go).

Of augmented imperfect forms I shall quote here only a few instances; the other imperfect forms will be found afterwards: *açrûdûm* 2nd pers. pl. middle v. Ys. 32, 3. you were heard of (from *çrû* to hear); *açperezata* Ys. 31, 16. 3rd pers. sg. middle v., he aspired after (from the root *çperez*); *aokhta*, 3rd pers. sg. middle v., he spoke; *apereçat*= *pereçat*, he asked; *advareñta* Vend. 19, 45. they ran; *adâunta*, they spoke (from *dvar*, to run, and *dav*, to speak, both terms ap-

* To both *â* is prefixed. It appears doubtful to me, whether this *â* is the preposition ort he lengthening of the augment *a*.

plied to the doings of evil spirits only) ; *apereçê*, I conversed, Vend. 2,2. In the Gâthas the augment is now and then used without any reference to the past time. So Yas. 30,2. *avaênatâ* which conveys evidently the sense of an imperative : look ye! and Ys. 44,14. *anâsê*, I may or shall drive away (from *nâs*).

(B.) Reduplication is the repetition of the whole root, if very short, or, if longer, of one consonant with a vowel at least. The vowel of the reduplicated syllable ought to be short, but we find it often long; the consonant differs sometimes from that of the root also. If the consonants of the root be a guttural : *k*, *g*, then, in the reduplication, we find always the corresponding palatal : *ch*, *j*; if it be a sibilant, generally *h* is used. The meaning attached to this reduplication is that of completing an action or state, expressing what is done and over, *i. e.* the past time. It forms, therefore, in the ancient Arian languages, such as Sanskrit, Zend, Latin, Greek, Gothic, &c., the real past tense, generally called, PERFECT ; e. g. *dâdareça*, I have seen, S. *dadarça*, Greek *dedorka* (from *dareç* to see), wholly distinct from the imperfect *dareçem*, I saw. The terminations of the Perfect differ from those of the present tense as well as from the Imperfect, yet they stand nearer to the latter. The terminations, as far as we can ascertain them from the scanty texts, are as follows :

Active v. sg. 1st and 3rd—*a*.

" " " 2nd *tha*.

" " " pl. 1st *ma* ; 2nd *tha* ; 3rd *us*.*

Dual. 3rd *âtare*.†

Middle sg. 1st and 3rd *ê*, 2nd *sa*.

" " dual 3rd *âitê*.‡

" pl. 3rd *are*, *ere*.

To this reduplicated form, however, the terminations of the Imperfect, with or without the augment, can be added ; then we

* Ys. 50,10 *aêurus* they have gone (from the root *ere*, *ir* to go).

† Ys. 13,4. *vaochâtarê* they two have spoken, *vâvarezâtarê*, they two have wrought.

‡ Ys. 13,4. *mamanâitê* they two have thought. These three dual forms belong to the Gâthâ dialect only.

obtain the pure PLUPERFECT, e. g. *ava-jaghnat*, Yt. 13,105. he had slain (from the root *jan*, a modification of *ghan*, to slay).

(C.) Composition of the verbal root with the past tense of *aç*, to be, makes a new tense altogether; it is according to its nature the most general past tense. The Greek grammarians call it the FIRST AORIST; in the Sanskrit grammar it is one of the many *Lung* forms; in Latin it is mixed up with the reduplicated past tenses, being no more a separate past tense; for instance, the reduplicated *tutudi* I have thrust, is the perfect of *tundo*, and *scrip-si*, I have written, that of *scribo*, I write. These forms are, however, in the usual Zend very scarce; in the Gâtha dialect which, being more ancient, shows a greater richness in forms, we find them now and then employed. The original *s* is sometimes changed into *h* or *ç*. Ex. *çtâoṇhat*, 3rd pers. sg. act., he placed (from *çtâ* to stand); *mãçta* 3rd pers. sing middle Vend. 2, 31. he thought; *mĕṅhâ (cha)* Ys. 13,5. 2nd pers sg. middle v., thou thoughtst; *mĕṅhî* 1st pers. sg. middle v. Yas. 43, 5. I thought; which three forms are traceable to the same root, *man*, to think, used in the Zend, as well as in the Sanscrit, exclusively in the middle voice. The literal meaning of these forms is: thinking was he, wast thou, was I, (*mãçta*=*man* and *açta* or *çta* middle of v. *aç* to be); other forms of this kind, which are found in the Gâtha dialect, are: *dâoṇhô* Ys. 34,1. 44,18. 2nd pers. sg. subjunct, middle v., that thou mightst give; the meaning of the past is not adhered to; in the corresponding *dâoṇhê*, 2nd pers. sg. middle v. Ys. 36,1. "thou putst," we find it kept; the root in both cases is *dâ*; *çĕṅghûs* 3rd pers. pl. Ys. 34, 7. they indicated, pointed out (from *çaṇh*, *çah* to say, promulgate; *h* of the root is changed into *g* on account of the *h* of the termination, two *h* never being allowed to meet). Now and then we find these forms used without any reference to the past; so Ys. 11, 18. *râhî* 1st pers. sg. middle (from *râ*, to give), means, "I give, present" you, and not "I gave."

## 16.—THE IMPERFECT.

Of all past tenses, the imperfect, which is most frequently used, is chiefly employed in describing past events, or state of things. I shall give here a list of these forms selected from the texts.

1st pers. sing. act. *dadhãm*, I created (from *dhâ*) ; *vîdhâraêm*, Ys. 13,2. I held, kept (from *dhar* to hold, keep).

1st pers. sg. middle *aguzê*, I concealed myself (from *guz*) ; *apereçê*, I conversed (from *pereç*).

2nd pers. sg. act. *pereçô*, thou askedst ; *apajaçô*, thou wentst away ; *irithyô* Yt. 22, 16. thou diedst ; 2nd sg. middle v. *mairyanuha* Yt. 22, 34. thou diedst (from *mar*, *mere* to die) ; *uçzayanha* Ys. 9, 13. thou wast born (root *zan*) ; 3rd pers. sg. act. *apereçat*, he asked, *ashnaot*, he reached, (from *ash* to reach, obtain), *frashûçat*, he stepped forward (root, *shûç*), *âç*, *aç*, he was (root *aç* to be) ; 3rd pers. sg. middle v. *fra-manyata*, he meditated, *ni-shaçta*, he sat down (root *sad* to sit), *uzdaçta*, he offered (r. *dâ*), *yazata*, he worshipped (r. *yaz*), *çtayata*, he placed (causal of *çtâ* to stand) ; 3rd pers. dual act. *apereçayatem* Ys. 12, 5. they two conversed, *fra-chaêshaêtem* Yt. 8, 38. they two searched after him (r. *chish*, to search, inquire); *pairi-avâtem* Yt. 13, 77. they two were helping ; 1st pers. pl. act. *fra-vaochâma*, we pronounced (r. *vach*, to speak) ; 2nd pl. act. *taurvayata*, you defeated ; 3rd act. *vaênen*, they saw, *anhen*, *hen*, they were (r. *aç* to be) ; 3rd middle v. *fraoreñta*, they professed (r. *var* to choose, profess a religion), *advarenta*, they ran (r. *dvar* to run).

---

## 17.—THE PERFECT AND PLUPERFECT.

The perfect, denoting the completion of an action, does not frequently occur, neither in the usual Zend, nor in the Gâtha dialect. Example : 1st pers. sg. act. : *dâdareça*, I have seen; *fra-dadâtha*, thou hast furthered; *vôiçta*,* thou knowest; 3rd pers. sing. *dadha*, he has created; *tatasha*, he has prepared (r. *tash* to cut, prepare); *vavacha*, he has spoken; *âoṇha*, he has been (r. *aç* to be); *tûtava*, he was able (r. *tu* to be able); *vîvaêdha* Yt. 13, 99. he has broken (r. *vidh* to break, S. *vyadh* to slay); *chakana* Yt. 22,11. he has loved (r. *kan* to love, like); *jighaurva*, has given a smell (root *ghaurv* S. *ghrâ* to smack). 1st pers. pl. act. *çuçruma* Yt. 13, 48. we have heard; *châkhrare*, they have done (r. *kar*, *kere*); *irîrithare*, they are dead (r. *irith* to die); *dâdhare* Yt. 19, 6. they have given. 1st pers. sg. middle v. *çuçruyê* Yt. 17,17. I have heard; 2nd sg. *urûrudhusa*, thou hast grown (root *rudh* to grow); 3rd. *tuthruyê*, has fashioned (root *thru* to form, fashion); *daidhê* Yt. 5, 130. has placed.

A peculiar perfect form is *yaêshê* Yt. 13, 99. where the reduplication is lost (the regular form would be *yêyêshê*) and, in order to compensate that loss, the vowel of the root lengthened. The root is here *yaç*, *yah* S. *yas*, to make efforts, handle, and to hurt, violate. In the passage alleged it means: he has damaged, hurt. Formations of this kind are frequent in Sanskrit, Latin, (*fregi* I have broken instead of *fafragi* from *frango*, I break) and the Teutonic (compare, for instance, the modern English *I held* with the gothic form *haihald* from *haldan* hold) languages.

The pluperfect is very rare; unmistakable instances are: *jaghmat* Yt. 19,12. he had come, *ava-jâghnât*, he had slain; *shushuyãm* Yt. 8,11. I had moved, *jaghmyãm*, I had come (both forms being in the potential mood).

## 18.—FUTURE TENSE.

The way of expressing future time being not so settled as that of expressing the ideas of the present and past, we find various contrivances employed for answering this purpose, the number of which is greater than in any other of the cognate languages. We meet

* Root: *vid* to know, *vaêda* I know. According to its terminations it is a mere perfect, but the meaning is that of the present; it corresponds exactly to the Greek *oida*, I know, 2nd pers. S. *oistha*.

with the forms applied in the Sanskrit, Greek and Litthuanian, as well as those used in Latin, and the ancient Teutonic languages.

The two future formations of the Sanskrit, the simple, consisting in the addition *sya* to the verbal root, and the periphrastic, compounded of a noun expressing the doer with an auxiliary verb (as for instance S. *kartâ smi* lit. I am a doer, means, I shall do), are to be met with in a few instances only. Ex. *vakhshyâ* Ys. 30,1. I shall tell (root *vach* to tell). It is more frequent in participle formations, e. g. *bûshyantya*, what is about to be, will be, *zãhyamâna*, what is about to be born (root *zan* to produce), *uzdâhyamana* what is about to be offered (root *dâ*), *haoshyañta* Vis p. 9, 3. what is about to be squeezed (r. *hu* to squeeze the Homa juice). Of the other Sanskrit future formation I know only one instance in the Zend texts ; *parsta* Vend 11,11. it will destroy, lit. is destroyer (root *pereth* to destroy).

Now and then we find one of the Aorists (that with *s*, *h*,) with the terminations of the present tense used for a future, e. g. *jënghaiti*, Ys. 31,14. it will come (r. *jam* to come).

In the frequent phrase Ys. 33,10. " who are, and who were, and who will be," we find the future expressed simply by *bavaiñti*, the pres. of *bû* to be. Even the imperfect of *bû* is used in that sense, e. g. *bvat*, in a shortened form, Vend 2, 5. he will be, *bun*, Vend 11, 2. they will be ; in composition with a participle : *pereçemnô bva*, Vend. 18, 29. I shall be asking, I shall ask.

The most common way of expressing futurity is, however, the application of the two kinds of subjunctives above mentioned (see pagg. 64.65.)

---

## 19.—PASSIVE FORMS.

The passive forms generally agree with those of the middle voice, except that the syllable *ya* is added to the roots. In the 3rd pers. sg. imperf. a peculiar form is to be observed, which, however, entirely agrees with the Sanskrit. Ex. *janyâontê*, they are slain (r. *jan*), *zayâontê*, they are born (r. *zan*), *vidhayêintê*, they are deposited (r. *dhâ*).

3rd pers. sg. imperf. *çrâvî*, it was heard (*çru* to hear); *avâchi*, it was spoken, said; (r. *vach*), *jaini*, he was slain (r. *jan*), *erenâvi*, was obtained, (r. *ere*, to go), *mraot*, Ys. 32,14. was told (root *mrû*, to tell).

---

## 20.—PARTICIPLES.

In participles the Zend is as rich as any of the sister languages. Grammatically all participles being subject to declension are considered as nouns.

*(a)*. Present participle, active voice.—It is made up by the addition of the syllable *at* (or in its fuller form *ant*) to the crude form of the present tense, as is the case in the sister languages, Sanskrit, Latin, etc. This crude form of the participle, in consequence of its always taking nominal terminations, except if forming part of a compound word, generally may be recognised not from its nominative, but from its oblique cases, or from its being part of a compound. Ex. *barat-zaothrem*, bringing an offering (consisting of sacred water), *tachat*, Vend. 8, 100. running, in running, when running (r. *tach*, to run), *bareñtem*, accus. sg. of *barat*, *barent*, bringing; the nominative termination in *ãç* e. g. *khshayãç* Ys. 49,12. ruling (r. *khshi* to rule), *yâçãc*, worshipping (instead of *yâç-ant-s*, *khshy-ant-s*, *s* being the sign of the nominative, compare Latin *amans*, loving, instead of *am-ant-s*). In the Gâthas we find now and then simply *aç*, e. g. *çtavaç* Ys. 45,6. praising (r. *çtu*). In the usual Zend the nominative sounds often *ô* only, e. g. *çrâvayô*, praying, *açrâvayô*, not praying (instead of *çrâvayãç* acc. *çrâvayantem*), *açâchayô* Vend. 18, 5. not teaching, *açikhshô*, not learning; before *cha*, *chit* this *ô* is changed into its original form, *aç*, e. g. *jvaçchit*, if living, (r. *jiv*) to live. Instead of the termination *ant* we meet now and then, chiefly in the Gâthas, with that in *an* only, e. g. *avaṇhan*, dat. *avaṇhânê*, helping, *mãthran* speaking, *çpaçânô* Vend 13,28. nom. pl. seeing (r. *çpaç* to see), *evindânô* nom. pl. not finding (r. *vind*, to find).

*(b.)* Past participle, active voice.—It is formed in the same way as in Sanskrit and Greek, by the addition of the syllable

*vat*, sounding in its nominative case, masculine gender, generally *vâo*, feminine gender *ushi*, in the oblique cases *vant* (as in the acc.), or *vat* (as in the instrumental) or *ush* to the root e. g. *vîd-vâo* knowing (lit. one who has acquired knowledge), fem. *vîd-ushi*, *vîdushê* dat. sing. to one knowing. Ex. *jaghnvâo* Yt. 10, 71. having slain, defeated (r. *jan*, *ghan*, to defeat); *mamanus* Yt. 8,39. having thought, resolved upon (root *man*), *chichithushîm* Vend. 18,69. acc. fem., having known (r. *chith* to know); *vaokushê* Yt. 13, 88. to him who has spoken (r. *vach*); *vâverezushê*, to him who has wrought (root *verez* to work); *biwivâo* Yt. 11, 5. 13, 41. having become afraid, frightened (r. *bî* to fear).

*(c.)* Participles of the future tense.—See above under the "future tense."

(*d.*) Present participles of the middle and passive voices.—Of these there are two formations, of very frequent use, the one adding *ana*, and the other *mana*, or *mena*, or *mna*, to the crude form of the present tense. Ex. *pereçmana*, carrying on a conversation (root *pereç*), *frabûidhyamana*, passive Vend. 18, 49. awakened, when being awakened (r. *budh* to awaken), *verezimna*, wrought, done, *aojanó*, saying (r. *aoj*=*vach* to say), *çrayanó*, begging (r. *çri* to go for), *âçtavana* Vend. 3, 40. invoking, praising (r. *çtu*).

(*e.*) Past participle passive voice.—It is formed by the addition of *ta* to the root. Its meaning is in the majority of cases a passive one; but we find it now and then used in a merely active sense, as is the case in modern Persian, also, e. g. *âçtûtó*, Vend. 3, 40. reciting, *varetó* Ys. 45, 1. choosing, professing (r. *var* to choose). Examples of the passive meaning are numerous: *chiçtó*, known (r. *chit* to know), *beretó*, carried, *baçta* bound (r. *band* to bind), *gerepta*, seized, taken (r. *gerew*, to take) &c.

---

## 21.—INFINITIVE.

The infinitive mood is expressed in various ways. In the Gâtha dialect we find the same means employed in expressing this mood, as in the Vedic language, viz. the forms ending in *dhyâi*, *dyâi* and *anhê*, S. *asê*, which are, as to their true nature, datives of abstract nouns, the former meaning "for making," and the latter "for being." In the usual Zend, these forms are very rare (see Vend. 2, 24. *vazaidhyâi*, to carry r. vaz S. *vah*); in their room we find the dative case of abstract nouns ending in *ti* or *na* used, or other means adopted for supplying the want of the old proper infinitives. Ex. from the Gâthas: *verezidyâi*, to work, *çrûidyâi*, to hear (roots *verez* and *çru*, *dazdyâi*, to give (r. *dâ* reduplicated, instead of *dad-dyâi*), *uziredyâi* Ys. 43,12. to step forward, to appear (r. *ere*, *ir*, to go), *mereñgedyâi* Ys. 46,11 to. kill (r. *mereñch*); *râshayanhê* Ys. 49, 3. to hurt, damage (r. *rash*, to hurt), *nipâonhê* Ys. 28, 12. in order to protect (r. *pâ*, to protect) &c. A peculiar form is *dâvôi* Ys. 28,3, to give (r. *dâ*). Examples from the usual Zend: *paitistâtêê* Vend 20, 3. to resist, withstand; *anumatayaêcha anukhtayaêcha* Ys. 8, 7. in order to think accordingly, and in order to speak accordingly (from *man* to think, and *vach* to speak); *ava-histêê*, in order to stand; *bavat perenê paçvãm*, Vend 2, 8. he was to fill (the earth) with cattle (r. *pere*, to fill).

Even some traces of the modern Persian infinitive in *tan*, the ancient form of which was *tana*, as we can ascertain from the ancient Persian cuneiform inscriptions, are occasionally met with, e. g. *añtare pâperetânê*,* in order to fight.

Now and then the middle voice participle is used to express the infinitive mood, e. g. *nâshemnâi* Ys. 9, 30. to remove, destroy, *çraêshemnô* Vend 13, 17. in order to attack.

---

## 22.—GERUNDIAL FORMS.

These are much fewer than in Sanskrit. The absolute indeclinable gerunds in *tvâ* or *ya*, so extremely frequent in Sanskrit, are never found in Zend; there the gerunds are used only as declinable words, qualifying substantives, or if they are without a

* The root is here not *peret*, but *pere*, to destroy, the intensive form of which sounds *pâpere*, to attempt, to destroy, fight a battle.

substantive, the neutral form is chosen. The termination of these forms is in *ya*. Ex. *yâ karshya* Vend 3, 24. which (the earth) is to be ploughed; *ayaozhdya bavaiñti* Vend. 3, 14. they are not to be purified; *paitirichya daithê* Ys. 11, 7. I put to be abandoned, (all bad things); *narem âçtârayañtîm âoṇhat* Vend. 5,7. it were to punish a man (*âçtâray*, causal of *çtere* to spread, means, to undergo a punishment, to atone); *bareçman frastairyât*, from the Barsom to be spread; *mâ mereñchainîs gaêthâo* Vend. 8, 21. the fields are not to be devastated.

---

## 23.—NOUNS (SUBSTANTIVES AND ADJECTIVES): THEIR FORMATION AND GENDERS.

Nouns are formed out of roots by addition of suffixes; now and then the root itself serves expressing the nominal idea, as we have shown above. There are three genders in Zend, as in the sister tongues, viz. masculine, feminine and neuter. Here I shall briefly enumerate the chief suffixes applied in the Zend to the formations of nouns; they agree wholly with those of the cognate languages.

*a*, one of the most common suffixes, forms substantives as well as adjectives; if its nominative case sounds *ô* (a change of *a-s*; *s* being the characteristic of the nominative sg.), it is a masculine; if it sounds *a* (instead of *â*), it is a feminine; if *em* (S. *am*, Latin *um*, Greek *on*), it is a neuter, e. g. *viçpa* all (S. *viçva*) masc. *vîçpô*, fem. *vîçpa* (instead of *vîçpâ*), neuter *vîçpem*; masc. *gaosh-ô*, ear, *maêgh-ô*, cloud, (the crude forms are *gaosh-a*, *maêgh-a*), *zaçt-ô*, hand, *daêvô* devil; fem. *çaoka*, light (r. *çuch* to light, shine), *îzha*, nourishment, *gena*, wife (S. *gnâ*, Greek *gyne*).

*i* forms substantives as well as adjectives, e. g. *gair-i* masc., a mountain, *zair-i* masc. gold; *khshathri*, fem. a lady, *daêna*, religion. In adjectives it is a feminine termination, e. g. *mâzdayaçni-s* fem. adj., "what refers to a Mazdayasna" or worshipper of Ahuramazda (the ancient name of the Parsees), *daêna zarathustri* adjec. fem., "what refers to Zarathustra"; *daēvi*, a female devil (S. devī).

*u* forms substantives and adjectives, e. g. *aṇhu*, life (r. *aç*, to be), *bâz-u*, arm *erez-u*, finger, *pour-u*, much (S. *pur-u*, Greek *poly*), *vour-u* wide (S. *ur-u*, Greek *eyry*), *voh-u*, good (S. *vas-u*).

*an* forms substantives expressing the doer, e. g. *tash-an*, cutter (r. *tash*, to cut), *urv-an*, soul, literal: breather (r. *vá* to blow, *ur-vá*, blow from the body, *i. e.* to breathe); their gender is masculine.

*ana* forms abstract nouns, neuter gender (nom. sg. therefore, sounding always *anem*, pl. *ana*), e. g. *maēth-ana*, building, *maç-ana*, greatness, *vaṇh-ana* excellence, *raoch-ana*, window.

*áni* forms feminines of masculines terminating in *a*; e. g. *ahur-âni* Ys. 68. a female genius, the feminine of *ahura** (compare the S. *Indrânî*, *Varunânî*, the respective wives of *Indra* and *Varuna*).

*aṇh*, sounding in the nominative always *ó*, forms abstract nouns in the neuter gender, e. g. *man-aṇh*, mind (nom. *manó*, genit. *manaṇhó*, S. *man-as*, Greek *men-os*, Latin *mens*), *nem-aṇh*, praise, worship, a bow, (r. *nam* to bow, turn, S. *namas*), *av-aṇh*, help, *rafen-aṇh*, pleasure. All these formations can be made adjectives by lengthening the *a* of *aṇh* (nom. sing. *áo*) e. g. *vach-áo*, speaking, from *vach-aṇh*, speech; *manáo*, minded, from *man-aṇh*, mind.

*are* corresponding as well as the preceding suffix *aṇh* to S. *as*, is confined to the nominative sg. only, while the oblique cases agree entirely with those of the nouns ending in *as*. Ex: *vad-are* Ys. 9, 30. a blow, stroke (S. *badha*), *zav-are*, strength, *râz-are*, rule, *daçv-are* gift, *vazdv-are*, possession, treasure.

*at*, *ant* forms adjectives; the feminine terminates in *ti*, e. g. *berez-at*, high, fem. *berez-ati*; in the nom. masc. *at*, with the characteristic *s* (*at-s*), is changed into *ó*, e. g. *berez-ó* Yt. 14,12.

* The word *Ahur-âni* does not mean a wife of *Ahuramazdaa*, *ahura* being in the Zend-Avesta an epithet, meaning living, immortal, and is applied to all genii indiscriminately and to heroes equally. The full name of God in the Zend-Avesta is always *Ahuramazda*; he is the only one, having no wife as the Hindoo deities.

This suffix is applied to the formation of participles, as we have seen above.

*in* forming substantives and adjectives, e. g. *kain-in*, nom. sing. *kain-is*, pl. *kain-înô*, girl; *peren-in*, pl. *peren-înô* Yt. 10, 119. winged (adject. from *perenem*, wing).

*ka* forms substantives, e. g. *mahr-ka*, death (r. *mare* to die), *pairi-ka*, a fairy, *mashyâ-ka*, a man (very likely diminutive) from *mashya*, man.

*ma, man*, of very frequent use, forms both abstract and concrete nouns; those formed by *ma* (nom. *mô*) are in the masc. gender, e. g. *dah-ma* (s. *das-ma*), a pious man,* and those which take *man* (nom. *ma)*, are in the neuter gender. Ex. *bareç-man* the Barsom, *maêç-man*, urine, *dâ-man* creature, *chash-man*, eye, (compare the Latin neuter nouns in *men* as *car-men*, a poem, *tenta-men*, a trial).

*na, nu* form substantives. Ex. *yaç-na*, prayer, worship, *varena*, choice, creed, *rash-nu*, righteousness, *taf-nu* heat, *baresh-nu* summit.

*ra* forms adjectives, e. g. *khrûra*, cruel.

*tha*, fem., *them*, neuter, form abstract nouns, e. g. *gaê-tha*, a field walled in, *gâ-tha*, song, *mahrka-them* killing, ruin, *frâda-them*, thriving; *ti* fem. makes abstract nouns as well as *thwem* (neuter), e. g. *yês-ti* worship (r. *yaç*), *anukh-ti* speaking accordingly, *ârmaiti* devotedness and the sacred name of the earth, *mã-thwem* thinking, *çtao-thwem*, praising, *vã-thwem* abundance, (in flocks).

*tu* (mostly masculine) forms concrete and abstract nouns, e. g. *ra-tu*, master, chief, *khra-tu*, intelleot, *zan-tu* a tribe, a town.

*tar*, masc. (nom. *ta*) characterises the doer of any thing, e. g. *dâ-ta* (*r*), giver, creator, *thrâ-ta* (*r*) protector, *pi-ta* (*r*) father (lit. protector, r. *pâ* to protect); compare the Latin and Greek nouns in *tor*, e. g. *da-tor* a giver. The feminine of these nouns is *thri-s* e. g. *dâthri-s*, a she giver.

* The Dustoors understand by it a "priest," in opposition to a layman.

*thra* makes masculines (*thró*) as well as neuter (*threm*) nouns, e. g. *puthró*, a son, *çrao-threm*, hearing, *gá-threm*, singing.

*tát* fem. forms abstract nouns e. g. *amere-tát* immortality, *drva-tát*, firmness, health, *ukhshyãç-tát* growth, *nerefçãç-tát* waning (compare the Latin abstract nouns in *tát* e. g. *veri-tas*, truth, gen. *veritat-is*).

*ya*, of very frequent occurrence, forms relative adjectives, pointing out a certain relationship to their substantives, e. g. *yêçnya* what refers to prayers, *áhúir-ya* what refers to ahura, *túir-ya*, the fourth, &c.

*vat*, *mat* (nom. masc. *váo*, fem. *vati*, neut. *vat*) very common, form adjectives, meaning "having, provided with," e. g. *haomavat*, having Homa, with Homa, *gao-mat* having milk, with milk, *amaváo* masc. *ama-vati* fem., *ama-vat*, neut. having strength, power, powerful.

---

## 24.—DEGREES OF COMPARISON.

### Comparatives and Superlatives.

There are two sets of suffixes employed for the formation of the degrees of comparison, which agree wholly with those used in the Sanskrit and Greek: *yaṇh* (nom. sg. *yáo*) m., *yahi* f., *yaṇh* n. (nom. sg. *yó*), and *tara* (nom. sg. *taró* m., *tara* f., *tarem* n.) for the comparatives; *ista* (nom. sg. *istó* m., *ista* f., *istem* n.) and *tema* (nom. sg. *temó* m., *tema* f., *temem* n.) for the superlatives.

Ex.: *vohu* good, comp.: *vahyáo* m. (in the Gâthas *vaqyáo*), *vahyêhi* f., *vahyó*, *vaňhó* n. better, sup.: *vahistó* m., *vahista* f., *vahistem* n. best; *maz*, *maç* great (S. *mah*, Latin *mag-nus*, Greek *meg-a*), comp.: *maçyáo* m., *maçyêhi* f., *maçyó* n., greater, sup.: *mazistó* m., *mazista* f., *mazistem* n., greatest; *kaçu*, little, comp.: *kaçyáo* m., *kaçyêhi* f., *kaçyó* n., less, fewer, sup.: *kaçistó*, *a*, *em* least; *çpan*, *çpen* (r. *çvi* to thrive) thriving, excellent, comp.: *çpanyáo* m., more excellent, *çpenistó* most excellent.

Examples of the other set of comparative and superlative suffixes are the following: *ushaç-tara* more eastward, *daoshaçtara* more westward, *jãthwó-tara* more baneful; *amavaç-tema* the strongest, *ápótema* most abundant in water, *yátumaç-tema*, being best conversant with sorcery, *urvaró-tema* having most of trees, &c.

## 25.—COMPOUND NOUNS.

The Zend language is as rich in compound words of various kinds as its ancient sister tongues, Sanskrit and Greek, but, on account of its standing nearest to the more simple Vedic idiom, less artificial in this respect than the classical Sanskrit. I forego the numerous compositions of prepositions with nouns which would more properly belong to a dictionary than to a short grammatical sketch. Following Sanskrit grammar we may bring these compound words under five heads.

1.—COPULATIVE COMPOUNDS (*Dvanda* in Sanskrit) of comparatively rare occurrence, e. g. *paçvîra* (dual) Yt. 13, 12. cattle (and) man (*paçu*, cattle, *vîra*, man), *Frashaostrâjâmâçpâ* Ys. 12, 7, Frashoster (and) Jâmâsp.*

2.—ADJECTIVE COMPOUNDS, being a composition of an adjective with a noun, e. g. *pouru-aênâo* Ys. 32, 6. many sins, evils; *daregâyû* 28, 7. two long lives (*darega*, long, *âyu* life, the life of the body and that of the soul.)

3.—COMPOUNDS OF DEPENDENCY, where one part, generally the first, depends upon the other. This class comprises combinations of nouns with nouns (the first then is to be resolved into the genitive case), *e. g. daṇhu-paiti*, master of the country, governor, (*daṇhu*, country, *paiti*, master, lord), *vîçpê-mazista* Ys. 33, 5. the greatest of all; or of nouns with present (or its equivalent) and past participles, e. g. *çraoshô-pâta* protected (*pâta*) by Serosh, *frâdat-gaêtha*, making the fields thrive (*frâdat*, making thrive, pres. partic.), *daêvô-zusta* loved by the devils, *mithah-vachâo*, telling lies, *erezh-vachâo*, telling the truth, *çpô-bereta*, carried by a dog. In these compounds we often observe the peculiarity of a vowel, which is *ô*, inserted between the first and second parts, e. g. *zrvô-dâta*, created in the time (*zrvô* is to be traced to *zarvan*, time), *baghô-bakhta* ordained by fate.†

* Both words are in the dual, and are wholly analogous to the Vedic compounds *Mitrâ-Varunâ*, *i. e*, Mitra (and) Varuna (gods).

† *Zrvô* and *baghô* are, as to the sense, to be taken in the instrumental case, *zrvô* therefore, stands instead of *zrva*, "through the time," and *baghô* is put instead of *bagha*, "through fate."

4.—POSSESSIVE COMPOUNDS, belong to any of the preceding classes, but are solely employed in qualifying substantives; they are, therefore, mere adjectives, e. g. *bareçmô-zaçta* having Barsom in his hand, *zairi-gaona*, of golden colour, gold coloured, *hazaṇrô-çtûnem* having thousand pillars (a palace), *vouru-gaoyaoitis* (in the Vedic Sanscrit *gavyûti* pasturage) having large pasturages, fields (an epithet of *Mithra*).

5.—PARTICLE-COMPOUNDS. I shall confine myself here to some remarks on certain inseparable prefixes and some adverbs only, and forego the prepositions which serve chiefly the purpose of modifying the verbal notions, expressed by the roots.

Among the inseparable prefixes stands foremost *a* or *an* (if the word, to which it is prefixed, commences with a vowel), the well known negative particle of the ancient Arian languages; it always negatives the existence of the idea, expressed by the word to which it is prefixed, e. g. *a-tbistô*, not to be hated, annoyed, i. e. friendly, peaceful, *a-çrâvayat*, not reciting (the sacred prayers) i. e. infidel; *an-aiwidrukhtô* one who does not belie (Mithra), *an-ashava* not religious, impious, *an-âhita* not polluted, i. e. clear (an epithet of the genius presiding over the waters).

*aç*, *as*, very, exceedingly, e. g. *aç-khratus* very intelligent, wise, *aç-varethrajãstemô* Yt. 10, 98. the most victorious, *as-frâyasti* with a great multitude, i. e. with a great many Yt. 10, 77.

*hu*, well, *dus*, ill (S. *su*, *dus*) e. g. *hu-matem* well thought, *dus-matem* ill-thought, *hûkhtem* (instead of *hu-ûkhtem*) well spoken, *duzh-ûkhtem* ill spoken, *hvarstem* (instead of *hu-varstem*) well done, *duzh-varstem*, ill done, *hu-kereta* well formed &c.

*frâyô*, often, repeatedly, always, e. g. *frâyô humatô* Yt. 11, 20. always thinking of good, *frâyô-hûkhtô*, always speaking of good.

*vî*, against, expresses a separation, removal, e. g. *vî-daêvô** against the devils, for the removal of the devils; *vî-âpôtemem*, most devoid of water.

*hama*, *hâma* (S. *sama*, *sâma*, Pers. *ham*), the same, equal, e. g. *hama-gaona* of the same colour, *hâma-takhma* equally swift.

* The first part of the word *Vendidâd* in Zend: *vî-daêvo-dâtem*, i. e. what is given in order to remove the devils, to be guarded against their influences.

## 26.—INFLECTION OF NOUNS; NUMBERS AND CASES.

The Zend, like Sanskrit and Greek, has besides the SINGULAR and PLURAL, a peculiar formation to express a duality, which is called DUAL. All these three numbers are modified in various ways by cases, of which we find exactly as many as in Sanskrit, viz. eight, including the vocative. In the sg. and pl. (except the vocative in pl., and the accus. in neuter nouns) each case has generally its own termination; but in the dual, one and the same form is used to express several different cases. In Sanskrit the eight cases are expressed in the dual by three forms only; but in Zend we find five forms, a richness to be discovered in no other language of the Arian stock. I shall enumerate them in the Sanskrit order. 1, the NOMINATIVE; 2, the ACCUSATIVE; 3, the INSTRUMENTAL, expressing the ideas of "with, through, by;" 4, the DATIVE; 5, the ABLATIVE, meaning "from, out of," pointing out the origin of a thing; 6, the GENITIVE; 7, the LOCATIVE, corresponding to "in, at, on;" 8, the VOCATIVE.

I shall illustrate the use of these by a few examples. Nom.: *mraot ahurô mazdâo*, Ahuramazda said. Acc.: *ahurem mazdãm yazamaidê*, Ahuramazda we worship. Instr.: *upazôit açpahê astraya*, he may beat (him) with a horsewhip; dat.: *fryô fryâi daidit*, a friend gave to a friend. Abl.: *têm khshathrât môithat*, Ys. 46, 4. him from possession (*khshatrât*) he turned out; *yûs daêvâ akât mananhô çtâ chithrem*, ye devils! you are offspring from the evil mind (*akât mananhô*). Gen.: *puthrô ahurahê mazdâo*, son of Ahuramazda (the fire); *dâtare gaêthanãm*, creator of the fields. Loc.: *tem yazata Zarathustrô manahi*, Yt. 14, 11. Zarathustra worshipped him in his mind; *viçpaêshu vanhushu* in all the good men. Voc.: *dâtare*, O creator! *Ardvi çûra anâhitê*, Ardooisoor Anâitis!

As to inflexion, all nouns may be divided into two chief classes, which have several sub-divisions; the first comprises all those nouns, the crude forms of which terminate in a consonant, the second those the crude forms of which end in a vowel. The terminations, if joined to the latter, must naturally undergo some changes; from which reason the true form of the cases can be ascertained from such nouns only as end in consonants. Chiefly according to this class of nouns, I shall give here a list of the terminations.

| | SINGULAR. | DUAL. | PLURAL. |
|---|---|---|---|
| Nom. | *s* | *a* | *ô (aç)* |
| Ac. | *em* | *a* | *ô, ãs* |
| Ins. | *a* | *bya* | *bis* |
| Dat. | *ê* | *bya* | *byô (byaç)* |
| Abl. | *at* | *âo* | *byô* |
| Gen. | *ô (aç)* | *âo* | *ãm* |
| Loc. | *i* | *yô* | *aêshu, aêshva, hva* |
| Voc. | like the nom. | „ | „ |

## 27.—DECLENSION OF NOUNS TERMINATING IN A CONSONANT.

(A). In a guttural or palatal sound. The palatal remains only before the terminations which commence with vowels, but if they begin with a consonant, it is to be changed into a corresponding guttural, viz. *kh* before *s*, and *gh* before *b*. Thus we obtain from the crude forms, *vâch*, voice, *druj*, destruction, the nominatives *vâkh-s*, *drukh*-s, while the accus. are *vâch-em*, *drujem*; in the dat. pl. *byô*, *vâch* inserts *zh*: *vaghzhe-byô*, Yt. 10, 88. to the voices, words. The other cases are generally supplied by the related *vachô* word.

(B). In a labial. *p* before the *s* of the nom. becomes *f*, e. g. *âf-s*, water (crude form *âp*, Latin *aqua*), acc. *âpem*; *âp-ô*, *apô*, gen. sing.; *âp-ô*, nom. and acc. pl.; *ap-ãm*, gen. pl.; *âpa* dual. *keref-s*, nom. sg. shape; flesh; acc. *kehrp-em*;* instr. *kehrp-a* (comp. Latin *corpus*). Before *y* the *p* can be further changed into *u*, e. g. *aiw-yô*, dat. pl. (a contraction of *aiwibyô* 'to the waters').

* The *h* is merely euphonical, serving no grammatical purpose.

(C). In a sibilant as *ç*, e. g. *víç* a village, a quarter (comp. Latin vicus, S. *viç*, Greek *oikos*, a house), acc. *víç-em*, dat. *víçê*, nom. pl. *víç-ó*, gen. pl. *víç-ãm*; before the soft *b*, *ç* is changed into the corresponding *zh*, e. g. *vízhibyó* (dat. pl.) Ys. 53, 8.

(D). In *aṇh*. This class is very frequent; all are of the neuter gender; the nom. terminates in *ó*, which becomes *aç* before the enclitic particle *cha* e. g. *manaçcha* "and the mind;" the oblique cases mostly end in *aṇh*. Ex. *man-aṇh*, mind, nom. and acc. *manó*; instr. *manaṇha*, dat. *manaṇhê*, gen. *mananhó*, abl. *manaṇhat*, loc. *manahi*; pl. nom. and acc. *çravâo* sayings (from the crude form *çravaṇh*, nom. sing. *çravó*), gen. *çravaṇhãm*, inst. *raochê-bis* (from *raochaṇh*, light), *çravâis* (from *çravaṇh*, as if *çrava* were the crude form,) *vachê-bis* (from *vachaṇh*, nom. *vachó*, word), loc. *raochó-hva*, Yt. 22, 15. (from *raoch-aṇh*). From these forms we may see, that *anh* is kept before such terminations only as commence with a vowel, before the terminations beginning with consonants, *ó* or *ê* being substituted. The nom. and acc. pl. is *âo*, a contraction of a fuller form.

· The adjective forms in *âo*, being always traceable to such an abstract in *aṇh*, follow the same rule; e. g. *raochâo*, having light, shining, from *raochaṇh* light, forms the acc. sg. masc. *raochaṇhem*, a termination which is never to be found in the abstract nouns in *aṇh* themselves on account of their being in the neuter gender.

(E). Masc. in *an*, *van*, e. g. *urvan* m. soul, *zarvan*, m. time, *ashavan* m. *ashaoni* f. (contraction of *ashavan-i*) adj. pious, religious. The chief peculiarity of the inflexion of the nouns consists in dropping the *a* and changing *v* into the vowel *u* before all the oblique cases of the singular, except the acc., and the oblique cases of the plural, except those, terminations of which commence with a consonant, like the dat. and instr. pl. In the nom. sing. the *n* drops, but the *a* remains; in the acc. sing. and nom. pl. both remain, *a* being then lengthened to *ã*.

Ex. *urvan*, soul, *zrvan*, *zarvan*, time, *adhwan*, path, *atharvan*, a priest, *ashavan*, religious, pure.

| | Singular. | Plural. |
|---|---|---|
| Nom. | *urva*, *zrva* (*zarva*), *âthrava* | *urvãnô* |
| Acc. | *urvânem*, *zrvânem*, *ashavanem* | *urunô* (*açcha*) |
| Inst. | *ashavana* | *urvôibyô* |
| Dat. | *urunê*, *ashaonê* (before *cha* : *aê*, *urunaêcha*) | *ashavabyô* |
| Abl. | *urunô*,-*aç* (*cha*), *ashaunat* | *ashavabyô* |
| Gen. | *urunô*, *athaurunô*, *zrvânahe** | *urunãm* |
| Loc. | *zruni*, Vend 19, 9 "in the time" | *ashaonãm* |

Dat. dual *ashavanaêibya*, Ys. 1, 11.

The feminine of *ashavan* is *ashaoni*, to be declined like a fem. in *i*; see below.

In *an*, *man*, (neuter and masc.); in the nom. and acc. sing. the final *n* drops always; the nom. and acc. pl. is either equal to the sg., or *i* (in which case the whole termination assumes the shape of *ẽni*, e. g. *nâmẽni*, names, from *nâman*, a name; compare. S. *âni* in *nâmâni*, the names, from *nâm-an*, a name), is added to *ãn*; now and then, *ãn* alone remains, e. g. *dâm-ãn*, creatures, from *dâm-a* (*n*) a creature, preserved in the modern Persian interrogative pronoun : *kudâm* i. e. what creature=who? which?

Ex. *bareç-man* Barsom, *nâm-an*, a name, *maêç-man* urine, *airyaman*, friend, associate, and a proper name.

| | Singular. | Plural. |
|---|---|---|
| Nom. | *bareçma*, n. *airyẽmâ*, m. | *bareçma*, *nâmẽni* |
| Acc. | *aîryamanem* | |
| Inst. | *bareçmana* | |
| Dat. | *bareçmainê* | *dâmabyô* |
| Abl. | *bareçman* | |
| Gen. | *bareçmanô* | *dâmanãm* |
| Loc. | *bareçman*, *ãnmaini* G., in the soul, | *bareçmôhu* |

* This genitive form (it ought to sound *zrunô* which I never met with) is to be traced to a crude form ending in *a*, *zrvâna*, derived from the original *zrvan* by means of the suffix *a*.

### Dual.

Nom. and acc. *raçmana,* the two battle lines; dat. and instr. *açmanaêibya** Visp. 10,2. to the two stones, loc. *raçmaoyó* in the two battle lines.

(G). In *ar, tar; a* is weak and often left out, as may be seen from the paradigma. In the nom. sg. the *r* is generally silent, always in such nouns, as denote the doer of an action and signify the nearest kinsmen, as *dá-tar,* creator, *pá-tar,* protector, *pi-tar,* father, *má-tar,* mother, *brátar,* brother, *qanh-ar* (S. *svasar*) sister, *dugh-dhar* daughter, the nom. sg. being *páta, pita, máta, qaṇha,* &c. In *átar* fire (its root is uncertain) the usual termination of the nom. sg. *s* is added to *ar,* as *átar-s* (modern Persian *atesh,* fire).

| | Singular. | Plural. |
|---|---|---|
| Nom. | *átars, dáta, pita, (ptá* G.) | *átaró, dátáró.* |
| Acc. | *átarem, dátárem, pitarem* | *átaró* |
| Inst. | *áthrá,* G. | |
| Dat. | *áthrê (aêcha), pithrê, bráthrê* | *áterebyó* |
| Abl. | *áthrat, pithre (ó)* G. | |
| Gen. | *áthró (açcha), dáthró* | *áthrãm, dáthranãm* |
| Loc. | | |
| Voc. | *átare, dátare,* in compounds *átare.* | |

Dual.

Nom. and acc. *pátára,* Yt. 14, 45. the two protectors.*
*thwórestára,* Ys. 42, 2, the two creators.†
*zámátara-qaçura,* Yt. 10, 116. the son-in-law (and) father-in-law.
*bráthra,* Yt. 10, 116. the two brothers.

(H) in *tát* fem. The final *t* is often dropped. In the nom. sg. the whole termination is left out, and *áo* substituted; e. g. the nom. sg. of *haurvatát,* wholesomeness, health, is *haurváo* (before *cha* " and": *haurváoçcha,* Ys. 34, 11), that of *drvatát* health, *drváo.* In the nom. and acc. pl. *tát* is now and then preserved; e. g. *ameretátaç-*

* The original meaning of *açman* is rock, stone, then the firmament; the modern Persian *asmán,* sky, is traced to it.

† These are the two creative powers, combined in Ormuzd, the Supreme deity, as we shall see in the 4th chapter.

*çha*, and the immortalities (crude form *ameretât*), Ys. 31, 6; but in *haurvatô* acc. pl., it is lost. The gen. sg. is *ameretâtô, haurvatâtô, drvatâtô*; acc. sg. *drvatâtem, ameretâtem*; loc. *ameretâiti* Ys. 45, 7. Pretty frequent is the nom. and acc. dual *haurvâtâ ameretâtâ* (a Dvandva compound) "health (and) immortality"; the dat. dual is *âmeretatbya*; the gen. dual *haurvatâoç* (*cha*) *ameretâtâo*, Visp. 9, 5.

(I) In *in*. The *n* drops in the nominative; the *i* is not made long as is the case in Sanskrit, but remains either short or is changed into *ê*.

Ex. *kainin*, a girl, *perenin*, winged; nom. sg. *kainê* (perhaps a contraction of *kanya*, acc. *kanyãm*); acc. sg. *kaininem*; gen. sg. *kaininô* and *kanyâo*, nom. pl. *pereninô, kainyô, kainîna*, Yt. 17, 54.; dative pl. *kainibyo*, Ys. 53, 5.

(K) In *ant, vant, mant*, see above the present participles, active voice. The nom. sg. m. of the adjectives in *vant, mant*, always terminates in *vâo, mâo*, the fem. is *vati, mati*, the neuter *vat, mat*. The acc. sg. masc. and the nom. pl. have the full form *ant* before the termination; in the other cases of the sg. *n* can be omitted, but chiefly in the present participle, it is often to be met with; in the oblique cases of the plural this *n* is generally left out.

Ex. *barant*, bearing, *dadant*, giving, *açtvant*, endowed with bodies, *bânumant* shining, *berezant* high, *dregvant* (nom. *vâo*), wicked (a word used in the Gâthas only), *hanant*, awarding, (r. *han*), *çaoshyant*, an ancient fire-priest, a prophet, *drvant*, running (applied to ghosts and evil spirits, r. *dru* to run).

| | Singular. | Plural. |
|---|---|---|
| Nom. | *dadãç, açtvâo, berezô, dregvâo çaoshyãç* | *çaoshyañtô, dregvañtô, berezañtô, berezañta* Yt. 5, 13. |
| Acc. | *bareñtem, açtvañtem, dregvañtem* | *çaoshyañtô, berezañta*, Yt. 10, 145, *çurunvataçcha* (those who have heard.) |

| | | |
|---|---|---|
| Inst. | *dregvâtá* G., *berezata* | *dregvôdebîs*, G. |
| Dat. | *haneñtê*, *dregvâitê* G., *dregvatâe* (*cha*) G., *drvataê* (*cha*) | *dregvôdebyó*. |
| Abl. | *açtvatat* | |
| Gen. | *açtvatô*, *bânumatô*, *berezatô* | *berezatãm*, *dregvatãm*, *drvatãm*, |
| Loc. | *bareñti*, *açtvaiñti* | *pishyaçu*,* Ys. 50, 2, in the seeing ones, *dregvaçu*, G. (instead of *dregvatçu*). |

(L) in *vaṇh*, *vas*, nom. *vâo* ; in the oblique cases *vas* is mostly changed into *ush*, e. g. *dadhvâo*, having created, then creator (a name of Ahuramazda), acc. *dadhvâoṇhem*, gen. sing. *dathushô* ; nom. *vîdvâo*, knowing, gen. *vîdushô* ; abl. *dathushat* ; dat. sg. *vîdushê*, *vaokushê* (from *vaochvâo*, one who has spoken); gen. pl. *vidvaêshãm* (formed according to the pronominal declension).

---

## 28.—DECLENSION OF NOUNS TERMINATING IN VOWELS.

### Masculine and Neuter Nouns in *a*.

The inflexion of the masculine and neuter nouns in *a*, differs in the nom. acc. of the sing. and pl. only, while all other cases are equal. In the neuter gender the nom. and acc. have always one and the same termination, in the sing. *em*, in the pl. *a*, as is the case in Sanskrit, Latin, and Greek also.

* Root *pish-yaç*, to see (*hvare-pishyaçû*, in those who see the sun i. e. live).

Singular.—The nom. terminates always in *ô*, which is a phonetical change of *a-s*; before the enclitical particle *cha*, which is generally affixed to a word, the original form in the shape of *aç* remains, e. g. *ahurô*, *ahuraçcha*. The acc. ends always in *em*; if the last syllable of the word be *ya*, it is contracted to *i*, if *aya*, it is made *ê*.

The instrumental terminates in the bare crude form, the termination being lost; the dat. has *âi*, before *cha*: *aê*; the abl. *ât*, *dat*.

The genitive termination differs from the preceding class; its termination is *ahya*, *aqya*, in the Gâthas (*asya* in S.), and *ahê* in the classical Zend; the loc. ends in *ê*. The vocative terminates in the crude form, e. g. *ahura!*

Dual: nom. and acc. *a* (in the Gâthas *â*), and *ê*, e. g. *pâdha*, the two feet, *zaçtê*, the two hands, *duyê çaitê*, two hundred; instr. *bya*, *zaçtaêibya*, with the two hands, *havanaêibya*, with the two Homa utensils (the mortar and beater); dative *aiwê*, e. g. *pâdhaiwê*, to the two feet, *gaoshaiwê*, to the two ears, Yt. 16, 7.; abl. *yâo*, e. g. *pâdhayâo*, from the two feet, *gaoshayâo* from the two ears, Yt. 10, 23.; gen. *yâo*, e. g. *vîrayâo* in the Dvandva: *paçvâo vîrayâo** of both cattle and men, Visp. 7, 3.; loc. *ayô*, as *zaçtayô*, into the two hands. From these statements we can see, that the Zend is richer in Dual forms than any other of the cognate languages; Sanskrit has only three and Greek only two, but Zend has five distinct forms for the cases of the dual.

Plural.—The nominative masculine terminates in *âoṇhô* (identical with *âsas* in the Vedic Sanskrit) and *a*; the neuter always in *a*. The acc. ends in *ã*, *ãn*, (*ãs*, *ãç*, before *cha*), *ē*, (*ēç* before *cha*) and simply *a*, e. g. *aêçmã*, pieces of wood, *haomãn*, the Homas, *puthrē*, children, *maziste* Visp. 3, 5. greatest, *ameshēçcha âpeñtē*, and the Amshashpands (archangels), *mashyãçcha* and the men.

In the Gâthas we find the peculiar form in *ēñg*, which is, I think, only a harsher pronunciation of *ãç*, e. g. *viçpēñg*, all, *daêvēñg* the devils, *mashyēñg* men, &c.

* The Dual is put twice, each part of the Dvandva (copulative compound) is provided with it, as is generally the case in such compounds, see page 90.

The instr. ends in *âis*, as in Sanskrit, e. g. *mãthrâis*, through the sacred prayers. The dative terminates in *byô*, which is identical with the first class of nouns. The gen. ends in *anãm* (S. *ân m*). The loc. termination is *aêshu*, *aêshva*, *fshva* (comp. *kamnafshvâ*, Ys. 46, 2. "among the few," from *kamna*, few). The vocative is identical with the nominative.

Ex.: *ahura*, living (a name of god), *mazda* (although the nom. is *mazdâo*, it is inflected like those nouns, the nominatives of which end in *ô*) creator,* *gaya*, possession, existence, *mashya*, man, *asha*, truth, *zarathustra*, Zoroaster, *dâta*, given, created, *çpitama*, the family name of Zoroaster, *khshathra*, rule, *urvâtem*, a revealed saying, *zaosha*, pleasure, *urvaêça*, end, *mithra*, friend, promise, *mareta*, mortal.

| | Singular. | Plural. |
|---|---|---|
| Nom. | *ahurô mazdâo, ashem, zarathustrô, mazdâoçcha* | *ahurâonhô*, Ys. 30, 9. *mazdâoṇhô*, Ys. 45, 1. *çpitamâoṇhô, daêva, urvâta* |
| Acc. | *ahurem, mazdãm, zarathustrem, mashîm, gaêm* | *haomã*, &c. see above. |
| Inst. | *asha, khshathra* | *khshathrâis, mashyâis, urvâtâis* |

* Burnouf's explanation of the name *mazdâo* by the Sanskrit *medhâs*, wise, which I followed myself also, did not prove satisfactory to me on further researches. That the word in phonetical respect is identical with the Sanskrit, *medhâs*, is not to be denied; but the original meaning of it is not "wise." Were it the case, we ought to suppose it to be a contraction of *maiti-dhâo*, "producing wisdom;" but *maiti* (thought, wisdom = S *mati*) is generally affixed, not prefixed to another word, e. g. *tarô-maiti*, perverse thought, i. e disobedience; but the word *mat* "with" is very frequently prefixed to other words. If added to *dhâo*, creating, it must be changed according to the phonetical laws into *mazdâo*. The general meaning of *mat* being "together, all" (see Visp. 14, 1.) the word *mazdâo* means either the joint creator, or the creator of all. That may be clearly seen from Ys. 45, 1.

| | | |
|---|---|---|
| Dat. | *ahurâi mazdâi, ashâi, zarathustrâi* | *mithrôibyô, maretaêibyô* |
| Abl | *ashât, ashâat* | *anâhitaêibyô*, Yt. 10, 38. (unpolluted) |
| Gen. | *mazdâo, ahurahyâ, ahurahê, ashahê, zarathustrahê* | *daêvanãm, vîçpanãm* |
| Loc. | *zaoshê, urvaêçê* | *mashyaêshu, naptyaêshu* (relations), *maretaêshu* |
| Voc. | *ahura, mazda, zarathustra,* | *daêva* |

On the dual see above.

---

## 29.—FEMININES IN *â*.

The *â* is made short in the nom. sing.; but in the acc. it is preserved in *ãm*; the terminations commencing with a vowel, as the instr. *a*, dat. *âi*, abl. *at*, genit. *âo*, insert *y* between these terminations and the crude forms, just as is the case in Sanskrit, e. g. *daêna-ya, daêna-yâi, daêna-yâo*, &c. from *daêna*, creed, religion; in the instr. the euphonical *y* is often left out, e. g. *hizvâ* G. instead of *hizvayâ*, through the tongue.

The locat. is rare; it terminates in *ê* as the mascul. in *a* do, e. g. *gaêthê*, in the world, from *gaêtha* Yas. 34, 2., *daênê* Yt 8, 23. in the creed. The vocative ends partially in *a*, and partially in *ê*, e. g. *ardvi çûra anâhitê*, Ardooisoor Anaitis! (nom. *anâhita*).

PLURAL.—The nom. and acc. end in *áo*, before *cha* in *áoç (cha)*; the instr. in *bîs*, *bis*; the dat. and abl. in *byô*; the genit. in *anãm*; the loc. in *áhu*, *áhva*. Dual forms of this class are not to be found in the texts.

Ex.: *gaêtha* (a) fold, (b) world; *gâtha* song; *daêna* (a) meditation or vision (b) creed, belief; *urvara*, tree (Lat. arbor), *gena*, wife, *hizva* tongue, *zaothra* consecrated water.

| | Singular. | Plural. |
|---|---|---|
| Nom. | *daêna, gaêtha, gátha* | *daênâo, gaêthâo, gâthâo* |
| Acc. | *daênãm, gaêthãm, gâthãm* | The same. |
| Instr. | *hizvá* G., *daênaya* | *genâbîs* G., *daênâbîs* |
| Dative | *daênayâi* | *daênâbyó, gâthâbyô* |
| Abl. | *zaothrayât* | *gaêthâbyô* |
| Gen. | *gaêthayâo* | *gaêthanãm, gâthanãm, zaothranãm, urvaranãm* |
| Loc. | *zaothrê, daênê, gaêthê* | *gâthahva* |
| Voc. | *anâhitê, mazdadhâitê, çûra* | Like the nom. |

## 30.—NOUNS TERMINATING IN *i* AND *u* OF ALL THE THREE GENDERS.

SINGULAR.—The nom. adds always *s* in nouns of masculine and feminine genders, but in certain adjectival feminine terminations *s* drops. In the acc. *i* and *u* are generally lengthened before the termination, *m*. In the instr. the termination, *a*, G. *á*, is partially added to *i* or *u* of the crude form, in which case these vowels are dissolved into their respectives emivowels *y* and *w*, e. g. *vaṇhuyá*, from *vaṇhví*, fem. good, *khrathwá*, from *khratu*, intelligence, and partially left out, in which case the instr. represents the bare crude form, e. g. *khratú*, *chiçté* G., knowledge, *çaçti*, by order, *yésti* with prayer. The dat. adds *ê* in the masculine, and *ái* in the feminines terminating in *i*; the *i* of the crude form is before the termination dissolved into *ay*, which is contracted often to *ê*, in which way we obtain theinflection *êê*, before *cha* generally *ayaêcha*, e. g. *paitistâtêê*, for withstanding, from *paitistâti*; *u* is either changed into the semivowels *v* and *w* e. g. *rathwê*, from *ratu*, chief, or it remains joined (by means of *y*) to the termination, e. g. *tanuyê* from *tanu* body. In the abl. we find the forms *ôit* and *aot* (wanting in Sanskrit). In the genit. there are various forms, the mascul. take *ôis*, *aos*, *êus*; the fem. *âo*, *ô*, in which case the vowel of the crude form is changed into *y* or *v*. The loc. is rare; it coincides entirely with the dat., e. g. *tanuyê* in or on the body (Vend. 4.); of the nouns in *u* we find now and then *âu* as in Sanskrit. In the voc. *i* is frequently changed into *ê*, and *u* into *ô*.

DUAL. nom. the vowel is lengthened, e. g. *mainyú* the two spirits, from *mainyu*; the dat. is *byá* G. (*ahubyá*, to the two lives from *ahu* life); the genit. is *âo*, *u* being dissolved into *v*, e. g. *mainivâo* of the two spirits, from *mainyu*, *ahvâo* of the two lives, from *ahu*, *bâzvâo* of the two arms, from *bâzu* (S. *bâhu* arm).

Plur. The nom. in *i* and *u* are dissolved into *ay* and *av* before the termination *ô* (*ayô*, *avô*). In the acc. a contraction takes place, which has crept now and then into the nom. also; we find, besides *ayô*, *avô*, the terminations, *îs*, *ûs*. The instr. is *ôibis* in masc., *ibis* in fem. The dat. abl. is *byô*, *byaç* (*cha*). The genit. is *ãm*, before which the termination *i* is to be changed into *y*, and *u* into *v*, e. g. *yâthwãm* from *yâtu* witch, *kaoyãm* from *kavi*, prophet, poet (used in the bad sense of a sorcerer). In order to preserve the original vowels *i* and *u*, an euphonical *n* is often inserted between them and the termination (*nãm*). The locat. is *shu*, *shva*.

Ex. *açtvaiti* the fem. of *açtvat*, endowed with bodies, *vaṇhus*, m., *vaṇuhi* f. *vohu* n., good; *gairi*, mountain, *mainyu*, m. spirit, *ârmaiti* f. genius of earth, *daqyu* G. *daṇhu*, m. country, province, *nâiri*, woman, *paçu* m. cattle, *açti* f. body, existence, *barethri* mother, womb, *khshathri*, lady, *chiçti* f. knowledge.

| | Singular. | Plural. |
|---|---|---|
| Nom. | *gairis, ratus, açtvaiti, vaṇuhi, vohu, mainyus* | *garayô, ratavô, açtayô, kâvayaçcha* |
| Acc. | *gairîm, ratûm, açtvaitîm, vaṇuhîm, mainyûm* | *gairîs, ratûs, paçûs, açtvaitîs, vaṇhûs* m. *vaṇuhîs*, f. |
| Inst. | *ashi, ârmaitî* G., *khrathwâ, mainyû* G. | *azdibis*, G. |
| Dat. | *paitistâtêê, rathwê, açtvaithyâi, tanuyê* | *nâiribyô, ratubyô, vaṇuhibyô* |
| Abl. | *barethryât, tanaot, vaṇhaot* | The same. |
| Gen. | *garôis, tanvô, manyêus, vanhêus*, m. *vaṇhuyâo*, f. *açtvaithyâo, nairyâo* | *gairinãm, daqyunãm, açtvaitinãm, yâthwãm, vohunãm* |
| Loc. | *tanuyê, aṇhvô, açtvainti, vaṇhâu, gara*, (Af. 1, 17.) | *barethrishva, vaṇhushu, khshathrishva* |
| Voc. | *ârmaitê, chiçtê* | |

## 31.—PECULIARITIES IN THE INFLEXION OF A FEW COMMON NOUNS.

*çpan*, dog, nom. sing. *çpá*, acc. *çpánem*, instr. *çpâna*, dative *çûnê*, gen. *çûnô*, loc. *çpânaê(cha)*; nom. pl. *çpánô*, gen. *çûnãm*.

*gâo*, animal, flesh; cow, milk; a poetical name of the earth; arm (chiefly in the dual), nom. *gâus*, acc. *gãm*, instr. *gava*, dative *gavê*, abl. *gaot*; dual, nom *gavôi*, instr. *gavaêibya*; pl. nom. *gavô*, acc. *gâo*, instr. *gaobîs*, gen. *gavãm*.

*hvare*, sun, nom. *hvare*, gen. *hûrô*.

*mâoṇh*, moon, nom. *mâo*, *mâoçcha* acc. *mâoṇhem*, dat. *mâoṇhâi*, gen. *mâoṇhahê*; pl. *mâoṇhô*.

*çtare*, star (Latin *stella*); in composition: *çtehr-paêçaṇh*, starlike, sg. acc. *çtârem*, gen. *çtârô*, *çtârahê*; nom. pl. *çtârô*, acc. *çtrêus*, dat. and abl. *çtarebyô*, gen. *çtârãm*, *çtrãm*.

*zâo*, *zem*, earth, nom. sg. *zâo*, acc. *zãm*, instr. *zemâ*, dat. *zemê*, abl. *zemât*, gen. *zemô*, loc. *zemâ*, *zemê*, *zemi*; nom. and acc. pl. *zemô*, instr. *zemâis* (in compounds only), gen. *zemãm*.

*nar*, man; nom. *nâ*, acc. *narem*, dat. *nairê*, *naraê* (*cha*), gen. *nars*, *neres* G., voc. *nare*; nom. dual, *nara*, dat. and abl. *nerebya* nom. pl. *narô*, acc. *narêus*, dat. *nerebyô*, loc. *nâshû* G., *nafshû* G.

*pañtan*, way; nom. sg. *panta*,* acc. *pañtãm*, instr. *patha*, loc. *pathâo*; nom. pl. *pañtânô*, acc. *pathô*, gen. *pathãm*.

*açan*, day, gen. sg. *açnô*, loc. *açni*, *açnê*, abl. *açnâat*; gen. pl. *açnãm*.

*khshapan*, night; nom. sg. *khshapa* acc. *khshapanem*, abl. *khshafnâat*, gen. *khshapô* (used in the loc. also), loc. *khshafnê*; uom. pl. *khshapanô* m., *khshafna* n., acc. *khshafnô*, gen. *khshafnãm* (*khshapara* n., known from the Vend., is a derivation from *khshapa* meaning "night time," like as *ayara* n., from *aya*. day, means "day time)."

* Vend. 16, 11. *panta vichinaêta*, a way may be chosen (by the *Mâzdayaçnas*).

## 32.—PRONOUNS.

### (A) Personal Pronouns.

The Zend, agreeing in this part of speech, even in anomalies, with the Sanskrit, has, like the other languages of the Arian stock, a separate form for the nominative in all numbers and a separate one for the oblique cases. We find, as in other old languages, proper pronouns of the first and second persons only, but not of the third, the place of which is generally occupied by a demonstrative pronoun. In the Gâtha dialect, there are some older forms to be found. The following table exhibits the personal pronouns of the first and second persons in both dialects.

| | Singular. | Dual. | Plural. |
|---|---|---|---|
| Nom. | 1 *azem*, I.<br>2 *tvĕm*, *túm*, *tú* thou | | 1 *vaêm*, we<br>2 *yúzhem*, you *yús*, G. |
| Acc. | 1 *mãm*, *má*, me<br>2 *thwãm*, *thwá*, thee | | 1 *ahma*, *nó*, *nĕ* G. |
| Instr. | 1 *má ?*<br>2 *thwá*, through thee | | |
| Dative | 1 *mói mé*, *maibyó* *maibyá*(*cha*) G. to me<br>2 *tói*, *tê*, to thee | | 1 *nó*; *nĕ* G., *ahmaibyácha*<br>2 *yúshmaibyá*, *vó*, *vĕ* G. |
| Abl. | 1 *mat*, from me<br>2 *thwat*; from thee | | *yúshmat* |
| Gen. | 1 *mana*, of me<br>2 *tava*, of thee | *náo*<br>*váo* | *ahmákem*, *nó*; *nĕ* G.<br>*yúshmákem*, *vó*; *vĕ* G. |

| Loc. | 1 *mê* G. in me<br>2 *thwê*, *thwôi* G. in thee | | |
|---|---|---|---|

In the Gâthas we meet often the peculiar forms in *khshma*, inflected exactly like *yûzhem* (abl. *khshmat*, gen. *khshmâkem*, &c). I explained them formerly as a secondary form for *yúzhem* conveying the same meaning "you"; but this contradicts all etymology and does not suit the passages where it is used. It is very likely a demonstrative pronoun signifying "that, such," (which is quite clear from Ys. 46,10), but used in the sense of a plural.

*hvô*=S. *sva*, himself, is often used in the Gâthas conveying the sense of an emphatic pronoun of the 3rd person sing., "he, himself."

POSSESSIVE PRONOUNS of the 1st and 2nd persons, are of two kinds, the one adding the terminations of the pronominal declension (see pag. 108) to the crude forms *ma*, *thwa*, the other taking the suffixes *ka* or *vat*. Of the former class oblique cases are only extant, as dat. *thwahmâi*, to thy, abl. *thwahmât*, from thy, gen. sg. *mahyâ* m., *magyâo* f., of my; *thwahyá* m., *thwaqyâo* f., of thy; loc. sing. *mahmî*, in my, *thwahmî*, in thy, loc. pl. *thwâhû* in thy. Of the latter class are, nom. sg. *thwvâvãç*, thine; dat. sg. *mavaitê*, to mine; acc. pl. *ahmâkĕng*, ours, instr. pl. *ahmâkâis*, through ours, dat. sg. *yûshmâkâi* to your, &c. Most of these forms are peculiar to the Gâthas.

Of *hvô*, "himself," we find a possessive pronoun formed also of which I notice the dative sing. *qaqyâi* f., to herself, and gen. sing. *qaqyâo*, f. of herself, her own, which is also found in the Gâthas.

Of *khshma*, "those, such," the forms *khshmâkai* to their, gen. sing. *khshmávatô*, of their, loc. plu. *khshmâvaçû* in their, &c. are frequently to be met with in these old songs.

## 33.—DEMONSTRATIVE, RELATIVE AND INTERROGATIVE PRONOUNS.

All these pronouns form their cases in one and the same way; the terminations of the cases are distinct from those of substantives and adjectives; we style it, therefore, the pronominal declension. The dat. sing., for instance, of the masculine is *hmái*, nom. pl. *é* gen. pl. *aēshām*, &c. as will be seen from the following list.

1 Demonstrative—*hó* m.; *há* f.; *tat* n., this.

2 Relative—*yó* m.; *yá* f.; *yat* n., which.

3 Interrogative—*kó* m.; *ká* f.; *kat* n., who? what?

| | Sing. m. n. | Sing. fem. | Plu. m. n. | Pl. fem. |
|---|---|---|---|---|
| Nom. | 1, m. *hó*, *hâu*, *adá*<br>2, *yó*; *yē* G.<br>3, *kô*; *kē* G.<br>n. *at*, *tat*; *yat*, *kat* | 1, *há*<br>2, *yá*<br>3, *yat* | 1, m. *tói*, m. *tá*, n.<br>2, *yói*, m. *tá*, n.<br>3, *kói*, m. *ká*, n. | 1, *táo*<br>2, *yáo*<br>3, *káo* |
| Acc. | 1, m. *tem*, *tēm* G.<br>2, *yim*, *yēm* G.<br>3, *kem*, *kēm* G. | 1, *tãm*<br>2, *yãm*<br>3, *kãm* | 1, *tã*, *tãs* *tēñg* G.<br>2, *yã*, *yãs*; *yēñg* G.<br>3, *kēñg* G. | Ditto |
| Instr. | 1, m. *tá*, *aná* G., *ana*<br>2, *yá*<br>3, *kaēná* G. *kana* | 1, *tayá*, *áya*<br>3, *kayá* | 1, m. *táis*, *aēibis*, *anáis*<br>2, *yáis*<br>3, *káis* | 1, *táis*; *ábis* G. |
| Dat. | 1, m. *ahmái*<br>2, *yahmái*<br>3, *kahmái* | 1, *aqyái* G.<br>3, *kahyái* | 1, *taēibyó*<br>2, *yaēibyó*<br>3, *kaēibyó* | 1, *ábyó*<br>2, *yábyó* |

| | | | | |
|---|---|---|---|---|
| Abl. | 1, m. *ahmât*<br>2, *yahmât*, *yât* G.<br>3, *kahmât* | 1, *anhât*<br>2, *yênhât* | Ditto | Ditto |
| Gen. | 1, m. *ahyâ* G.; *ahê*<br>2, *yêhyâ* G. *yênhê*<br>3, *kah yâ* G.; *kanhê* | 1, *aqyâo*, G. *anhâo*<br>2, *yênhâo*<br>3, *kanhâo* | 1, *aêshãm*<br>2, *yaêshãm* | 1, *anaês-hãm, âonhãm*<br>2, *yâonhãm* |
| Loc. | 1, *ahmi*<br>2, *yahmi*<br>3, *kahmi* | 1, *ahmya*<br>2, *yahmya*<br>3, *kuthra* where | 1, *aêshva*<br>2, *yaêshu*<br>*kuthra* | 1, *âhva*<br>2, *yâhva* |

Dual: nom. 1, *hâ* (these two, Ys. 30, 3), *tâ*; 2, *yâ*.
Ditto; gen. 1, *ayâo*; 2, *yayâo*.

DEMONSTRATIVES.—Besides the demonstrative pronoun *hô* and the two others (the crude forms *a* and *ana*) which supply some cases to the former, as will be seen from the preceding table, forms of other pronominal roots are frequently in use to express the idea "this, that."

*ava*, that, nom. sg. *aom* m., *ava* f., *avat* n., acc. *aom* m., *avãm* f., *avat* n.; dat. *avaqyâi* f. (Yt. 10,78. refers to *danhu* f. country) gen. *avanhâo* f.; dual nom. *avâ*; pl. nom. and acc. *ava*, *avê* m., *avâo* f.; instr. *avâis*, abl. *avatbyô*, gen. *avaêshãm*.

*i*, *ima* this, sing. nom. *aêm* m., *îm* f., *imat* n.; acc. *imãm* f.; pl. nom. *imâo* f., *imâ* n. G., acc. *imãm*; *imâo* f.

*aêsha* this, sg. nom. *aêshô* m., *aêsha* f., *aêtat* n.; *aêtem* m., *aêtãm* f.; instr. *aêta* m., *aêtaya* f.; dat. *aêtahmâi* m., *aêtahmât* n., *aêtanhâo* f.; gen. *aêtahê* m., *aêtanhâo*, *aêtayâo* f; loc. *aêtahmi* m.; pl. nom. *aêtê* m., *aêtaô* f.; acc. *aêta*, m. n., *aêtâo* f.; gen. *aêtaêshãm* m., *aêtanhãm* f.; loc. *aêtaêshva* m. dual gen. *aêtayâo*.

Besides these demonstratives, here enumerated, we meet (chiefly in the Gâthas) with several oblique cases of other pronominal roots, which are used rather as enclitics, being appended to other stronger words, than as full independent words; one may style them "accentless pronouns." Of the root *da* we find the acc. sg. *dim* after particles as *á* (to), *paiti* (again), *nôit* (not), in the meaning of "him;" its neuter is *dit* it (Afr. 1,4); acc. pl. *dís*, them.

*î*, *îm*, *ît** are in the Gâthas often added to other words, chiefly to the relative pronoun *ya*, or the negative particle *nôit*, not, in order to make it more emphatical. In most cases it has no meaning which may be expressed by words in the modern languages; now and then it conveys the sense of an oblique case of a pronoun e. g. *îm* Ys. 46,5 "him;" *îs* acc. pl. "them."

Of the root *si*, *hi*, we find *hê*, *hôi* (*sê* only after vowels e. g. *yêzi sê*) in the sense of a genitive: of it, of him, and *hîm* as an acc. sg. "him."

INTERROGATIVES.—Besides the root *ha* we find the secondary form *cha*, *chi*, applied in putting direct and indirect questions; but it is more frequently used in combination with another word in order to generalise its sense, as we shall see (pg. 111). Nom. sg. m. f. *chis* who? *chit* n. what, acc. *chim*, dat. *chahmâi*, abl. *chôit*, gen. *chahya*. In the oblique cases it means, "one, any one," (compare the Latin *quis* who? used instead of *aliquis* any one). *Chvat*, how much? pl. *chvañtô* how many?

---

## 34.—OTHER PRONOMINAL FORMS.

### CORRELATIVE PRONOMINAL ADJECTIVES MEANING ONE OUT OF TWO.

These are formed out of the crude forms of the demonstrative, relative and interrogative pronouns by means of the comparative termination *tara*, viz. *atara* either, *yatára* whether, *katára*, whether G. The neutral form *katárem* introduces now and then, like the Latin *utrum* a question referring to the

* These little words are to be found in the same meaning in the Vedic language also, but not in the classical Sanskrit.

preference of one thing to another, e. g. Ys. 31,17. : *katârem ashavâ vâ dregvâo vâ verenvaitê mazyô* ? whether, the pious or the wicked teaches the greater (thing) ?

CORRELATIVES EXPRESSING "KIND, MANNER."

*avat*, such, nom. sg. *avâo* m., *avaiti* f., *avat* n.; acc. *avâoñtem*, *avavat* nom. sg., *avavaiti* f. this much, such; instr. *avavata* gen. *avavatô*; gen. *avavatãm*.

*tâtâo* f. Yt. 5,15, acc. pl. "such,"—*yavan*, *yavat*, for how long a time, see Yt. 15,40.: *yat nmânô-paitîm viñdâma yavânem* (acc. sing. m.) *çraêsta kehrpa yô nô huberetãm barat yavata* (instr. sing m.) *gaya jvâva*, that we may have the house father go long (living) in the best health, to bestow boons upon us during how long a time we both (the father on the one side, the children on the other) may live.

INDEFINITE PRONOUNS.

These are formed, as mentioned above, by the addition of *cha*, *chis* or *chit* to another pronoun or an adverb, e. g. *kaçchit*, any one, every one (declined like *kô*, who ? e. g. dat. *kahmâichit* to every one); *chischa* whosever; *naêchis* none, *mâchis*, no body (the latter is chiefly used, in prohibitive sentences).

*chit* can be added to nouns, substantives and adjectives also, in order to generalise the meaning, and may often be best translated by "whatever," e. g. *daêvachit* whatever devils. Exactly in the same sense *china* (S. *chana*) is now and then added to a word.

PRONOMINAL ADJECTIVES.

These, as for instance, *viçpa* all, *anya* another, follow partially the peculiarities of the pronominal declension; nom. pl. *viçpê*, *anyê*, gen. pl. *viçpaêshãm*, *anyaêshãm*.

---

## 35.—NUMERALS.

1. *aêva* (nom. and in composition *aêvô*); 2 *dva*, *va*, *duyê*, *uyê* and *bi*, if formingpart of a compound ;* 3 *thri* (nom. *thrâyô*);

* Instead of these different forms of *dva*, the dual nom. *ubê* (Lat. *ambo*, S. *ubhê*), instr. and dat *ubôibyâ*, gen. *ubôyô* "both" is used, chiefly in the Gâtha dialect.

4 *chathware*, *chathru* in compounds (nom. *chathwârô*) ; 6 *pañcha*, *meñda* G. ; 6 *khshvas*, *khshvîdem* G. ; 7 *hapta* ; 8 *asta* ; 9 *nava* ; 10 *daça* ; 11 *aêvañdaça* ; 12 *dvadaça*, 13 *thridaça* ; 14 *chathrudaça* ; 15 *pañchadaça* ; 16 *khshvasdaça* ; 17 *haptadaça* ; 18 *astadaça* ; 19 *navadaça* ; 20 *vîçaiti* ; 30 *thriçãç* (*cha*), *thriçatem*, ; 40 *chathwareçatem* ; 50 *pañchâçat*, *panchâçatem* ; 60 *khshvasti* ; 70 *haptâithi* ; 80 *astaiti* ; 90 *navaiti* ; 100 *çatem* (dat. sg. *çatêê* ; in composition *çata* and *çatô*), 200 *duyê çaitê*, 400 *chathware çata* ; 500 *pancha çata* etc ; 1000 *hazañra* ; 10,000 *baêvare* ; 100,000 *ahãkhsta*.

The ordinals are : *paoirya*, *frakhstya* first ; *bitya* second ; *thritya* third ; *khtûirya*, *tûirya** fourth ; *pukhdha* fifth ; *khstva*, sixth ; *haptatha* seventh ; *astema* eighth ; *nâuma* ninth ; *daçema* tenth ; *aêvañdaça* (nom. *aêvañdaçô*) eleventh ; *navadaça* (*çô*) nineteenth.

*Multiplication numerals* are formed by addition of *keret* and *vat* (nom. mas. sg. *vâo*) *hakeret* once, *bis*, *bizhvat* twice, *thris*, *thrizhvat* thrice ; *vîçaitivâo* 20 fold, *thriçathwâo* 30 fold, *chathwareçathwâo* 40 fold, *haptaithivâo* 70 fold ; *çatâyus* hundred fold ; *hazanrâis* thousand fold ; *baêvarôis* ten thousand fold.

---

## 35.—PARTICLES.

A complete enumeration and exact description of the particles belonging more properly to the dictionary than to the grammar, I shall confine myself to making some remarks only.

ADVERBS : *athra* there, *idha*, *idâ* G. here, *tadha* there ; *yathra* where, *kuthra*, *katha* where ? *avathra* there ; *yatha* as, like as, *kutha* how ? *inja* here, *tinja* there, *upairi* above, *adhairi* below, down, *uiti* so, thus. *nû*, *nu*, now ; *yava* ever (Yt. 22,10), *yavat* how long ; *yadhôit* whence ; *bâ* certainly ; *moshu* soon ; *bâdha* quickly, surely, *bâdhistem* soonest ; *frakhsni* in direction of,

* The nom. sg. m. of all these ordinals in *ya* ends in *yô*, the acc. in *îm*, e. g. *paoirîm bitîm* etc.

towards; *aiwitó* round about, *para* before, *paçcha* afterwards, *paitis* in presence (*pesh* in modern Pers.) etc.—There are several negatives: *nôit* not (from *na it*), *má* not (prohibitive); *naêdha*, *nava*, *navât* (instead of *na-vá*; *na-vâ-at*) neither, nor.

PREPOSITIONS.—We find the same as in the Sanscrit; they are, as to their position, used very freely; if forming a part of the verb, they may be separated from it, as is the case in the Vedic and Homeric languages (not in the usual Sanscrit and Greek); often they are put twice, once without the verb and then with the verb; they can be placed before and after the noun; if the noun is qualified by an adjective or participle, the preposition is generally put between them. They govern, if put to a noun, different cases, some take the accusative as *upa* in, at, *avi* to, towards; some the instrumental as *mat* with; some the dative as *pairi* round, against; some the ablative as *paiti* in, at, during; some the locative as *aibi* in, about, *paiti* in, upon, at, etc.; but most of them can govern several cases, as is the case in Latin and Greek also.

Two prepositions deserve a peculiar attention, *â* and *hacha*. *â* S. *á*, means to, towards, and governs in this meaning the accusative; but together with *hacha* it is applied to express the idea "from—to," in which case both govern the ablative; *á* serves in this case, expressing "to, up to" and *hacha* "from" e. g. *hacha gayât marathnât âçaoshyañtât verethraghnât* Yt. 13,145. from Gayomart (the first man, Adam) to Sosiosh Verethraghna (the prophet and redeemer, expected by the Parsees at the end of the word); *hachâ hô-vakhshât â hû-frâshmô-dâitôit* Yt. 5,91 from sunrise to sunset. *Hacha* governs the ablat. and instrum. in the meaning 'from': *apâkhtarât hacha nmânât* from the northern country; *hacha ushaçtara Heñdva avi daoshaçtarem* from the eastern India to the western. If added to the accusative, it means "for, in favour.'

CONJUNCTIONS *cha* (always affixed to another word) and, also, *uta* and, also; *at* so, *atha*, then, thus; *yêzi*, *yêidhi* if; *zi* then, therefore; *viçpem â ahmât* for the purpose, in order to, that; *vâ* or; *vâ-vâ* either—or, etc.

## 36.—THE TWO DIALECTS OF THE ZEND LANGUAGE.

After having pointed out in the preceding paragraphs of the outlines of a Zend grammar, in each particular case, the differences of the Gâtha language from the common Zend, I shall now briefly state my views on the relationship in which they stand to each other. The chief question arising here is, whether they represent the same language in two different periods of age, or two contemporary dialects, spoken in two different regions of the territories of the ancient Bactrian empire. Our knowledge of the dialects of the Iranian tongues and the periods of their development at the time previous to the Christian era is so limited, that it is extremely difficult to decide this question in a satisfactory way.

The differences between these two dialects are both of a phonetical and grammatical nature. Were the deviations merely of the former kind, we should be fully entitled to ascribe them to two different ways of pronouncing certain vowels and consonants, as generally happens in different districts with nations speaking the same language; but should we discover in one of them more full and ancient forms, in the other evidently younger and more contracted ones, then the difference between the Gâtha language and the usual Zend is to be ascribed to different periods of age.

The phonetical differences of the Gâtha language from that of the other books are at the first glance so considerable as to induce one to trace them to different localities of the same country, and not to different ages. But on a closer inquiry (see pag. 54.) we find that several of these phonetical peculiarities, as the constant lengthening of vowels at the end, the severing of one syllable into two, as for instances, of *yâ* (nom. pl. neutr. relat. pronoun), into *ëeâ* are attributable to the original singing of the Gâthas, and the other smaller pieces constituting the older Yasna (see the 3rd Essay), and are not to be traced to dialectical differences. Only the change of one vowel into another, such as that of final *ô*, or initial *a*, into *ĕ*, e. g. *kĕ* = *kô* who? *ĕmavat* strong, instead of *amavat*, and some consonantal changes, as *t* into *ç*, e. g. *çtavaç* praising, instead of *çtavat*, or the softening of harsh consonants as *âdrĕñg* (acc. pl. of *âtar* fire), instead of *âthrãç*, etc. are suggestive of dialectical differences. But these deviations being of no great importance, no great weight can be attached to them. These deviations are merely of such a nature as might exist between the idioms even of neighbouring villages or towns of the same district. That these peculiarities, notwithstanding their insignificance, have been preserved so well, and not been dissolved and changed into the current Bactrian language, which is preserved in the largest portion of the Zend-Avesta, indicate the high reverence in which those songs stood in the eyes of the Zoroastrians. In consideration, that (besides other reasons) the Gâthas contain the undoubted teaching of Zarathustra himself, we do not hesitate to believe this peculiar language used in the Gâthas to have been the dialect of his town or village.

As to grammatical forms, the Gâtha dialect shows not a few deviations from the current Zend language. Most of them represent evidently a more primitive state of the Bactrian language, nearer to its Arian source; some might be considered as merely dialectical peculiarities. The genit. sg. of the mascul. in *a* (see pag. 99) ends nearly throughout in the Gâthas in *ahyâ*, whilst in the common Zend language there is always *ahê*, apparently a contraction of *ahya* which exactly corresponds with the Sanscrit genitive termination *asya* (e. g. g. *daêvahyâ*, Z. *daêvahê*, S. *devasya*); the first pers. imperat. expressing intention, volition (see pag. 69), requires only *â*, *âi*, whereas in the common Zend language the derived termination *âni* which is used in Sanscrit also, prevails; the usual infinitive formation in the Gâthas is that in *dyâi* which is so extremely frequent in the Vedic dialect, while it is nearly unknown to the common Zend, and totally to the classical Sanscrit. In the pronouns chiefly, the language of the songs shows more ancient forms, than we find in any other part of the Zend Avesta, e. g. *maibyâ* " to me" which original form, agreeing so well with the Sanscrit *mahyam*, Lat. *mihi* (to me), is nowhere to be found in the common Zend; *mahyâ* m., compare further *maqyâo* f. of me, etc. (see pag. 107). The frequent use of the enclitic pronominal particles *î*, *îm*, *hîm*, etc. (see pag. 110), which is a peculiar feature of the Vedic dialect, distinguishing it from the classical Sanscrit, and the great liberty of separating the preposition from its verb, a chief characteristic of the most ancient forms of the Sanscrit (in the Vedas), and the Grecian languages (in Homer), indicate a more ancient stage of language in the Gâtha dialect, than we can discover in the common Zend, where these traces of a more floating and not quite settled form of expression are much fewer, and only in poetical pieces occasionally to be met with.

According to these remarks, there seems to be no doubt, that the dialect of the Gâthas shows some traces of a higher antiquity than we can claim for the classical Zend. But the differences are not so great as between the Vedic and the classical Sanscrit, and the Greek of Homer and that of the Attic dialect; the two dialects of the Zend-Avesta being much closer to each other. They represent one and the same language with such changes as might be brought about within the space of one or two centuries. The Gâtha dialect is therefore only 100 or, at the utmost, 200 years older than the classical Zend which was the standard language of the ancient Iranian empire as depicted in the earlier parts of the Shâhnâmeh.

---

## 37.—ZEND IN ITS AFFINITY TO SANSCRIT.

Every one who is but slightly acquainted with Sanscrit and Persian will, after the perusal of this sketch of the Zend grammar, be wholly convinced of the close affinity, in which the Zend language stands to both. Its relation to the most ancient Sanscrit, the so-called Vedic dialect,* is as close, as that of the different dialects of the Grecian language (Aeolic, Ionic, Doric, Attic) to each other. The language of the sacred songs of the Brahmans, and that of the Parsee are nothing but two dialects of two or more tribes of one and the same nation. As the Ionians, Dorians, Aetolians, etc. are different tribes of the Grecian nation, whose general name was "Hellenes," the ancient Brahmans and Parsees are only two tribes of the nation which is called *Aryas* both in Veda and Zend Avesta, the former to be compared with the Ionians, the latter with the Dorians. The most striking feature perceptible in comparing both Zend dialects with Sanscrit is, that they are related to the Vedic form of Sanscrit only, not to the classical. In verbal forms, chiefly moods, and tenses, the classical Sanscrit, though very rich in comparison with modern language, is much poorer than its more primitive form preserved in the Vedas only, having lost, for instance, various forms of the subjunctive mood, most tenses of all other moods, except Indicative (in the Imperative and Potential moods only the present tense is preserved), the manifold forms expressing the infinitive mood,† etc. whereas all these formations in the greatest completeness are to be met with in the Vedas, Zend Avesta, and the Homeric Greek. The syntactical structure is in the Vedic Sanscrit and the Zend simple enough, and verbal forms are much more frequently made use of than in the classical Sanscrit. There is no doubt, the classical Sanscrit was formed long after the separation of the Iranians from the Hindus.

* It is distinct from the usual Sanscrit which alone is studied by the Brahmans now-a-days. The most learned Pandits of the present Brahmanic community who are perfectly acquainted with the classical Sanscrit language, are utterly unable to explain the more ancient portions of the Vedas, which consist chiefly of songs, and speculations on the meaning of rites, their effects, ect. They learn them parrot-like by heart, but do not care a bit about understanding their prayers. If they are requested to tell the meaning, they resort to a commentary made several hundred years ago by a highly celebrated Brahman (Sâyana), but which on a closer enquiry proves to be entirely insufficient (it is made without critical judgement, and without reference to parallels), to arrive at a complete insight into the Vedic antiquity.

† In the Vedic language there are eleven to be observed which are reduced in the classical Sanscrit to one only.

The differences between the Vedic Sanscrit and the Zend languages are very little in grammar, but are chiefly of a phonetical and lexicographical nature, as the difference is between German and Dutch. There are certain regular changes of sounds, and other phonetical peculiarities perceptible, the knowledge of which enables the philologist to make the Zend word easily a pure Sanscrit one. The most remarkable changes are as follows :—

initial *s* in Sanscrit is in the Zend changed into *h;* ex. : *soma* (the sacred drink of the Brahmans)= *homa ; sama* together, the same = *hama ; sa* demonstrat. "he" = *ha ; sach* to follow (Latin *sequi*) = *hach*. In the word itself the same change takes place, e. g. *aṇhu* = S. *asu* life, except now and then in the last syllable, where *s* is preserved e. g. *yazaê-sa* thou shalt worship. At the end it remains, except if preceded by *a* in which case both (*as*) are changed into *ô ;* only before the enclitic particle *cha* the sibilant is kept, e. g. *ahurô*, (S. *asura-s*) living, instead of *ahura-s*, but *ahuraçcha* (and the living).

*h* of Sanscrit where it is no original, but only a derived sound, never remains in Zend. It is generally changed into *z*, e. g. *zi* "then, therefore" = S. *hi*, *zima* winter = S. *hima*, *zbê* (root) to invoke = S. *hvê*. *z* is further equivalent to S. *j*, e. g. *zan* (mod. Pers. *zâdan*) to produce = S. *jan* (Lat. *gigno*), *hizva* tongue = *jihvâ*. On the peculiar sound *q* which corresponds with S. *sv* see pag. 55.

In comparing Zend with Sanscrit words, we observe often a nasal sound in the former which is wanting in the latter. This is chiefly the case before *h*, e. g. *aṇhu* = *asu*.

Instead of Sanscrit *çv* we meet in Zend with *çp* e. g. *açpa* a horse = S. *açva* (Late. *equus*, Greek *hippos*), *viçpa* all = S. *viçva*, *çpâ* a dog = S. *çvâ*.

In the place of the Sanscrit *ṛt* we find, besides the regular change *aret* (the vowel *ṛ* in Sanscrit is in Zend always represented by *are*, *ere* ; *ṛt* itself is a corruption of *art*) that in *ash* e. g. *mashya* man = S. *martya* (Lat. *mortalis*, Greek *brotos*), *asha* true, sincere = S. *ṛta*.

These are the most remarkable phonetical differences existing between Sanscrit and Zend. By means of them it is very simple to find the corresponding word in Sanscrit, and in strictly adhering to them we can discover a large number of Vedic words and forms. There are, of course, now and then (as is always the case in the dialects of every language) peculiar words to be found in Zend, but always traceable to Sanscrit roots.

A comparison of the grammatical forms of Zend and Sanscrit can be dispensed with here. They are so very near, and in many cases entirely identical, that they suggest themselves by itself to any one who has but a slight acquaintance with Sanscrit. The strongest proof for the original identity of Sanscrit and Zend forms, as regards grammar, is the harmony of both even in irregularities. So, for instance, the deviations of the pronominal declensions from that of the nouns, are in both languages the same, e. g. Z. *ahmái* to him = S. *asmâi*, *kahmâi* to whom = S. *kasmâi*, *yaêshãm* of whom (pls) = S. *yeshâm*. The declension of irregular nouns as Z. *çpan* a dog = S. *çvan* Z. *pantan* way = S. *pathin* (path) is the same : nom. sg. Z. *çpá* = S. *çvá* ; acc. *çpánem* = *çvánam* ; dat. *çúnê* = *çunê* ; gen. *çúnó* = *çunas* ; nom. pl, *çpánó* = *çvánas*, gen. *çúnãm* = *çunâm* ; nom. sg. *pañta* = *panthâs* ; instr. *patha* = *pathá* ; nom. pl. *pañtánó* = *panthánas* ; acc. *pathó* = *pathas* ; gen. *pathãm* = *pathâm*.

The extremely close affinity of Zend to the Vedic Sanscrit is chiefly to be seen from some present tense forms which differ in the classical Sanscrit from the Vedic ; compare, for instance, Z. *kerenaomi*, I make, with the Vedic *kṛnomi* and the S. *karomi* ; Z. *jamaiti* (instead of *gamaiti*). Ved. *gamati*, S. *gacchati* he goes ; Z. *gerewnámi*, Ved. *gṛbhnámi*, S. *gṛhnámi* I take.

# III.

# THE ZEND AVESTA

OR

# THE SCRIPTURE OF THE PARSEES.

---

IN this essay I intend to give a brief statement of the contents of the whole of the Zend-Avesta together with translations of some important or interesting pieces contained therein, which will enable the reader to form a judgment of the true character of the sacred books of the Parsees. As to the arrangement of the matter, I think it most suitable to treat, after some preliminary remarks, about the name, extent, and preservation of the sacred books, of the separate parts which make up the present Parsee scripture, and finally attempt to give a short critical and historical sketch of this religious literature.

## 1.—NAME OF THE PARSEE SCRIPTURE.

The sacred writings of the Parsees are called Zend-Avesta.* This position of the two words ought to be inverted, for in the Pehlevi books always the order "Avesta-Zend" is used. That this order is the only right and correct one, is corroborated by the traditional as well as the critical and historical explanations of both terms. In the opinion of the present Parsee priests,

* The whole question is fully treated in my paper "on the names Avesta, Zend, and Pazend" published in the Journal of the German Oriental Society Vol. IX. pgg. 694-703.

*Avesta* means the original text of the sacred books, and *Zend* denotes the Pehlevi translation. This view is, however, not quite correct, though it is not wholly unfounded. It is true, many passages may be alleged from Pehlevi books, whence to gather clearly, that Zend simply means "translation" or "commentary." The only objection to be raised against the priestly opinion, is, that "Zend" cannot mean the Pehlevi-translation; for, in the Pehlevi translation of the Yasna, the scripture is, if mentioned, always denoted by *Avesta-Zand** which circumstance evidently shows, that the "Zand" was regarded by the translators as forming part of the scripture. Were the name "Zand" applicable to the Pehlevi-translation only, it would be a gross self-conceit on the part of the translators, had they styled their own work a part of the scripture believed to have been revealed to Zarathustra by Ahuramazda. From this use made of the denomination "Avesta u Zand" by the Pehlevi-translators we are fully entitled to gather that "Zand" was a translation or commentary on the Avesta, known as a sacred book to those learned Parsee-priests, to whose labours we owe the translation of the present scripture of the Parsees into the Pehlevi-language. We, therefore, may suppose that the scripture, they undertook to translate, comprised both parts. This scripture being the same as that which is extant now-a-days, we dare say that Zand as well as Avesta is preserved to a certain extent, and to be found in the texts, which now go by the name Zend-Avesta. What parts of these texts form the Avesta or the original text, and what make up the Zend or the commentary, will be seen from the statement of the contents of the several books, and the short historical sketch of the Zend literature to be given at the end of this essay. From this the reader will learn, that the Avesta is to be found chiefly in Yasna (or Izeshne), while all the other books represent pre-eminently (not exclusively) the proper Zend literature.

* See Ys. 30, 1. 31, 1. where "*urvâta*," which is translated by "two speeches" is explained by "Avesta Zend." The Supreme Dustoor Neriosengh, in his Sanscrit translation of the larger portion of the Yasna, renders the word "Zand" by *artha* i. e. meaning.

It is, therefore, a wholly erroneous innovation which has been adopted by some European scholars to call the scripture of the Parsees simply " Avesta."* It is true, this word is used in Parsee-books of later date, as in the Pehlevi-translation of the Vendidâd, and in the Bundehesh in the meaning of " text, scripture," or in that of " passage from the sacred text ;" but in such cases it is only an abbreviation for quoting the scripture; each Avesta or sacred text being supposed to have its time hallowed interpretation, called Zend.†

The meaning of the term " Zend" varied at different periods. Originally it meant the interpretation of the sacred texts descended from Zarathustra and his disciples by the successors of the prophet. In the course of time these interpretations being regarded as equally sacred with the original texts, both were then called Avesta. Both having become unintelligible, to the majority of the Zoroastrians, in consequence of their language having died out, they required, in order to become intelligible, a Zend or explanation again. This new Zend was furnished by the most learned priests of the Sassanian period in the shape of a translation into the vernacular language of Persia (Pehlevi) in those days, which translation, being the only source to the priests of the present time whence to derive any knowledge of the old texts, is therefore, the only Zend or explanation they know of.

The word " Zend," however, implied originally more than a mere commentary on the Avesta or sacred texts. The interpretation of the scripture gave rise to new doctrines, the whole of which were called Zend doctrine (*Zandi-âgâhi*), as we

* Its Pehlevi form is *apistak*. As to its origin *(ava-sthâ)* it means simply " text, scripture." In the sacred texts themselves the word is not used. It is in all probability identical with *pustak* book, used in the late Sanscrit and Marathi, where it is evidently a foreign word, borrowed from the middle age Persian.

† This word is never to be met with in the texts, is to be traced to the root *zan* = S. *jnâ* Greek *gno*, to know, whence it is derived by means of the abstract suffix *ti* .(see pag. 88); its original form, therefore, was *zanti*, conveying the general sense of " knowledge," applicable to interpretations of any kind whatever. It is the explanation of what is contained in the Avesta, which, as being regarded as the word of God himself, is unintelligible to men without interpretation.

can see from the opening verse of the Pehlevi book Bundehesh, which runs as follows :

"The Zend doctrine (treats) first of the creations of Hormuzd, and those of his adversary, the evil spirit, then of the creatures from their creation to the time of the other body (resurrection)."

And in fact we find in the Bundehesh doctrines propounded which in their very germs only are to be found in the original Avesta, for instance, the creation of the world within six periods, the duration of the world for 12,000 years, the particulars about the resurrection of the dead, etc. These doctrines being known already to Grecian writers (see pag. 6), who lived before the Christian era, we are fully entitled to suppose the Zend doctrine to have been completely developed for about 500 years before the Sassanids.

The name *Pazend* to be met with frequently in connection with Avesta and Zend, denotes the further explanation of the Zend doctrine (see the passage of Masûdi, quoted above pag. 11).

---

## 2.—THE ORIGINAL EXTENT OF THE ZEND AVESTA. THE NOSKS.

From the ancient classical writers as well as from the traditional reports of the Parsees, we learn, that the religious literature of the ancient Persians was of a considerable extent, whilst the Zend-Avesta in its present state is a comparatively small book. This circumstance necessarily leads us to the conclusion, that the sacred literature of the Zoroastrians has experienced very heavy losses. Thus Pliny reports, on the authority of Hermippos, the Grecian philosopher (see pag. 5), that Zoroaster composed two millions of verses, and an Arabic historian ABU JAFIR ATTAVARI* assures us, that Zoroaster's writings comprised twelve thousand cowskins (parchments). These reports might appear, at the first glance, to be exaggerations, but for the enor-

* Hyde de religione veterum Persarum pag. 318.

mous extent of the sacred books of other oriental nations,* there is sufficient reason of believing, that the number and extent of the books, ascribed to Zoroaster by his followers, was very considerable. The loss of most of these books, known to the ancient Greeks, is ascribed by the Parsees mainly to direct persecution by Alexander the Great, who is said to have ordered all the sacred books of the Persians, which he could obtain, to be burnt, except those which treated of medicine and astronomy. This report, although it be the unanimous belief of the Parsees up to this time, is certainly unfounded; because it contradicts entirely all that we know of the enlightened policy of the great Macedonian conqueror in his treatment of nations conquered by him. To burn books, in order to uproot a religion, resembles rather Mohammedan fanaticism than Grecian policy; we, therefore, may consider this Parsee report to be based on confounding the Macedonian conquest with that achieved by the Mohammedans. But at that time most of the ancient literature was already lost. The real cause of this loss was, that in consequence of the Macedonian conquest Greecian civilization began to spread in Persia, which proved detrimental to the ancient religion. For 500 years (from the Macedonian conquest 335 B. C. to the Sassanian accession to the throne of Iran 235 A. D.), the Zoroastrian religion seems not to have been supported by any kings, in consequence of which neglect it gradually decayed. During that period the greater portion of the ancient literature, which, on account of its language being dying out, had become unintelligible to the majority even of the priests, was lost. The Sassanids, then, in their endeavours to revive the Zoroastrian faith, were searching after all the fragments which still were extant and to their exertions we owe in the main that condition

* Thus for instance, comprises, the text of the sacred books of the southern Buddhists (Cylon, Birma, etc.), according to Turnour's computation, 4500 leaves, each page being about two feet long, and containing nine lines. The lines being written without any space between the words, we may conclude, that in one line there are at least as many as ten lines of any ordinary poetical measure. Thus 4500 × 2 × 9 = 81,000 lines of ordinary measure. Again the commentary exten is to a greater length, than the texts, so that there must be nearly 2,000,000 lines in the whole of the sacred books.

and extent of the Zend-Avesta, in which it has reached our time.

The names of all the books together with short summaries of their contents are, however, extant. According to the reports relating to them, the whole scripture consisted of twenty-one parts, called *Nosks*,* each containing Avesta and Zend i. e. an original text and a commentary on it. The number "twenty-one" was to correspond to the twenty-one words, of which the most sacred prayer of the Zoroastrians "*yatha ahû vairyô*" (commonly called *Honovar*) was composed. This division is artificial, and apparently, made for the purpose of bringing the whole of the once very extensive scripture into accordance with the number of the words of that most sacred prayer; each section of it to be headed by one of those holy words to which a supernatural power is ascribed. That such a division into 21 sections really existed, cannot be doubted; for the names of the several sections together with the number of chapters they comprise, and a short statement of the chief contents, are still extant. I shall enumerate them according to the reports of them to be found in two *Rivâyats*.†

1. *Setudtar* or *setud-yashts* (Zend: *çtaota, çtûiti* praise, worship) comprised 33 chapters, containing the praise and worship of the *Yazatas* or angels.

* The word occurs in the Zend-Avesta itself Yas. 9,22 in the compound: *naçkô-fraçdonhô* studying the Nosks, that is to say, the different parts of the Scripture. Its origin is uncertain, and I doubt whether it is of Arian origin. Undoubtedly the Arabic *nuskhah*, pl. *nusakh*, transcript, copy of a book, is identical with it; but this word seems to be strange to the Arabic also; because its supposed root *nasakha* bears in the Semitic languages the meaning of 'sweeping away,' abolishing, which has nothing to do with writing.

† The *Rivâyats* are collections of correspondences and decisions of Destoors in matters concerning the religion. In the excellent library of my friend Nushirvanjee Jamaspjee, High-priest of the Parsees at Poona, there are two collections of this kind, one called *Barzu qivâm eddîn* (collected about 250 years ago,) the other going by the name *Shapoor Baroochee* (about 125 years ago.) From these two collections my remarks on the Nosks are taken. The younger brother of Nushirvanjee, Destoor Hoshengjee from Mhow, who lived for some time at Poona, was kind enough to furnish me with some extracts from these books. He is an excellent Persian scholar and well versed in all books relating to religion.

2. *Setudgar*, 22 chapters, containing prayers and instructions to men about good actions, chiefly those called *jadângôi* i. e. to induce another to assist a fellowman.

3. *Vahista mâthra*, 22 chapters, treating of abstinence, piety, religion, qualities of Zoroaster, etc.

4. *Bagha*, 21 chapters, containing an explanation of the religious duties, the orders and commandments of God and obedience of men, how to guard against hell and to reach heaven.

5. *Dâm dât*, 22 chapters; contents: knowledge of this and that world (the future life), qualities of their inhabitants; the revelations of God concerning heaven, earth, water, trees, fire, men and beasts; the resurrection of the dead and the passing of the bridge *chinvat* (the way to heaven).

6. *Nâdur*, 35 chapters, containing astronomy, geography, astrology, translated into Arabic under the name *Yûntâl*; and known to the Persians by the name *fawâmas jân*.

7. *Pacham*, 22 chapters, treating of what food is allowed or prohibited, of the reward to be obtained in the other world for keeping the six *Gahanbârs** and the *Fravardagan*.†

8. *Ratushtâi*, 50 chapters (at the time of Alexander the Great only 13 were extant), treated of the different *ratus* or heads in the creation, such as kings, High-priests, Ministers, and gave statements as to what fishes are Ormuzd's and what Ahriman's; there was besides a geopraphical section in it.

9. *Burush*, 60 chapters (thirteen of which only were extant at the time of Alexander the Great), contents: the code of law for kings, governors, etc.; workmanship of various kinds; the sin of lying.

10. *Koshusarub*, 60 ch. (at Alexander's times 15 only were extant), treated of metaphysics, natural philosophy, divinity, etc.

11. *Vishtasp Nosk*, 60 ch. (at Alexander's time only 10),

* The festivals to be observed in the commemoration of the creation of the world. Originally they represent the six seasons of the year.

† The five last days of the year and the five first ones of the new year. During these ten days the *Farvars* (*Fravashi*) or souls of the deceased are believed to appear in the houses. The days, therefore, are called *Fravardagan*.

on the reign of king Gustasp and his conversion to the religion and its propagation by him through the world.

12. *Chidrusht*, 22 ch., was divided into six parts: 1st on the nature of the divine being, the Zoroastrian faith, the duties enjoined by it; 2nd, on obedience due to the king; 3rd, on the reward for good actions in the other world, and how to be saved from hell; 4th, on the structure of the world, agriculture, botany, etc.; 5th, on the four classes of which a nation consists, viz. rulers, warriors, agriculturists, traders and workmen (the contents of the sixth division are left out).

13. *Safand*, 60 ch., on the miracles of Zoroaster, the Gahânbar, etc.

14. *Jarasht*, 22 ch., on the human life, from the birth to its end and up to the day of resurrection; on the causes of man's birth, why some are born in wealth, others in poverty.

15. *Baghan Yesh*, 17 ch., containing the praise of high angel-like men.

16. *Naydrum*, 54 ch., code of law, stating what is allowed, and what prohibited.

17. *Húsparûm*, 64 ch., on medicine, astronomy, midwifery, etc.

18. *Domasarûb*, 65 ch., on the marriages between the nearest relatives (called *qaetvo-datha*); Zoology and treatment of animals.

19, *Húskarûm*, 52 ch., treating of the civil and criminal law; of the boundaries of the country, of the resurrection.

20. *Vendidâd*, 22 ch., on removal of uncleanliness of every description from which great defects arise in the world.

21. *Hadokht*, 30 ch., on the creation, its wonders, structure, etc.

---

## 3.—THE BOOKS NOW EXTANT. THE SUPPOSED ZOROASTRIAN AUTHORSHIP.

Of these twenty-one sections, which have been enumerated, only one, the *Vendidad*, is completely preserved; of some of the others, as the *Vishtasp Nosk, Bagh** fragments only are extant, the far larger number of these ancient sacred books having been lost for ever. There are, however, in the *Zend Avesta* as used by the Parsee-priests now-a-days, besides the Vendidâd other books extant which are in the foregoing list either not mentioned at all, as *Yaçna* (*Izeshne*) and *Visparad*, or not clearly enough indicated as the *Yashts*. These latter very likely were comprised in the first, and fifteenth Nosk, as well as the smaller prayers (*Nyâyish, Afrîgân, Gâhs, Sîrozah*).

As to *Izeshne* and *Visparad*, they cannot be found out in one of these twenty one Nosks, if we examine the statements of their contents. They were separate from them altogether, occupying in regard to these Nosks the same rank as the Vedas in the Brahmanic literature in reference to the Shâstras, and Purânas. That Izeshne is the most sacred book of the whole Zend-Avesta may be easily ascertained from perusing and comparing it with the other books contained in this scripture of the Parsees now-a-days, where (as in Vendidâd) many verses from it are quoted as most sacred and scriptural.

The difference between *Yaçna* and the *Avesta-Zend* said to have been contained in the twenty-one Nosks is about the same as that between the five Mosaic books (Pentateuch) which always were believed by the Jews to be the most sacred part of the Old Testament,† and the other books of the Old Testament together with the different parts of the extensive *Talmud.*‡ There is no doubt and the present state of the only Nosk now completely extant, viz. that of the Vendidad, seems to prove it, that by far the larger bulk of the various contents of these books, contained Zend or the explanation of an ancient sacred text, called Avesta.

* In the library of Destoor Nushirvanjee there is a small fragment of this Nosk, which is not known as yet in Europe; it is about treatment of a dead body and the fate of the soul immediately after death.

† The Samaritan Jews acknowledge up to this day the five books of Moses only as scripture.

‡ Some portions of this enormously large work which may be said even to surpass as to bigness the original extent of the twenty-one Nosks, chiefly those called *Halakah* i. e. rule, are as authoritative for the Jews as the Thorah (5 books of Moses) itself.

A good deal of the contents of those Zend books is in all probability extant in the Pehlevi literature, as yet very imperfectly known in Europe.

From the contents of the Noaks, as given above, we clearly see that they must represent the whole religious and scientific literature current throughout the ancient Persian empire; for they treated not only of religious topics, but of medicine, astronomy, agriculture, botany, philosophy, etc. That the contents of those Zoroastrian books which were known to the Greeks and Romans, were of such a various character, undoubtedly follows from their reports which have reached our time. Indices of them, like those catalogues of the ancient literature known to Parsee priests now-a-days, were extant at the time of Alexander the Great; because Hermippos (see p. 5) is said to have read and perused such a catalogue. This extensive ancient literature, which in all probability was complete already in 400 B. C. (see the 27th paragraph of this Essay) shows the great activity and scientific interest exhibited by the priests of the Zoroastrian religion in olden times. Such a comprehensive literature was of course the work of centuries, chiefly if one takes into consideration the scarcity and expensiveness of fit writing materials,* the clumsiness of the ancient characters used (in all probability a kind of cuneiform), and the long time which orientals require for an original composition. The sacred literature of the Jews to be dated from the early times of Moses (either 1300 or 1500 B. C.) down to the close of the Talmudic literature (960 A. D.), comprises a space of about 2,400 years. Were we to apply the same calculation to the Zoroastrian literature, its beginning were to be placed at such an early period as 2800 B. C. which would not contradict in the least the statements made by the Greeks† about the age in which the founder

* They used cowskins which were prepared for that purpose. In the fragments of the ancient literature, as extant in the Zend-Avesta, no where a word of the meaning "to write" is to be found. That is merely fortuitous; because systematical books on scientific matters can never be composed without the aid of writing. That the art of writing in the shape of an alphabet, like that used now by the European nations, was perfectly known to the Persians in the 6th century before the Christian era, we know now from the inscriptions of the kings of the Achemenidian dynasty, such as Cyrus and Darius.

† See the 4th Essay.

of the Parsee religion is said by them to have been living. At all events this much seems to be certain, that at least a thousand years must have elapsed, before such a various and bulky sacred literature could grow up out of the seeds sown by the great founder of the Parsee creed, Zarathustra Spitama.

As to the authorship of these books, they were ascribed by the ancient Greeks and Romans, and are, by the present Parsees, to Zoroaster himself. This opinion being so old as to have been known to the Greeks several centuries previous to the commencement of the Christian era, we may presume, that it is not without foundation, though, on the other hand, it is impossible for a modern critic to believe that such an extensive literature as this, treating of such various topics, was the work of a single man. The Parsee tradition, it is true, gets over this difficulty by asserting, that all the 21 Nosks, were written by God himself, and given to Zoroaster as his prophet to forward them to mankind. But such assertions being inadmissible in modern criticism, which tries to solve a problem by appeal to reason not to miracles of the most extraordinary character, we must dispense with it entirely, the more as such claims to God's immediate authorship of the whole Zend-Avesta never are made in any one of the books which are now extant. They claim to divine revelation (only the Yaçna, not the Vendidâd) but not in such a form as to exclude all activity from the part of the receiving prophet. As to the nature of this revelation, the reader may best learn it from the second Gâtha of which I shall give a translation in this essay, in the seventh paragraph. He will see that the prophet was believed to have held conversations with God himself, questioning the Supreme Being about all matters of importance and receiving always the right answers to his questions. The prophet accordingly, after having been instructed, communicated these contents of his conversations with God to his disciples and the public at large. Who wrote them down, is quite uncertain; for in the old books no mention of this circumstance is made. The scanty pieces which can be traced to the founder himself, were very likely not written down by him, but learnt by heart by his disciples as was the case with the numerous Vedic songs which for centuries were handed down orally only. To the European reader it may be somewhat astonishing to hear that such large books as the Vedas could be faithfully and accurately retained in the memory for centuries; but considering that up to the present day thousands of Brahmans are living who are able to recite parrot-like with the greatest accuracy, even as to accents, without any mistake the whole of one of the Vedas, we are driven to admit that the same could have been the case at those early times to which we must trace the origin of the Zoroastrian religion. As long as the language of the songs or prayers repeated was a living one and perfectly intelligible, there was no need of committing them to writing; but as soon as it had become dead, the aid of writing was required in order to guard the sacred prayers against corruption and mutilation. That was, in all probability, the case already 1,000 years before the beginning of our era.

To revert to the supposed Zoroastrian authorship of the whole Zend-Avesta, believed by the ancient Greeks as well as by the modern Parsees, the solution of the difficulty is simple, if we take the name "Zarathustra" (Zoroaster) not as the proper name of only one individual, but as that of the spiritual heads of the religious community of the ancient Persians in general. That this was really the case the reader will see from the 4th Essay. The founder is distinguished by the name "Spitama." The High-priest of the whole Parsee community was believed to be the successor of the great founder *Zarathustra Spitama*, and to have inherited his spirit. His sayings and decisions, therefore, were listened to with the greatest reverence, and in the course of time believed to be as sacred and divine as those which are with reason to be ascribed to the founder alone. The meaning of the supposed Zoroastrian authorship of the whole Zend-Avesta is, that the scripture is the joint work of the High-priests in the ancient Persian empire and other priests nearest to them in rank, compiled in the course of centuries. This circumstance throws light upon the fact, that only the Destoors or present High-priests are required to understand the meaning of the Zend-Avesta, and none who has not thoroughly studied it can be acknowledged as a real Destoor.

The pieces extant now, and collected for the first time in Westergoard's valuable edition comprise the following books: YASNA (Izeshne), VISPORATU (Visparad,) VENDIDAD, and 24 sections, called YASHTS, including fragments of the Hadokht (No. 22 in West. edition) and Vistasp Nosks (No. 24); to these are added some small prayers of different kinds, called: AFRIGAN (3), NYAYISH (6), GAH (5), with some miscellaneous fragments (9), and the SIROZAH (30 days) or calendar. We shall treat of each of them in particular.

---

## 4.—YASNA.

The word "Yaçna"* corresponds entirely to the S. *yajna* "sacrifice," and does not signify only mere prayers, like the Nyâyish, but prayers referring to sacrificial rites including the performance of the latter. The solemn recital of the Yasna before the fire is always connected with ceremonies, to which several of the prayers, contained in the Yasna, allude. So they require consecrated water *zaothra*, a kind of bread, *qaretem* i. e. food in Zend, butter, called *gâus hudhâo*, fresh milk, called *gâus jîvya*, meat (*myazda*,)† the branches of the *Homa* plant together with one of the pomegranate (*hadhânaèpâta*), the juice of the Homa plant, (*para-haoma*), hair of an ox (*varaça*), and a bundle of twigs, (*bareçma*, now-a-days *barsom*), which are tied together by means of a reed. Without these implements, which are evidently the remnants of sacrifices, agreeing to a certain extent withthose of

* *Izeshne* is the Pehlevi form of it; the root is *yaz*, *yaç*, to worship, by means of acrifices and prayers; *na* forms abstract nouns in the Zend (see pag. 88.), and in Pehlevi *sne*, *shne* answers the same purpose.

† The Dustoors now-a-days understand by it "fruit," which they use when performing the Izeshne ceremony. But originally it meant "flesh," as may be clearly seen from the cognate Armenian *mis* meat; comp. Sanscr. *mânsa* being identical with "meat."

the Brahmans, as we shall see in the 4th Essay, no Izeshne can be performed by the priest. All these things must be in readiness, except the prepared Homa juice, and placed on a table of marble opposite to the fire of the *Dâdgâh* or the common hearth of the temple (not before the sacred fires *Aderan* or *Behrâm*), before the Izeshne ceremony can be commenced.

The Yasna at the present time comprises 72 chapters, which number (6 times 12) is very likely to represent the six *gahânbârs* or seasons, during which Ahuramazda is said to have created the world. At all events the extension of the several sections of the Yasna, called *Hâ* (from *hâta* in Zend) to the number 72, is not fortuitous, but was purposely made, as we may ascertain easily from the fact, that several chapters occur twice within the compass of those 72. For instance, the 61st and 72nd chapter are the same ; the 18th contains nothing but verses from the Gâtha portion of the Yasna.

On a closer enquiry we find it really consisting of at least two different parts, distinguishable by considerable difference as to language and contents. One part we may call " the old," the other " the younger Yasna." The old Yasna is written in a peculiar dialect, styled by me the Gâtha dialect in the 2nd Essay, where its chief peculiarities have been pointed out.

All pieces written in this peculiar dialect* formed originally a separate book, which was believed to be sacred even at the time of the composition of all other books, contained in the present Zend-Avesta. The original name of this collection was, in all likelihood, *mãthra çpeñta* (called *Mansarspend* in Persian writings) i. e. the holy word, several times mentioned in Vendidâd (4, 44.) in the meaning of " Scripture." Its different parts were known by different names, as *Gâthas* or songs, *Yasna haptanhaiti* or the Yasna of seven chapters, which often are quoted in the other books, as Ys. 57, 8. (where the angel Serosh is said to have first recited the five Gâthas of Zarathustra

* These are the five Gâthas : Ys. 28—34. ; 43—46 ; 47—50 ; 51 ; 53 ; *Yasna haptanhaiti* (Yasna of seven chapters) 35—41, and some other smaller pieces, as Ys. 4, 27 ; 11, 9. 17. 18 ; 12 ; 13 ; 14 ; 15, 2. 3. ; 27, 13. 14 ; 56 ; 58.

Spitama), 71, 11. 12. 18. (where the Gâthas, the sacrificial prayers, and Yasna haptanhaiti, are distinguished, and a collection of all prayers is mentioned besides). In Vendidâd, chiefly in its 10th chapter, many sacred prayers are quoted, which all are to be found in the old Yasna, written in the peculiar Gâtha dialect.

In the 1st chapter of Visparad, we find a series of sacred prayers (or rather their angels*) invoked. This passage being of the greatest importance for the history of the Zend literature, I shall point out here all that refers therein to this matter. As sacred prayers and sacred literature in general the following pieces are there enumerated : 1, the three most sacred small prayers : *Yathâ ahu vairyô* (Yas. 27, 13.), *ashem vohû* (Yas. 27, 14), and *yênhê hâtam*† (Yas. 4, 27.) ; 2, the *Gâtha ahunavaiti* (Yas. 28—34.) ; 3, *Yaçna haptanhaitis* (Yas. 35-41) ; 4, *Gâtha ustavaiti* (Yas. 43-46.) ; 5, *Gâtha çpeñtâ-mainyus* (47-50.) ; 6, *Gâtha vohu-khshathra* (51) ; 7, *Gâtha vahistôistis* (53) ; 8, *Dahmi vanuhi* and *âfriti* (the *Dahman Afrigân* Yas. 60, the principal prayer for the deceased pious Zoroastrians, called *dahma*) ; 9, *Airyama ishyô* (Yas. 54, a short prayer, now used at the time of the solemnization of a marriage) ; 10, *Fshûsômãthra* (Yas. 58, a prayer for prosperity) ; 11, *Berezô hadaokhdha* (perhaps Yas. 15) ; 12, the conversations with,

* According to the Zoroastrian ideas every thing of the good creation, being animated or inanimated, is presided over by an angel, as the reader will learn from the eleventh paragraph of this chapter.

† These three prayers are very short ; it is, therefore, somewhat hazardous to venture a translation of them. The words themselves do not offer much difficulty, but the context does. The commencement of the first means : Both the two lives *(ahû)* and the master of every pure thing *(ratus ashâtchît hacha)* are to be believed in *(vairyô* lit. to be chosen). These two lives, to which frequently allusions are made, are either that of the body, and that of the soul, or this life, and that to come. The 'master of every pure thing' is an idea quite peculiar to the Zoroastrian theology. Every thing in creation is placed under a ruler, see the remarks in the eleventh paragraph. *Ashem vohu* means : 'the truth is good' ; it refers to the truth in thought, word and deed, which is the principle of the whole Zoroastrian moral. The five *Gathas* have their names from their respective beginning words except the first, which is called by the prayer *yathâ ahû vairyô*, which precedes this Gâtha.

and teaching of Ahuramazda, as imparted to the King and Chief High-priest (*Zarathustrôtemô* i. e. the highest Zarathustra) of a whole country, by which a book like the Vendidâd is to be understood, as we shall see afterwards.

In Vendidâd 18, 51. three classes of sacred writings are enumerated in the following order : Gâthas, Yasna (by which very likely the Yasna haptanhaiti is to be understood), and a sacred tradition in a conversational form (called *paitiparsta—çravaṇhem*), which appears to be a work like the present Vendidâd.

From these passages we may gather with certainty, that the old Yasna i. e. that part of the present Yasna, which is written in the peculiar Gâtha dialect, is the most ancient of the whole Zend-Avesta, being known as scripture already to the younger Yasna, the Visparat and Vendidâd. All other pieces in the Yasna, written in the common Zend language, are evidently of a younger date ; we may call them, therefore, the younger Yasna. I proceed now to the contents of the chief parts of the old Yasna, the Gathas.

---

## 5.—GATHAS.

The Gâthas, five in number, are comparatively small collections of metrical pieces, containing small prayers, songs, and hymns, which exhibit generally philosophical and abstract thoughts about metaphysical subjects. The name "Gâtha" well known in the Sanscrit and Pâli literature also, means "song" (chiefly a stanza which contains allusions to historical facts, as living in the mouth of the ancient bards), from the root *gâi*, to sing. That they were sung, is not to be doubted, as we may learn from Grecian reports (see pag. 8.), and from their being metrical compositions, the recital of which is always designated by a separate word: *fraçrâvayêiti.** At present the priests do not make any distinction as to the way of repeating the different parts of the Zend-Avesta; they recite them equally in a singing tone. That is not to be wondered at, the different constituents of the Yasna being unknown to the present priests, which was not the case in ancients times.

As to the metres, used in the Gâthas, we find them of the same nature as those which are to be found in the Vedic hymns. No rhyme is observed, only the syllables are counted, without much attention being paid to their quantity. The five collections, into which the Gâthas have been brought, exhibit each a different metre. Verses of the same metre were put together, irrespective of their contents. So the first Gâtha contains verses, each of which consists of 48 syllables; in the second the metre is of 55 syllables, in the third of 44, etc. The number of syllables is not always strictly observed; we find, now and then, one less or one more. To give the reader an idea of this poetry, I shall quote some instances. In the first Gâtha (called ahunavaiti), each verse consists of 3 lines, each comprising 16 syllables, as may be seen from the following example (Yas. 31,8.):

*At thwâ meṇhî paourvîm mazdâ yazûm çtôi mananhâ*<br>
so thee I thought first mazda great in creation, in mind,

*Vaṇhĕus ptarĕm manaṇhô hyat thwâ hĕm chashmainî*<br>
of the good father mind therefore thee together in the eye

*hĕñgrabem haithîm ashahyâ dâmîm aṇhĕus ahurem skyaothanaĕshû*†<br>
I seized (perceived) true of purity creator of life living in actions

In this verse the cesura is after the seventh syllable; the second half of each line comprises then nine syllables. Were

* There are three expressions used for the recital of the sacred texts, viz. *mar* to repeat, *dreñj* (or *framru*), to recite with a low voice, and *çrâvay*, *fraçrâvay* to recite with a loud voice, with observation of musical accents. The first expression conveys the most general meaning, viz. to repeat from memory (*mar* = S. *smar* to recollect), which was very likely done in the same way, as the Brahmans repeat the verses of Rigveda, with the observation of the accents in general. *Dreñj* means evidently a peculiar way of recital; it is chiefly applied to spells, to be compared with the recital of the verses of the Yajurveda, which is done with a low voice, and monotonously; *fraçrâvay* is then the solemn recital in form of a very simple tune, comparable to the way of singing Sâmaveda by the Brahmans. This expression is pre-eminently applied to the Gâthas. Comp. Yas. 19,6. Vend. 4,45. Yt. 13,20.

† See a more free translation pag. 144.

the cesura after the 8th syllable, and should the whole verse comprise only 32, instead of 48 syllables, this metre would correspond to the Sanscrit shloka, consisting of four half verses (padas), each comprising 8 syllables, which metre is preserved in some fragments of epic songs in the Zend Avesta, as we shall see afterwards. It stands nearest to the Gâyatrî metre, which consists of 24 syllables, divisible into 3 padas, each comprising 8 syllables.

In the second Gâtha (called *ustavaiti,* from the beginning words, *ustâ ahmâi* hail him !) there are five lines in each stanza, consisting of eleven syllables, for instance (Yas. 44,3.) :

*Tat* *thwâ* *pereçâ* *eres* *môi* *vaochâ* *ahurâ!*
That thee I will ask right me tell living!

*Kaçna* *zāthâ* *ptâ* *ashahyâ* *paouruyô?*
What man creator father of purity first?

*Kaçnâ* *qèng* *çtaremchâ* *dât* *advânem?*
What man sun and stars made path

*Kê* *yâ* *mâo* *ukhshyêitî* *nerefçaitî* *thwat?**
Who (makes) that the moon increases (and) wanes besides thee?

*tâchît* *mazdâ* *vaçemî* *anyâchâ* *vîduyê*
such things mazda! I wish and other to know

This metre is very near to the Vedic *Trishtubh* (which is sacred to the God Indra), which consists of 4 padas, each comprising 11 syllables, which makes 44 in all. That of the ustavaiti Gâtha exceeds it by one pada of 11 syllables only. In the 3rd Gâtha, called *çpeñtâ-mainyus,* however, it is completely extant, each verse there comprising 4 padas, each of 11 syllables, in all 44, just as many as the Trishtubh is composed of.† To obtain the number

* *Thwat* is the ablative case, dependent on *kê (kô)* who ? The meaning "besides, else," here absolutely required for a translation into modern languages, lies implied in the context.—*vîduyê* is a peculiar infinitive form of the root *vid* to know.

† To illustrate this assertion, I subjoin a specimen of this metre taken from Rigveda 1, 189, 1.

*Agne* *naya* *supathâ râyê* *asmân*
O fire god! bring on the good way to wealth us

*viçvâni* *deva* *vayunâni* *vidvân*
all O God! arts knowing!

*yuyodhy* *asmaj* *juhurânam* *enô*
remove from us wrath kindled sin

*bhûyishthâm* *tê* *nama-uktim* *vidhema*
utmost on thee worship-hymn let us bestow!

(Agni! provide us with riches by luck! O thou god, who knowest all arts of obtaining wealth! Remove from us all faults at which thou hast felt angry with us; let us prepare for thee the most excellent hymn for thy worship!).

of syllables which is required for each pada or foot in the specimen quoted above *(tat thwâ pereçâ)*, as well as in other verses of the Gâthas, the sound *ere*, corresponding to the Sanscrit *r* vowel, makes only one syllable, the short *e* (in *vaçemi* S. *vaçmi* I want, wish) being a mere auxiliary vowel, and *u* in *vîduyê* (instead of *vîdyê*) being of the same kind, are not to be counted. The syllables *va* and *ya*, *yê* are often made liquid, as is the case in the Vedic metres also, that is to say, they are pronounced as two syllables like *ua*, *ia iye*. The verse quoted above is, therefore, to be read as follows:

*Tat thwâ perçâ ers môi vochâ ahurâ.*
*kaçnâ zãthâ ptâ ashahyâ pouruyô.*
*kaçnâ qẽñg çtâremchâ dât aduânem.*
*kê yâ mâo ukhshiyêitî nerfçâitî thwat.*
*tâchît mazdâ vaçmî anyâchâ vîdyê.*

In the fourth Gâtha each stanza comprises 3 verses, or 6 pâdas or feet, each consisting of 7 syllables, which makes in all 42. In the fifth Gâtha there are various metres used which I must forego here.

The five Gâthas are expressly designated as the "five Gâthas of Zarathustra" (Yas. 57,8), in order to distinguish them from other Gâthas or songs, as for instance, those devoted to the praise of Homa (Yas. 10). That they really contain the sayings and teaching of the great founder of the Parsee religion, Zarathustra Spitama himself, cannot be doubted, as the reader will perceive from a perusal of the larger portion of them, which will be found in the following paragraphs.

---

## 6.—GATHA AHUNAVAITI.*

It is divided into seven chapters (Yas. chapt. 28-34. West.), which comprise 101 verses, all of them being composed in the same metre, which I described above (pag.136). As to its contents,

* To the explanation of this Gâtha the whole of the first volume of my German work on the Gâthas (pagg. 246) is devoted.

this Gâtha resembles more a collection of scattered verses, than one continuous whole. It is even doubtful, whether the author is always the same, the style being now and then different. But because of one and the same spirit pervading the whole Gâtha, we must allow it to belong to one age only. We have in it, in all probability, the sayings and songs of Zarathustra himself, mixed with those of his disciples *Jâmâçpa*, *Vistaçpa*, and *Frashaostra*. Thus, for instance, the following verse (Yas. 28,7.) must be considered as the composition of one of the disciples of the prophet:

"Come with the good mind, grant prosperity for life long, by means of thy mighty words, o thou Wise! give both, Zarathustra and us, thy powerful assistance to put down the assaults of our enemy."

Here Zarathustra being spoken of in the third, and the author in the first person, we are fully entitled to ascribe the verse to one of his followers, not to him.

The heading of this Gâtha "the revealed thought, the revealed word, the revealed deed of the holy Zarathustra; the arch-angels first sang the Gâthas"* is of high interest; because it does not refer to this Gâtha alone, but to all five indiscriminately. These introductory remarks are written not in the peculiar Gâtha dialect, but in the common Zend language, which circumstance shows clearly, that they proceed not from one of the authors, but from a subsequent collector of these sacred verses. We learn from it, that the Gâthas were believed to contain all that has been revealed† to Zarathustra Spitama; that he learnt them from the choir of the archangels who sang them to his mental ears, when, in a state of ecstasy, his mind was raised to heaven.

I shall present to the reader translations of some parts of this Gâtha. In its second section (chapt. 29), it is related that the *Geus urvâ* i. e., the soul of the animated creation, was crying

* The chapters of the Yasna are called Hâs, which is a corruption of the Zend word *hâta*.

† A full explanation of this heading is given in my German work on the Gâthas vol. I. pag. 41-46.

aloud in consequence of* attacks made upon his life, and imploring the assistance of the archangels. The murderer, frightened by this crying, asked one of the archangels, *Asha* (Ardibehesht), as to who had been appointed to protect this soul of the earth. Asha referred him to Mazda, who is "the most wise, and the giver of oracles." Mazda answered, that *Gêus urvâ* was being cut into pieces for the benefit of the agriculturist. Mazda now deliberated with Asha, as to who might be fit to communicate this declaration of the heavenly council to mankind. Asha answered, that there is only one man who heard the orders issued by the celestial councillors, viz. Zarathustra Spitama; he, therefore, was to be endowed with eloquence to bring their messages to the world.

*Gêus urvâ* means the universal soul of earth, the cause of all life and growth. The literal meaning of the word "soul of the cow" implies a simile; for the earth is compared to a cow.† By its cutting and dividing, ploughing is to be understood. The sense of that decree, issued by Ahurmazda and the heavenly council is, that the soil is to be tilled; it, therefore, enjoins

* The term in the original is *yânîm*, which does not signify "good, happy," as the Dustoors mean, but any thing seen when in a state of ecstacy. This meaning is even preserved in the modern Persian word *yân*, a reverie of a fanatic, a trance. The literal meaning is "a walk," as may be seen from its use in the Vedic Sanscrit (root *yâ* to go), but applied to the gesticulations of a prophet or seer, when in ecstacy, it means what he perceives with his mental eye in such an extraordinary frame of mind. The word "to see" is really used in reference to revelation in the Gâthas (see Yas. 43,5. 31,8 28,6.) This application of the word is wholly in accordance with its meaning in the Vedas, where is stated that the sacred songs *(mantra)* have been seen by the Rishis.

† In the Parsee or Pazend language, the name is corrupted to *goshûrûn*, which is very likely preserved in the modern Persian *gawhar* "nature." According to the tradition, he was the first animated creature in the shape of an ox, which after having been killed and cut into pieces, the whole living creation is said to have sprung from his body. The slaughterer of this primary ox, the supposed ancestor of the whole animal kingdom, is often alluded to by the name *gêus tashan* i. e. cutter of the cow. Who was the killer of this ox, is not said in the Zend-Avesta: the tradition charges with this murder, of course, *Angrô-mainyus*, the devil. This legend about the origin of the animated creation apparently refers to sacrificial rites, the creation of the world being considered by several ancient nations as a sacrifice, by the Brahmans as that of Brahma himself, by the ancient Scandinavians, the people of the Edda, as that of the primary giant *Bör*.

agriculture as a religious duty. Zarathustra, when encouraging men by the order of Ahwramazda to cultivate the earth, acts as a prophet of agriculture and civilization. In this capacity we shall find also him afterwards.

In the third section of this Gâtha (Yas. 30) one of the most important pieces of the Gâtha literature is presented to us. It is a metrical speech, delivered by Zarathustra Spitama himself, when standing before the sacred fire, to a numerously attended meeting of his countrymen. The chief tendency of this speech is to induce his countrymen to leave the worship of the devas or gods i. e. polytheism, to bow only before Ahuramazda, and to separate themselves entirely from the idolators. In order to gain his object wished for, he propounds the great difference which exists between the two religions, Monotheism, and Polytheism, showing that, whereas the former is the fountain of all prosperity both in this and the other life, the latter is utterly ruinous to mankind. He attempts further to explain the origin of both these religions so diametrically opposed to each other, and finds it in the existence of two primeval causes, called "existence" and "non-existence." But this merely philosophical doctrine is not to be confounded with his theology, according to which he acknowledged only one God, as will be clearly seen from the second Gâtha. In the following I submit to the reader a translation of the whole of this inaugural speech of Zarathustra.

1. I will now tell you who are assembled here, the wise sayings of the most wise, the praises of the living God, and the songs of the good spirit, the sublime truth which I see arising out of these sacred flames.

2. You shall, therefore, hearken to the soul of nature†

* *Gâus* has in Sanscrit the two meanings "cow," and "earth." In Greek *gê*, earth, is to be traced to this word. In the Vâmadeva songs (4th book of the Rigveda), the *Ribhus* (comparable to the elves of the Teutonic mythology) who represent the creative powers in nature, are said to "have cut the cow and made fertile the earth." The term evidently refers to the cultivation of the soil.

† *Gêus urvâ*, see pag. 140. It is here evidently an allusion made to that legend reported above.

(i. e. to plough and cultivate the earth); contemplate the beams of fire with a most pious mind! Every one, both men and women, ought to-day to choose his creed (between the Deva and the Ahura religion). Ye offspring of renowned ancestors awake to agree with us (i. e. to approve of my lore, to be delivered to you at this moment.)!

(The prophet begins to deliver the words, revealed to him through the sacred flames).

3. In the beginning there was a pair of twins, two spirits, each of a peculiar activity; these are the good, and the base in thought, word and deed. Choose one of these two spirits! Be good, not base!

4. And these two spirits united created the first (the material things); one, the reality, the other, the non-reality. To the liars (the worshippers of the devas i. e. gods) existence will become bad, whilst the believer in the true God enjoys prosperity.

5. Of these two spirits you must choose one, either the evil, the originator of the worst actions, or the true holy spirit. Some may wish to have the hardest lot (i. e. those who will not leave the polytheistic devareligion), others adore Ahuramazda by means of sincere actions.

6. You cannot belong to both of them (i. e. you cannot be worshippers of the one true god, and of many gods at the same time). One of the devas, against whom we are fighting, might overtake you, when in deliberation (what faith you are to embrace), whispering you to choose the naught mind.* Then the devas flock together to assault the two lives (the life of the body, and that of the soul), praised by the prophets.

7. And to succour this life (to increase it), Armaitis† came with wealth, the good and true mind; but the soul, as to time, the first cause among created beings, was with Thee.

8. But when he (the evil spirit) comes with one of these

* *Akem manô* (superlat. *achistem manô)* means literally: naught mind. It is a philosophical term applied by Zarathustra to designate his principle of non-existence, non-reality, which is the cause of all evils.

† She is the genius of earth, and the personification of the prayers.

evils (to sow ill weed among the believers), then thou hast the power through the good mind of punishing them who break their promises, o true spirit !*

9. Thus let us be such as help the life of the future.† The wise living spirits‡ are the greatest supporters of it. The prudent man wishes only to be there where wisdom is at home.

10. Wisdom is the shelter from lies, the annihilation of the destroyer (the evil spirit). All perfect things are garnered up in the splendid residence of the good mind (Vohu-manô), the Wise (Mazda), and the True (Asha)¶ who are known as the best beings.

11. Therefore perform ye the commandments which, pronounced by the Wise (God) himself, have been given to mankind; for they are a nuisance and perdition to liars, but prosperity to the believer in the truth; they are the fountain of happiness.

In the fourth section of the first *Gátha* (Yas. 31) we have a collection of *urvátas* i. e. sayings of Ahuramazda, revealed to his prophet Zarathustra, for the purpose of protecting the good creation from the attacks of the wicked men and evil spirits. The chief means of checking evil influences is the cultivation of the soil. I give some of these verses in translation.

7. He (Ahuramazda) first created through his inborn lustre§ the multitude of celestial bodies, and through his intellect the good creatures, governed by the inborn good mind. Thou living spirit, who art everlasting, makest them (the good creatures) grow.

* That is to say: those who give to-day the solemn promise to leave the polytheistic religion, and to follow that preached by Zarathustra, will be punished by God, should they break their promise.

† In this passage we have the germs of the doctrine of the resurrection of the dead body; see my German work on the Gáthas vol. I. pagg. 109-112.

‡ These are the archangels (Amshaspands).

¶ Three names of archangels.

§ *qáthrá* "by means of his own fire." Ahuramazda as the source of light, which most resembles him and where he appears to his prophet, is called *qáthrô* i. e. having his own light (not borrowed).

8. When my eyes beheld Thee, the essence of truth, the creator of life, who manifests his life in his works, then I knew Thee to be the primeval spirit, thou Wise, so high in mind as to create the world, and the father of the good mind.*

9. In Thee was Armaiti (genius of earth), in Thee the very wise fertiliser of the soil,† o thou wise living Spirit ! when thou hast made her paths that she might go from the tiller of the soil to him who does not cultivate it.‡

10. Of these two (the agriculturist and the herdsman), she chose the pious cultivator, the propagator of life, whom she blessed with the riches produced by the good mind. All that do not till her, but *continue to* worship the devas (devils), have no share in her good tidings (the fruits produced by her, and the blessings of civilization).

11. When thou madest the world with its bodies, and (gavest them) motions and speeches, then thou Wise ! hast created at first through thy mind the gaêthas (estates fenced in), and the sacred visions (*daênâo*), and intellects.¶

18. Do not listen to the sayings and precepts of the wicked (the evil spirit), because he has given to distruction house, vil-

* *Vohu-manô.* He represents the life in men and animals, the principle of vitality. If Ahuramazda is called the father of *Vohu-manô*, it means, that all vital powers in the animated beings have sprung out of him, as the supreme being.

† Literally : the cutter of the cow *(gêus tashâ)* see above pag. 140.

‡ The meaning is, that Armaiti, the genius of earth, is wandering from spot to spot to convert deserts and wildernesses into fruit-fields. She goes from the agriculturist to the shepherd who still adheres to the ancestoral nomadic life to call upon him to cultivate the soil also.

¶ By *gaêthas*, frequently mentioned in the Zend Avesta, the ancient settlements of the Iranian agriculturists are to be understood. Ahuramazda is constantly called their creator, that means, that these settlements belong to a very remote antiquity, and that they form the basis of the Ahura religion, or the religion of the agriculturists. The *daênas* are the revelations communicated to the prophets through visions. The root of the word is *dî*, to see (preserved in the modern Persian *dîdan* to see ; it is related to the Sanscrit root *dhyâi* to think, thinking being considered to be a seeing by means of the mental eyes). Afterwards it passed into the more general meaning of " religion, creed" and is kept in the form *dîn* up to this day in Persian, whence it was incorporated to Arabic, like many other Iranian words, at the time anterior to Mohammed. This word is to be found in the Litthuanian language (a link of the Arian stock) also in the form *dainô*, meaning a song (the mental fiction of the poet).

lage, district and province. Therefore kill them (the wicked) with the sword !

The fifth section (Hâ) of this Gâthas (Yas. 32.) is one of the most difficult pieces of the whole Yasna. It depicts in glowing colours idolatry, and its evil consequences. The prophet directs his speech against the devas or gods in the following manner.

3. Ye devas have sprung out of the evil spirit who takes possession of you by intoxication (Soma), teaching you manifold arts to deceive and destroy mankind, for which arts you are notorious every where.

4. Inspired by this evil spirit you have invented spells, which are applied by the most wicked pleasing the devas only, but rejected by the good spirit ; but the wicked perish through the wisdom and holiness of the living wise spirit.

5. Ye gods and thou evil spirit ! ye by means of your base mind, your base words, your base actions rob mankind of its earthly and immortal welfare by raising the wicked to power.

Of the sixth and seventh Has (Yas. 33-34) I give only a few verses in translation.

33,2. Who are opposed in their thoughts, words and actions to the wicked, and think of the welfare of creation,* their efforts will be crowned by success through the mercy of Ahuramazda.

3. Whether of two lords, of two yeomen, of two bondmen,† behaves himself well towards a religious man (an adherent to the Zoroastrian religion), and furthers the works of life by tilling the soil : that one will *once* be in the fields of the True and Good (i. e. in paradise).

4. But by means of prayer I will remove from thee (thy community), Mazda ! the irreligiosity and wickedness, the disobedi-

* The term in Zend is *açti* existence. It is the consequence of the adherence to the good principle.

† These three names of the members of the ancient Iranian community are very frequently used in the gâthas, but not in the other books of Zend Avesta. The word for " lord" is : *qaêtus* i. e. owner, that for yeoman : *airyama* i. e. associate, friend, that for bondman *verezena* i. e. workman, labourer.

ence of the lord and the falsehood of the servant belonging to him and his yeoman, and frustrate the most wicked designs plotted for destroying the fields.

14. Among the priests Zarathustra maintains the opinion, that the peculiar nature of each body (living creature) subsists through the wisdom of the good mind, through the sincerity of action, and the hearing of, and keeping to, the revealed word.

34,1. Immortality, truth, wealth, health, all these gifts to be granted in consequence of (pious) actions, words, and worshipping, to these *men* (who pray here), are plentiful in thy possession, Ahuramazda!

---

## 7.—GATHA USTAVAITI (Yasna 43-46).*

Whilst the first Gatha appears to be a mere collection of fragments of songs and scattered verses made without any other plan than to transmit to posterity what was believed to be the true and genuine sayings of the prophet, in this second gâtha we may observe a certain scheme carried out. Although it contains, with the exception of a few verses only (46, 13-17), all sayings of Zarathustra himself, yet they have not been put together, as is the case in many other instances, irrespective of their contents, but in a certain order with the view of presenting the followers of the prophet a true image of the mission, activity, and teaching of their great master. In the first section of this gâtha (43), his mission by the order of Ahuramazda, is announced, in the second (44) he receives instructions from the supreme Being about the highest matters of human speculation, in the third (45) he appears as a prophet before a large assembly of his countrymen to propound to them his new doctrines, and in the fourth or last section (46), we find different verses referring to the fate of the prophet, the congregation which he established and his most eminent friends and supporters.

* See the text with a literal latin translation in my larger work on the Gathas II. pp. 2-18, and the commentary on it II. pp. 59-154.

This gâtha being the most important piece of the whole Zend Avesta, from which to obtain an accurate knowledge of Zarathustra's teaching and activity, I submit to the reader in the following pages a translation of the whole of it.

1 (43.)

1. Blessed is he, blessed are all men, to whom the living wise god of his own command should grant those two everlasting powers (wholesomeness and immortality). For this very good I beseech Thee (Ahuramazda). Mayest thou through thy angel of piety (Armaiti) give me happiness, the good true things, and the possession of the good mind!

2. I believe Thee to be the best being of all, the source of light for the world. Every body shall choose Thee (believe in thee) as the source of light, Thee, Thee, holiest spirit Mazda! Thou createst all good true things by means of the power of thy good mind at any time, and promisest us (who believe in Thee) a long life.

3. This very man (Sraosha, Serosh), may go (and lead us) to Paradise, he who used to show us the right paths of happiness both in the earthly life and in that of the soul, in the present creations, where thy spirit dwells, the living, the faithful, the generous, the holy, Mazda!

4. I will believe Thee to be the powerful holy (god) Mazda! For thou givest with thy hand, filled with helps, good to the pious man, as well as to the impious, by means of the warmth of the fire* strengthening the good things. From this reason the vigour of the good mind has fallen to my lot.

5. Thus I believed in Thee as the holy God, thou living Wise! Because, I beheld Thee to be the primeval cause of life in the creation. For thou hast made (instituted) holy customs and words, thou hast given a bad fortune (emptiness) to the base, and a good to the good man. I will believe in Thee, thou glorious God! in the last (future) period of creation.

* The fire is supposed in the Zend-Avesta and the Vedas to be spread everywhere as the cause of all life.

6. In whatever period of my life I believed in Thee, living Wise ! in that thou camest with wealth and with the good mind through the actions of which our manours thrive. To these (men who are present) Armaiti* tells the everlasting laws, given by thy intellect, which nobody may abolish.

7. Thus I believed in Thee, thou holy living wise Spirit ! therefore he (Sraosha) came to me and asked : who art thou ? whose son art thou ? How dost thou at present think to increase and improve thy estates and their beings (to increase the power of the good mind in all thy territories where thou appearest)?

8. I replied to him : Firstly, I am Zarathustra. I will show myself as a destroyer to the liars as well as be the comforter for the religious men. As long as I can praise and glorify Thee, thou Wise ! I shall enlighten and awaken all that aspire to property (who wish to separate themselves from the nomadic tribes and become settlers in a certain country).

9. Thus I believed in Thee, the holy one, thou living Wise ! therefore he came to me with the good mind (and I asked him) : To whom dost thou wish the increase of this life should be communicated ? Standing at thy fire amongst thy worshippers who pray to Thee, I will be mindful of the truth (to improve all good things) as long as I shall be able.

10. Thus mayest thou grant me the truth. Then I shall call myself, if accompanied by the angel of piety, a pious obedient man. And I will ask in the behalf of both of us† whatever thou mayest be asked. For the king will, as it is only allowed to mighty men, make Thee for thy answers a mighty fire (to cause thy glory and adoration to be spread over many countries like the splendour of a blazing large flame).

11. Thus I believed in Thee, the holy one, thou living Wise ! Therefore he (the angel Sraosha) came to me, with the good mind. For because I, who am your most obedient servant amongst

* The genius of earth.

† Refers to Zarathustra and Kava Vistaspa, for whose welfare and renown the prophet is here praying.

men, am ready to destroy the enemies first by the recital of your* words : so tell me the best to be done.

12. And when thou camest to instruct me, and toldst me the true things ; then thou gavest me thy command not to appear (before large assemblies as a prophet) without having received a (special) revelation, before the angel Sraosha endowed with the sublime truth, which may impart your good true things to the two friction woods (by means of which the holiest fire, the source of all good in the creation, is produced) for the benefit (of all beings) have come to me.

13. Then I believed in Thee, the holy one, thou living Wise ! Therefore he came to me with the good mind. Let me obtain the things which I wished for ; grant me the gift of a long life ; none of you may detain it from me for the benefit of the good creation subject to thy dominion.

14. Therefore the powerful proprietor *of all goods* (Sraosha) communicated to me, his friend, knowledge of thy helps (thy powers) ; for endowed with all the gifts granted by Thee, as to the various kinds of speech, like all other men, who recite thy prayers, I was resolved upon making my appearance in *public as a prophet.*

15. Thus I believed in Thee, thou holy one, thou living Wise ! There he came to me with the good mind. May the greatest happiness brightly blaze out of these flames ! may the number of the worshippers of the liar (bad spirit) diminish ! may all those (that are here present) address themselves to the priests of the holy fire !

16. Thus prays, living Wise ! Zarathustra and every holy (pure) man for all that choose (as their guide) the holiest spirit. Essence and truth (the foundations of the good creation) may become predominant in the world ! In every being, which beholds the sun's light, Armaiti (the genius of piety) may reside ! She who causes by her actions through the good mind all growth.

2 (44.)

1. That I will ask Thee, tell me it right, thou living God !

* Refers to Ahuramazda and the archangels, forming the celestial council.

whether your friend (Sraosha) be willing to recite his own hymn as prayer to my friend (Frashaostra or Vistâçpa), thou Wise! and whether he should come to us with the good mind, to perform for us true actions of friendship.*

2. That I will ask Thee, tell me it right, thou living God! How arose the best *present* life (this world)? By what means are the present things (the world) to be supported? That spirit, the holy, (Vohu mano) o true wise spirit! is the guardian of the beings to ward off from them every evil, he is the promoter of all life.

3. That I will ask Thee, tell me it right, thou living God! Who was in the beginning the father and creator of truth? Who made the sun and stars the way? Who causes the moon to increase and wane if not thou? This I wish to know except what I already know.

4. That I will ask Thee, tell me it right, thou living God! Who is holding the earth and the skies above it? Who made the waters and the trees of the field? Who is in the winds and storms that they so quickly run? Who is the creator of the good minded beings, thou Wise?

5. That I will ask Thee, tell me it right, thou living God! Who made the lights of good effect and the darkness? Who made the sleep of good effect and the activity? Who made morning, noon and night, reminding always the priest of his duties?

6. That I will ask Thee, tell me it, thou living God! what verses I shall recite, if the following ones have been recited :† (a) Piety doubles the truth by her actions. (b,) He collects wealth with the good mind. (c,) Whom hast thou made for the imperishable cow Rânyôskereti ?‡

7. That I will ask Thee, tell me it right, thou living God!

* The meaning is: the prophet wants to ascertain from Ahuramazda, whether or not the Genius Serosh would make communications to his (the prophet's) friend.

† Here are quoted the beginning words of three certainly ancient prayers which are no longer known.

‡ This is a mythological name of the earth to be found in the Gâthas only. It means "producing the two friction woods (two wooden sticks, by means of rubbing which fire was produced)." See my work on the Gâthas vol. II. pag. 91-92.

Who has prepared the Bactrian (*berekhdha*) home with its properties? Who fashioned, moving up and down, like a weaver, the excellent son out of the father ?* To become acquainted with these things, I approach Thee, wise, holy spirit! creator of all beings!

8. That I will ask Thee, tell me it right, thou living God! What soul (what guardian angel) may tell me good things, to perform five times (a day)† the duties which are enjoined by thyself, thou Wise! and to recite those prayers which are communicated for the welfare *of all beings* by the good mind. What good, intended for the increase of life, is to be had: that may come to me.

9. That I will ask Thee, tell me it right, thou living God! How shall I bless that creed which thy friend (Serosh) who protects it with a true and good mind in the assembly of *the heavenly spirits*, ought to promulgate to the mighty king.

10. That I will ask Thee, instruct me right, thou living God! in the faith which, being the best of all, may protect my possession and may really produce the good things, by means of the words, and actions of the angel of the earth. My heart wishes (it is my lively desire), that I may know Thee, thou Wise!

11. That I will ask Thee, tell me it right, thou living God! how the angel of earth‡ may visit those men to whom the belief in Thee is preached. By these there I am acknowledged *as a prophet*; but all dissenters are regarded as my enemies.

12. That I will ask Thee, tell me it right thou living God! who is the religious man and who the impious, after whom I wish to inquire? With whom of both is the black *spirit*, and with whom the bright one? Is it not right to consider the impious man who attacks me or Thee to be a black one?

* This refers to the production of fire by means of two wooden sticks, which was in ancient times the most sacred way of bringing into existence the fire, commonly called 'Ahuramazda's son. See my work on the Gâthas II. pag. 81-82.

† The so-called five gâhs: Hâvânîm from 6-10 A. M., Rapithwan 10 A. M—3 P. M., Uzayêirina from 3 P. M—6 (sunset), Aiwiçrûthrema from 6-12 P. M., Ushahina from 12-6 A. M.

‡ This refers to the wanderings of Armaiti, the genius of earth, by which is to be understood the progress of agriculture and the arts of a more civilized life.

13. That I will ask Thee, tell me it right thou living God! How shall we drive away the destruction (destroyer) from this place to those, who full of disobedience do not respect the truth in keeping it, nor care about the thriving of the good mind (that it may be diffused all over the earth).

14. That I will ask Thee, tell me it right, thou living God! How shall I deliver the destroyer to the hands of truth to be annihilated by means of the hymns for thy praise? If thou Wise! communicatest to me an efficacious spell to be applied against the impious man, then I will destroy every difficulty and every misfortune.

15. That I will ask Thee, tell me it right, thou living God! When or to whom of the Lords givest thou as proprietor this fat flock (of sheep), two armies being gathered for a combat in silence, by means of those sayings which thou Wise! art desirous of pronouncing?

16. That I will ask Thee, tell me it right, thou living God! who killed the hostile demons of different shapes, to enable me to become acquainted with the rules established for the course of the two lives (physical and spiritual)? So may the angel Serosh, assisted by the good mind, shine for every one towards whom thou art propitious.

17. That I will ask Thee, tell me it right, thou living God! How may I come to your (of God and the angels) dwelling place to hear you sing? Aloud I express my wish to obtain the help of the angel of integrity, and that of immortality, by means of that song which is a treasure of truth.

18. That I will ask Thee, tell me it right, thou living God! How shall I, thou true! spend this gift, ten pregnant mares and even more* to obtain in future the two powers of integrity (wholesomeness) and immortality, in the same way as thou hast granted them to these men (to others known to the prophets)?

19. That I will ask Thee, tell me it right, thou living God!

* Refers to a sacrifice. Sacrifices of animals were customary at Zarathustra's time.

How is the first intellect* of that man, who does not return *what he has received* to the offerer of this gift,† of him, who does not grant any thing to the speaker of truth ; for the last intellect of this man (his doing) is already known to me.

20. What are, thou good ruler Mazda ! the devas (bad spirits) ? Thus I might ask Thee for those who attack the good existence (the good beings), by whose means the priest and prophet of the idols expose the earth (the cultivated countries) to destruction ; and *I wish to know besides* what the false prophet has gained by doing so. Do not, o true God ! grant him a field to fence it in (to make it his own property).

## 3 (45.)

1. All ye, who have come from nigh and far, listen now and hearken *to my speech.* Now I will tell you all about that pair of spirits how it is known to the wise. Neither the ill-speaker (the devil) shall destroy the second (spiritual) life, nor that man, who being a liar with his tongue, professes the false (idolatrous) belief.

2. I will tell you of the two primeval spirits of life, one of whom, the white one, told to the black : Do not follow me, the thoughts, the words, the intellects, the lores, the sayings, the actions, the meditations, the souls ?‡

3. I will tell you the first thought of this life which the living Wise communicated to me, to those among you who do not live according to the sayings (of God and his angels) as I think and pronounce them : to these men the end of life (experience) may be a help.§

4. Thus I will tell which is the best substance of this life. The Wise, who created it, possesses it by means of truth; *I will*

* The first and second intellects are notions of the Zoroastrian philosophy ; see the fourth Essay. The first intellect is that which is innate to the soul which came from heaven, the second is that one which man himself acquired by experience.

† That is to say 'who is ungrateful towards god.'

‡ All things are now following me, I am the only real master and lord, thy empire is nothing but illusion.

§ The meaning is : experience will convince them of the truth of the prophet's words.

*speak of him*, the father of the good active sense (mind), whose daughter Armaiti is endowed with good actions. Not is the being, who creates all, to be deceived.

5. I will tell what the holiest (God) delivered to me, the word, the best to be heard by men, to all who pay me attention and who have come here for this purpose. Wholesomeness and immortality are by means of the good mind's actions in the possession of the living Wise.

6. Thus I will tell you of the greatest of all (Sraosha), who is praising the truth, and doing good, and of all who are gathered round him (to assist him) by order of the holy spirit (Ahuramazda). The living Wise may hear me; by means of his goodness the good mind increases (in the world). He may lead me with the best of his wisdom.

7. By means of his power and his rule the generations gone by subsisted, and also those to come will subsist on him. The sincere man's mind is aspiring to the everlasting immortality, the destroyer of the wicked; she is in the possession of the living Wise, the Lord of the creatures.

8. Him, whom I desire to worship and celebrate with my hymns, I beheld just now with my eyes, him, who knows the truth, him, the living Wise, as the source of the good mind, the good action and the good word. So let us put down our gifts of praise in the dwelling place of the *heavenly* singers (angels).*

9. Him will I adore with our good mind, him, who is always propitious to us at day and night; he, the living Wise, who by his own labour is making the properties (to the religious men), may advance the thriving of our cattle and our men, and through the sublimity of the good mind protect the truth.

10. Him will I adore with the prayers of our devotion, who is known alone to be the living Wise; because he is acknowledged as intelligent and endowed with the true good mind. In his empire there are wholesomeness and immortality; he grants this world these two everlasting powers.

* The meaning is: our prayers, offered here, may go up to heaven, to be heard before the throne of God.

11. He, who thinks the idols and, besides, all those men who think of mischief only, to be base, and distinguishes such people from those who think of the right : his friend, brother or father is Ahuramazda himself. Thus is the saying of the Supreme fire priest.

4. (46).

1. To what country shall I go ? where shall I take my refuge? what country is sheltering tho master (Zarathustra) and his companion ? None of the servants pays reverence to me nor the wicked rulers of the country. How shall I worship Thee further, living Wise ?

2. I know that I am helpless. Look at me being amongst few men, for I have few men (I have lost my followers or they have left me) ; I implore Thee weeping, thou living god who grantest happiness as a friend gives *a present* to his friend. The good of the good mind is in thy own possession thou True* !

4. The wicked man enjoys the fields of the angel of truth who is protecting the earth in the district as well as in the province ; but by choosing evil, instead of good, he can not succeed in his deeds. Who drives him out of his dominion, or out of his property, thou Wise ! he is going further on the paths of good intellect.†

5. If in future a ruler takes hold of one who trespasses the law, or if a noble man takes hold of one who violates the bonds of friendship, or if a religious man living righteously takes hold of a wicked man : he shall, then, having learnt it, inform the master : into distress and utter want he shall be thrown to be unhappy.‡

6. But who, although he may be able, does not go to him

* These two verses (1. 2.) refer evidently to Zarathustra's persecution. I omit the third verse consisting of several sentences which seem not to be connected with each other. See my work on the Gâthas II pag. 130.31.

† It is considered to be a good work to destroy the enemies of agriculture, because by laying waste the cultivated soil they cause great damage to the good creation.

‡ This and the following verses refer to the breaking of solemn promises (called *mithra* see Vend.4) and apostasy.

(the chief of the community), he may, however, follow the customs of the untruth now prevailing.* For *he* is a wicked man whom another wicked considers to be the best one, and he is a religious man whose friend the religious one is. Such sayings of old hast thou revealed, o Wise!

7. Who† is appointed protector of my property, Wise! when the wicked endeavour to hurt me? who else, if not thy fire, and thy mind, through which thou hast created the existence (good beings), thou living God! Tell me the power necessary for holding up the religion.

8. Who spoils my estates, and does not choose me by bowing before my fire (the symbol of the deity), retribution may be made to him for his person in the same way. He shall be excluded from every good possession, but not from a bad one filled up with evils, o thou Wise!

9. Who is that man, who whilst supporting me, made me first acquainted with thee as the most venerable being as the living true God‡? The true sayings revealed by the maker of the earth§ come to my hands by means of thy good mind.

10. What man or what woman, thou living Wise! performs the best actions, known to thee, for the benefit of this (earthly) life, promoting thus the truth for the angel of truth, and spreading thy rule through the good mind, as well as gratifying all those men, who are gathered round me, to adore *the heavenly spirits*: all these I will lead over the bridge of the gatherer (heavenly bridge)¶ *to paradise.*

11. The sway is given into the hands of the priests and pro-

* The meaning is: that man, who does not assist in punishing such crimes as apostasy and promise breaking are, is himself an infidel and not more to be recognized as a member of the Zoroastrian community.

† This verse is one of the most celebrated prayers used by the Parsees now-a-days. It is the so called *Serosh bâj*.

‡ This refers very likely to the *gêus urva* 'the soul of earth' to whose oracles the prophet was constantly listening.

§ Lit. the cutter of the cow; see pag. 139. 40.

¶ None can enter Paradise without having first passed the 'bridge of the Gatherer' (called *Chinvat*), the passing of which can be facilitated to the deceased by prayers recited for him.

phets of idols, who by their *atrocious* actions, endeavour to destroy the human life. Actuated by their own spirit and mind, they ought to avoid the bridge of the gatherer to remain for ever in the dwelling place of destruction (hell).

12. When after the defeat of the enemy Fryâna the true rites (fire-worship and agriculture) arose amongst the (Iranian) tribes, and their allies, thou fenced'st with stakes the earth's estates. Thus the living Wise having fenced them all, he assigned them to those men (his worshippers) as property.*

13. Who amongst men pays zealously reverence to Zarathustra Spitama, such one is fit to deliver in public his lore. To him (Zarathustra) the living Wise entrusted the life (the existence of all good beings to protect them); for him he established through the good mind the estates; him we think to be your (of thyself and thy angels) good friend, thou True!

14. Zarathustra! Who is thy sincere friend *to assist in performing* the great work? Or, who will deliver it in public? The very man to do it, is Kavâ Vîstâspa. I will worship through the words of the good mind all those whom thou hast elected at the *heavenly* meeting.

15. Ye sons of Hêchataspa Spitama! to you I will speak; because you distinguish right from wrong. By means of your actions, the truth, *contained* in the ancient commandments of the living God, has been founded.

16. Venerable Frashostra! Go thou with those helpers whom we both have elected for the benefit of the world (the good beings) to that field where Piety resides, attended by Truth, where the stores of the Good Mind may be acquired, where is the dwelling place of the living Wise (i. e. Paradise).

17. Where from you only blessings not curses,† venerable

* Here the origin of the so called *gaêthas* i. e. possessions, estates, so very frequently alluded to in the Zendavesta, is described. We must understand by them the original settlements of the Iranians exposed to constant attacks from the part of nomadic tribes.

† When on earth, they used to pronounce curses as well as blessings. But in Paradise only good no bad words can be heard from them. They were celebrated magicians *(magavas)*.

wise Jâmâspas ! are to be heard, always (protecting) the goods of the leader and performer of the sacred rites, namely of the living Wise himself, endowed with great intellectual power.

18. For him, who bestowed most favours on me, I collect all the best of my goods *acquired* through the Good Mind. But to their last shifts I will put all those, thou Wise, True ! who have put us to them. I will beseech you to assist me. Such is my decision conceived according to my intellect and under standing.

19. Who makes increase this very life by means of truth to the utmost for me, who am Zarathustra myself, to such one the first (earthly) and the other (spiritual) life will be granted as a reward together with all goods to be had on the imperishable earth. Thou, living Wise ! art the very owner of all these things to the greatest extent, thou, who art my friend, Wise !

## 8.

## THE THREE LAST GATHAS (SPENTA-MAINYUS YS. 47-50; VOHU-KHSHATHREM 51; VAHISTOISTIS 53.) *

These three collections of ancient songs are much smaller, than the two first; the fourth and fifth consist, each of one Hâ, (chapter) only. I give here only a short account of them together with a translation of a few verses. The several chapters, except the last of the third Gâtha (50), form, as regards composition, nowhere a whole, but are, on an average, mere collections of detached verses, which were pronounced at different occasions either by Zarathustra himself, or his disciples. While in the two first Gâthas the majority of verses can be traced to Zarathustra himself, in these three last Gâthas, most verses appear to be the work of the master's disciples, such as Jâmâspa, Frashostra, Vîstâspa, others perhaps even that of their pupils, because all of them are spoken of (chiefly 51) with high reverence.

47,1. Ahuramazda gives through the white (holy) Spirit,

* See my German work vol. II. pagg. 20—38, and 155—217.

appearing in the best thought, the truth of speech, and the sincerity of action, to this world (universe) wholesomeness (Haurvatât), and immortality (Ameretât), wealth (Khshathra) and devotion (Armaiti).*

2. From his (Ahuramazda's) holiest spirit all good has sprung in the words, which are pronounced by the tongue of the Good Mind (*Vohumano*), and the works wrought by the hands of Armaiti (angel of the earth). By means of such a knowledge Mazda himself is the father of all truth (in thought, word, and deed).

48,4. He who created, by means of his wisdom, the good and naught mind in thinking, words, and deeds, rewards his obedient followers with prosperity. Art thou (Mazda !) not he, in whom is the last cause of both intellects (good, and evil) *hidden ?*

48,10. When will appear, thou Wise ! the men of vigour and courage to pollute that intoxicating liquor (the Soma) ? This diabolical art makes the idol priests so overbearing, and the evil spirit, reigning in the countries, increases *this pride.*†

49,4. Those poor (wretches) who, instigated by their base minds, cause mischief and ruin to the wealthy (settlers) through the spells uttered by their tongues, who are devoid of all good works and find delight in evil doings only,—such men produce the devils *(devas)* by means of their pernicious thoughts.

5. Mazda himself, and the prayers *offered by men*, and every one who is a truly noble son of Armaiti (the earth), as well as all that are in thy dominions, O living ! will protect this faith (Zoroastrian religion) by means of the good *inborn* mind.

* Ahuramazda is in this and the following two verses described as the only God and Spirit, in whom good and evil likewise originates. All the Amesha Spentas (archangels) of the latter Parseeism are only his gifts.

† This verse refers to the Brahmanic Soma worship, which, as the cause of so much evil, was cursed by Zarathustra. See the 2nd paragraph in the 4th Essay.

11. The spirits *of the deceased** are fighting against the wicked, ill-minded, ill-speaking, evil doing, evil thinking, disbelievers (in the true god, Ahuramazda). Such men will go to Hell!

50,6. Zarathustra is the prophet who, through his wisdom† and truth, utters in words the sacred thoughts (mantras). Through his tongue he makes known to the world, the laws given by my‡ intellect, the mysteries hidden in my mind.

10. All the luminaries with their bright appearances, all that is endowed with a radiant eye by the good mind, stars and the sun, the day's foreteller, wander *in their spheres* to thy praise, thou living, true, wise Spirit!

51,6. The living Wise bestows, through his power, the best of all upon him who brings offerings to please him; but the worst of all will fall to the lot of him who does not worship God in the last time of the world (when the good is engaged in a hard struggle against the bad).

7. Thou who hast created earth, water and trees, give me immortality (Ameretât), and prosperity (Haurvatât), holiest spirit! Those everlasting powers I will praise with a good mind.

15. Zarathustra assigned in times of yore as a reward to the Magavas§ the Paradise, where first of all Mazda himself was gone! You, *immortal saints!* have in your hands through your good and true mind those two powers¶ (to obtain everlasting life).

* In the original: *urvāçnô* i. e. souls. In the other books the common name of the spirits of the deceased pious Zorastrians, who are fighting against the attacks, made by the hellish empire upon the kingdom of light and goodness, is *Fravashis* i. e. protectors, which name is, however, never to be met with in the Gâthas.

† Lit. "through *mazda*" which word is, now and then, used in the appellative sense "wisdom."

‡ The speaker in this verse, as well as in the whole 50th chapter, is the *gēus urvā*.

§ This word is the original form of "Magi," which name was given in later times to all the Persian priests. Its form in the cuneiform inscriptions is *magush*. According to this verse it seems to have denoted the earliest followers of Zarathustra.

¶ These are *Ameretât*, and *Haurvatât*, the two last of the 7 Archangels in the Parseeism of later periods.

16. Kavâ Vîstâspa obtained through the possession of the spiritual power (*maga*), and through the verses, which the good mind had revealed, that knowledge which the living Wise himself, as the cause of truth, has invented.

17. Frashostra, the noble, wished to see my Highland (*berekhdha Armaiti* i. e. Bactria) to propagate there the good religion. Ahuramazda may bless this undertaking ! cry aloud that they must aspire after truth !

51,18. The wise Jâmâspas, the noble, illustrious, who have the good mind with truth, prefer the settled life*, saying : let me have it, because I cling to thee, Mazda !

53,1. It is reported that Zarathustra Spitama possessed the best good ; for Ahuramazda granted him all, that may be obtained by means of a sincere worship, for ever, all that promotes the good life, and he is giving the same to all those, who keep the words, and perform the actions enjoined by the good religion.

## 9.

## YASNA HAPTANHAITI AND THE OTHER MINOR PIECES OF THE OLD YASNA.

The *Yaçna haptanhaiti* or, as its name indicates, the Yasna, composed of 7 Has (comprising the sections from Yas. 35—41), is, though written in the Gâtha dialect, to be distinguished from the Gâthas. It is undoubtedly very old, but there is no sufficient evidence to trace it to Zarathustra himself. Its contents are simple prayers, in prose, which are to be offered to Ahuramazda, the Amesha spentas, the Fravashis, to the fire, as the symbol of Ahuramazda, who appears in its blazing flame (Yas. 36,1.), to the earth and other female genii (called *genâ* i. e. wife, Greek *gynê*, see Yas. 38,1.), as the angel, presiding over food (*izhâ* corresponding to *ila*, a name of earth, in the Veda), devotion, speech, etc. ; to the waters, to the animating spirit of creation, and to all

* This can be understood only, if one bears in mind, that the Zoroastrian religion has arisen at the time of transition from the pastoral life to agriculture. The kindred Brahmanic tribes, who were inimical to this new mode of life continued to lead the pastoral life of their ancestors. Agriculture was considered as a religious duty by the ancient Zoroastrians.

beings of the good creation. Compared with the Gâthas, they represent the Zoroastrian religion not in its original unaltered, but in a somewhat developed and altered state. The high philosophical ideas which are laid down in Zarathustra's own songs, are partially abandoned, and partially personified, and the philosophical, theological and moral doctrines have given way to the custom, which has remained up to this time, of addressing prayers to all beings of the good nature, irrespective of their being mere abstract nouns, as *Asha* i. e., truth, growth, *Vohû manô*, good mind, or real objects, as waters, trees, fire. The formula, by which here and in the younger Yasna, to which the Yasna haptanhaiti has undoubtedly furnished the model, the prayers begin, viz. *yazamaidê*, we worship, is entirely strange to the Gâthas, as well as the invocation of waters, female genii, etc.; even the names 'Amesha Spenta' (except in the heading of 28,1. see pag. 139) as the general term for the highest angels, and Fravashi, which is so extremely frequent in the later Zend literature, are never to be met with in those metrical pieces.

Although they are younger than the Gâthas, still they have just claims to be considered as more ancient and original than the pieces of the younger Yasna. A very striking proof, besides the difference of dialect, is, that the objects of worship are much fewer than in the younger prayers, that, for instance, the six seasons, the five divisions of the day, the five Gâthas, Zoroaster, the sacred branches (Barsom), the sacred drink (Homa) etc. never are mentioned in "Yasna of seven chapters." It formed originally a separate book, was very likely composed by one of the earliest successors of Zoroaster, and stands in the middle between the Gâthas, and the younger Yasna.

In the following I shall give some extracts from it.

35,1. We worship Ahuramazda the pure, the master of purity. We worship the Amesha spentas (the archangels), the possessors of good, the givers of good. We worship the whole creation of the true spirit, both the spiritual and terrestrial, all that supports (raises) the welfare of the good creation, and the spread of the good Mazdayasna religion.

2. We praise all good thoughts, all good words, all good deeds, which are and will be (which are being done and which have been done)* and we likewise keep clean and pure all that is good.

3. O Ahuramazda, thou true, happy being! we strive to think, to speak, and to do only what of all actions might be best fitted to promote the two lives (that of the body and of the soul).

4. We beseech the spirit of earth by means of these best works (agriculture), to grant us beautiful and fertile fields, to the believer as well as to the unbeliever, to him who has riches as well as to him who has no possession.

37,1. Thus we worship Ahuramazda who created and furthered the spirit of earth, and who created the good waters and trees and the luminaries and the earth and all good things.

2. Him we worship by the first prayers which were made by the spirit of earth, because of his power and greatness and good works.

3. We worship him in calling him by the Ahura names which were chosen by Mazda himself and which are the most sacred. We worship him with our bodies and souls. We worship him as *being united with* the spirits (Fravashis) of the pure men and women.

4. We worship the promotion of all good (Ashem vahistem) all that is very beautiful, shining, immortal, bright, every thing that is good.

## YASNA 12.

This chapter written in the Gatha dialect, contains a formula, by which the ancient Iranians who were weary of worshipping the Devas (Brahmanic gods) and the nomadic life, were received into the new religious community, established by Zarathustra Spitama.

1. I cease to be a Deva *worshipper*. I profess to be

* The words: *verezyamnanãmcha vãverezyamnanãmcha* (see pag. 81. 84. are evidently only an explanatory note of the rare words *yadacha* (yet) now, and *anyadacha*, not now i. e. either in future, or in past.

a Zoroastrian Mazdayasna (worshipper of Ahuramazda), an enemy of the Devas, and a devotee to Ahura, a praiser of the immortal saints (Amesha spentas), a worshipper of the immortal saints. I ascribe all good things to Ahuramazda, who is good, and has good, who is true, lucid, shining, who is the originator of all the best things, of the spirit in nature (*gâus*), of the growth in nature, of the luminaries and the self shining brightness which is in the luminaries.

2. I choose (follow, profess) the holy Armaiti, the good; she may be mine! I abominate all fraud and injury committed on the spirit of earth, and all damage and destruction of the quarters of the Mazdayasnas.

3. I allow the good spirits who reside on this earth in the good animals (as cows, sheep etc.) to go and roam about free according to their pleasure. I praise, besides, all that is offered with prayer to promote the growth of life. I shall cause neither damage nor destruction to the quarters of the Mazdayasnas, neither with my body nor my soul.

4. I forsake the Devas, the wicked, bad, false, untrue, the originators of mischief, who are most baneful, destructive, the basest of all beings. I forsake the Devas and those who are Devas-like, the witches and their like, and any being whatever of such a kind. I forsake them with thoughts, words and deeds; I forsake them hereby publicly and declare that all lie and falsehood is to be done away with.

5. 6. In the same way as Zarathustra at the time when Ahuramazda was holding conversations and meetings with him and both were conversing with each other, forsook the Devas: so do I forsake the Devas, as the holy Zarathustra did.

7. To what party the waters belong, to what party the trees, and the animating spirit of nature, to what party Ahuramazda belongs, who has created this spirit and the pure man; to what party Zarathustra, and Kavâ Vîstâspa and Frashostra and Jâmâspa were, of what party all the ancient firepriests (Soshyañtô) were, the pious, who were spreading the truth: of the same party and creed *am I*.

8. I am a Mazdayasna, a Zoroastrian Mazdayasna. I profess

this religion by praising and preferring it to others (the Deva* religion). I praise the thought, which is good, I praise the word which is good, I praise the work, which is good.

9. I praise the Mazdayasna religion, and the pure brotherhood, which it establishes, and defends against enemies, the Zoroastrian Ahura religion, which is the greatest, best, and most prosperous of all that are, and that will be. I ascribe all good to Ahuramazda. This shall be the praise (profession) of the Mazdayasna religion.

## 10.—THE YOUNGER YASNA.

This part of the Yasna, which is written in the common Zend language, is, as to the history of the Zoroastrian religion, of much less importance than the older Yasna. Its contents are, however, of a various nature, and form evidently either parts of other books, or existed independently. So, for instance, the chapters 1—8, contain the preliminary prayers to the Izeshne ceremony (see page 132), 9—11 refer to the preparation and drinking of the Homa juice, 57 is a Yasht or sacrificial prayer, addressed to the genius Serosh, 19—21 are a commentary (Zend) on the most sacred prayers : *Yathâ ahu vairyô*, *Ashem vohu*, and *Yênhê hâtãm.*

I must refrain here from giving a full account of it, and notice only some remarkable passages, and pieces.

In 18, 5—8 there is a small piece of prayer, concluding with a benediction by the Highpriest, the two last verses of which are of a particular interest. The Highpriest who calls himself Zarathustra (see page 170), addresses all the heads of the various divisions of the Iranian empire as follows :

7. I, who am Zarathustra, exhort the heads† of the houses, of the villages, towns, and countries to think and speak and act according to the good Zoroastrian Ahuramazda religion.

* The word used is *varana, varena* lit. choice (Z. *var.* to choose); it is, then, applied to religion.

† The word used is *fratema* S. *prathama* first. It is one of the Persian words which are to be found in the Old Testament. Its form there is *partemim* (*im* is the Hebrew plural), by which the grandees, of the Persian empire are meant. In the sense of head, chief the word *ratu* is more usual in Zend.

8. I bless the splendour and vigour of the whole good creation, and I curse* the distress and wretchedness of the whole bad creation. What is good and true, that is the best of all.

## (A) HOMA YASHT.

Chapters 9 and 10 which compose the so-called *Homa Yasht*, are, strictly speaking, no part of the Yasna, but belong to that extensive class of Zend literature, which is known by the name of Yashts, or sacrificial invocations of a special divine being. We shall treat afterwards of them. As to style, these two chapters contain no prose, but on a closer inquiry we find them to be verses and at the end (10, 19.) they are even called gâthâo i. e. songs. The metre itself is near the Sanscrit Anushtubh (4 times 8 syllables, with the cesura in the middle of every half verse), which has given origin to the common Shlokas, but it is apparently often disturbed. Each half verse consists of 7-9 syllables, the normal measure being limited to 8.

To give the reader an idea of this ancient metre I subjoin here the commencement of this Yasht.†

| | |
|---|---|
| *Hâvanîm â ratûm â*<br>morning prayer at time at | *Haomô upâit Zarathustrem*<br>Homa came to Zarathustra |
| *âtarem pairi yaozhdathentem*<br>(who was) fire everywhere cleaning | *gâthâoçcha çrâvayañtem.*<br>and the songs singing |
| *â dim pereçat Zarathustrô:*<br>Him asked Zarathustra | *Kô nare ahi yim azem*<br>who, man art thou? whom I |
| *vîçpahê aṇhêus açtvatô*<br>of the whole life endowed with bodies | *çraêstem dâdareça qahê*<br>the best (I) have seen of his own |
| *gayêhê qanvatô ameshahê?*<br>body, brilliant, immortal | *âat mê aêm paiti—aokhta*<br>Then to me that (man) answered |
| *Haomô ashava dûraoshô:*<br>Haoma pure evil-removing: | *Azem ahmi Zarathustra*<br>I am Zarathustra |
| *Haomô ashava dûraoshô;*<br>Homa, the pure, evil-removing | *â mâm yaçaṇuha çpitama!*<br>To me bring worship, spitama! |
| *Frâ mãm hunvaṇuha qaretêê*<br>me squeeze out to taste (me); | *Avi mãm çtaomaini çtûidhi*<br>on me in praise praise |
| *Yatha mâ aparachit*<br>as me the other all | *çaoshyañtô çtavãn*<br>Fire priests praised. |

The word *Homa*, which is identical with the Vedic word *Soma*, is used in two meanings in the Zend-Avesta. First it means

* For blessing and cursing one and the same word is used: *â frinâmi*. The same peculiarity is to be observed in the old Hebrew word *bérék*, to give a blessing, and to curse.

† *ere* is to be read as monosyllabic: *er*; the short *e* does generally not constitute a separate syllable.

the branches of a particular tree,* the juice of which is extracted and drunk before the fire ; secondly they understand by it a genius who has poured his life and vigour into that particular plant. There were many stories current in ancient times about the miraculous effects of the drinking of the Homa juice (a panacea for all diseases), which led to the belief, that the performance of this ceremony, which is nothing but the very much reformed and refined Soma worship of the Brahmans, proves highly beneficial to body and soul. These stories were embodied in a song (preserved in Yas. 9.), which being an enumeration of the miracles, effected by Homa, are his praise. Because of their legendary interest I give here a brief account of them.

Zarathustra, when once engaged at morning time in cleaning and feeding the sacred fire, and singing the sacred hymns, was visited by Homa, who appeared before him with a brilliant supernatural body. Being asked by the prophet, who he was, he told that he was Homa, and requested him to worship him in the same way as the ancient sages and prophets had done. Zarathustra began now a conversation with the angel, as to what men had worshipped him by extracting and drinking the juice of the Homa plant, and what reward they had obtained by it. Homa answered, that the first man who had been worshipping him, was *Vivanhâo* (see paragraph 1, (b) in the 4th Essay). His reward was the birth of *Yima*, the king,† the happy ruler of men in the golden age, under whose reign there was no death, no scorching heat, no benumbing cold, but all happiness, life, immortality (see the 2nd fargard of the Vendidad). The second who obtained a reward for his Homa worship, was *Athwya* (*Abtîn* in the Shâhnâmah). To him was born *Thraêtonô* (*Ferîdûm* in the Shâhnâmah), who slew the dragon, called *Azhi dahâka* (*Zohak*) with three mouths, three tails, six eyes, thousand scales (rings), which was destroying the good creation.

The third, who worshipped Homa was *Thrita* (*Trita* in the

* The Dustoors obtain them from Persia in a dried state. On their preparation see paragraph 1, (c) in the 4th Essay.

† *Yima* has the constant epithet "*Khshaêta*" i. e. king, ruler. The name *Jam-shid* in the Shahnâmah, is nothing but curruption of *Yima-khshaêta*.

Veda), the strongest of the Sâma family, of which the hero Rustem was an offspring. His reward was the birth of two sons: *Urvâkhshaya* and *Keresâspa* (Gershâsp in the Shâhnâmah, *Kriçâçva* in the Veda). *Keresâspa* became a great hero. He killed the dragon Sruvara which had been devouring horses and men.

The fourth benefited by my worship, says Homa at last, was your father Pourushaspa. He was rewarded by your birth. As soon as you were born, he adds further, you recited the sacred prayer, *yathâ ahû vairyô*, which frightened all devils (devas) so much as to make them hide themselves beneath the earth.

Zarathustra, after having attentively listened to the angel's reports, bowed before him and commenced to consecrate the branches of the Homa plant which were before him, in order to put into them secret powers. Then he walked six times round the sacred fire, asking at every turn Homa for a blessing, and sang his praise, that he, for instance, procures to old maids good and rich husbands, and is bestowing blessings of all kinds upon his devotees. He invoked him, at length, to drive away all evil spirits, and guard against all demonical influence.

In the following chapter (10), which is also a metrical composition, the praise of Homa, whose branches are meanwhile being bruised and water poured over them, is continued. "I praise the cloud, and the rain, which make grow thy body on the summits of mountains. I praise the high mountains, where thou hast grown Homa! I praise the earth, the wide, which is full of ways, labouring, thy mother, Homa!" etc.

From the contents of this Homa Yasht one may clearly see, that the Homa worship was not instituted by Zarathustra, but was known at a much earlier period. Zarathustra is only said to have adopted it. But in the second paragraph of the 4th Essay, to which I must refer here the reader, we shall see that he was fighting against the Brahmanic Soma worship and trying to overthrow it.

### (B.) Yas. 19.

This chapter, written in prose, is a kind of theological commentary on the most sacred prayer *Ahunavairya* (Honovar). I give some of its most interesting passages in translation.

1. 2. Zarathustra asked Ahuramazda : Ahuramazda ! holiest spirit ! creator of all the territories which are endowed with bodies (filled with living beings), thou pure ! Which was thy word, Ahuramazda, that thou spokest unto me before there were the heavens, and the waters, and the earth, and the animals, and trees, and the fire, the son of Ahuramazda, before there were the pious man, and the devils (devas), and carnivorous evil spirits (khrafçtra) and men, before there was the whole living creation endowed with bodies, which is created by Mazda, and all good things of a pure appearance ?

3. 4. Ahuramazda then answered : This word were the parts of the Ahuna vairya prayer, O Zarathustra Spitama ! which I spoke unto thee, before there were the heavens, and the waters, etc.

6. Who, in this my world, which is endowed with bodies, repeats, O Zarathustra Spitama ! one part of the Ahuna vairya prayer, or in the course of repeating, mutters it (as spells are muttered), or in the course of muttering sings it, or in the course of singing prays to it*—his soul shall I, who am Ahuramazda, carry all three times over the bridge to paradise (*Vahista*, *Behesht* in Pers.).

7. But who in this my world, which is endowed with bodies, O Zarathustra Spitama ! takes off in muttering a part of the Ahura vairya prayer, either the half, or a third, or a fourth, or a fifth of it (i. e. who mutilates the prayer), his soul shall I, who am Ahuramazda, take out of paradise and carry round about the earth in its full length and breadth.

8. I speak continuously this *sacred* word, which was life, and was a master (one of the heads of the good creation), before the creation of the day, before the waters, earth, trees, the four footed animals, before the birth of the pure man, before the

* Here the different ways of recital are mentioned see about them pag. 136. After singing or reciting sacred verses one prays to them (the verse, or song being considered as a being) by the formula : *Yazamaidê* (we worship, pray) : *Ahunem vairîm* (the Ahuna vairya prayer).

creation of the archangels (Ameshaspentas) with their beautiful bodies.

9. The white (holy) of my two Spirits* has continuously spoken it, in order to produce the works of life for Mazda (me) in the whole good creation, which is, was, and will be.

18. Who are the heads† contained in it? The head of the family, the head of the village, the head of the town (a tribe), the head of the country, and Zarathustra as the fifth in all countries except the Zoroastrian Raji‡ (the country Ragha). The Zoroastrian Ragha namely has four heads only. Who are these heads? The head of the family, of the village, of the town, and Zarathustra as the fourth.

## (C.) YAS. 57.

This chapter is devoted to the praise of the angel Sraosha (Serosh); it is, therefore, called the Serosh Yasht. He is the personification of the whole divine worship of the Parsees. This Yasht is to be recited at the commencement of the night time.

2. We worship *the angel* Serosh, the sincere, the beautiful, the victorious, who protects our territories, the true, the master of truth, who of Ahuramazda's creatures first worshipped Ahuramazda by means of spreading the sacred twigs (Barsom), who worshipped the Ameshaspentas (the archangels), who worshipped the two masters, the two creators§ (*thwôrestâra*), who create all things.

3. For his splendour and beauty, for his power and victory, for his praying to the angels *in our behalf*, I will worship him with an audible prayer and with the offering of consecrated

* The two spirits, united in Ahuramazda, as the only God, are: *çpentô mainyus* (the white) and *angrô mainyus* (the black).

† In the 16th verse was said, that it contains five heads.

‡ The word *rajôit* (ablat. of a crude form *raji*) is evidently nothing but a feminine formation (in *i*) of Ragha. Its original form was *raghyi* i. e. what appertains to Ragha, the Ragha territory; before *yi* which has the power of changing gutterals (*k, g*) into palatals (*ch, j*), the *gh* was changed into *j*.

§ These are: spentô-mainyus, and angrômainyus; see above.

water (*zaothra*). He may come to help us, he, the victorious sincere Serosh.

6. He first spread the bundle of sacred twigs (Barsom), that with three, and that with five, and that with seven, and that with nine stalks, those which were as long as to go up to the knees, and those which went as far as the middle of the breast, (he spread them) to worship, to praise, to satisfy and extol the archangels.

7. He first sang the five Gâthas of Zarathustra Spitama according to their stanzas, and their sentences, distinguishing their high and low tones.

10. He wounds after sunset with his drawn sword the cruel demon Aêshemô (i. e. attack, rapine).

15 18. He slays the demon of destruction (*devî-drukhs*) who prevents the growth of nature, and murders its life. He is the guardian and protector of the whole world here below.* He, who never slumbers and is always awake, protects the creatures of Ahuramazda; he guards with his sword drawn, the whole world endowed with bodies, after sunset, *against the attacks of the demons.* He never enjoyed sleep since the two spirits, the white, and the black, have created *the world*; he is watching the territories of the good creation and fighting, at day and night against the Devas (demons) of Mazenderan.† He is never frightened nor runs away if struggling with the demons; but all the demons must flee from him and hide themselves in darkness.

21. He has a palace with 1000 pillars erected on the highest summit of the mountain Alborj.‡ It has its own light from in-

* In the original: *fravôis* (see the same Yt. 10,103.) which is of the same origin as the modern Persian *farû*, *farûd* down, downwards. The Pelhevi translators (they have *panij* i. e. for, before) misunderstood the rare word.

† In the original: *mâzanya*. These Mazanian devas, several times alluded to in the Zend Avesta, are evidently the Divs of Mazenderan, so well known to the readers of the Shâhnâmah.

‡ In Zend: *Harô berezaiti*, i. e. the high mountain.

side, and from outside it is decorated with stars. His victorious sword is the sacred prayer Ahuna vairya, and the Yasna of seven chapters (see above), and the Fshûsa-prayer (Yas. 58), and all the sections of Yasna.

24. He walks teaching the religion round about the world. Ahuramazda, Vohu-mano, Ashem Vahistem, Khshathra vairya, Spenta Armaitis, Haurvatât and Ameretat,* the Ahuric question, and the Ahuric creed (i. e. their respective angels) believed in it (the religion taught by Serosh).

25. Protect our two lives, that of the body and that of the soul, O Serosh! against death, against the attacks of evil spirits. Give us strength, etc.

## 11. VISPARAD.

The name "Visparad" (Zend : *viçpê ratavô*) means "all heads." By this name a collection of prayers, composed of 23 chapters, is meant. They are written in the usual Zend language, and bear, as to their contents, a great resemblance to the first part of the younger Yasna (chapt. 1-27). They refer to the same ceremony, as that part, viz. to the preparation of sacred water, and consecration of certain offerings, such as sacred bread, the branches of Homa, with a branch of the pomegrante tree, and the juice obtained from them (called *Parahoma*), fruits, butter, hair, fresh milk, flesh, which are carried round about the sacred fire, and after having been shown to it, eaten by the priest, or by the man, in whose favour the ceremony is performed. These offerings, which are nothing but a remnant of the ancient Arian sacrifices, so carefully preserved up to this day by the Brahmans (see paragraph 1 (c) in the 4th Essay), represent a meal, given to all the heads or chiefs (called *ratus*) of both the visible and invisible world, who are all severally invoked. In Yasna (chapt. 1) there are a good many more enumerated than in the first chapter of Visparad. In Yasna the enumeration of "the heads" is begun by Ahuramazda, and the archangels, while

* The six names after that of Ahuramazda are those of the archangels.

in Visparad (1) the invitation* is introduced by the heads of the invisible, spiritual (*mainyava*), and visible, terrestrial (*gaêthya*) world, the chiefs of all that is on heaven, in water, born out of eggs, of what is walking on its face, of quadrupeds, of water crabs.† In this rough division of the created living beings (of the good creation only), the whole animal kingdom is comprised. The primary type of each class is its respective ratu or head. After the heads of the animals, the six heads of the year, or the six seasons,‡ are enumerated, which are now called Gâhânbârs. These are believed to have been instituted by Ahuramazda in commemoration of the six periods, during which, according to the Zoroastrian doctrine, the world has been created, and are strictly observed by the Parsees up to this day. The names of these six seasons are : 1, *Maidhyô-zaremya* (now Medio-zarem, mid-summer), 2, *Maidhyô-shema* (now Medioshem, mid-winter), 3. *Paitis-hahya* (now Paytashem, spring) ; 4. *Ayâthrema* (now Yathrem, rainy season) ; 5. *Maidhyâirya* (now Mediarem, the middle of the year) ; 6. *Hamaspathmaêdaya* (now Hamashpatmâdîm), the season at which great expiatory sacrifices were being brought for the growth of the whole creation§ in the two last months of the year.¶

After the six seasons, the heads of all the sacred prayers, (which are believed to be angels), including chiefly the Gâthas, are invited together with the female genii (*ghena*

* The formula is : *nivaêdhayêmi hañkârayêmi*, i. e. I invite and prepare for, etc. (I prepare a meal and invite to it). To *nivaêdhayêmi* compare the *naivedya* of the Brahmans, i. e. the food given to the gods. By the word "*aham karishye*, i. e. I shall perform a ceremony," the Brahmans begin all their ceremonies.

† *Chaṇra-hâch*, i. e. who follow the order *chanra*, mod. *Pers. changâr*, a crab. That the crabs are creatures of Ahuramazda, is already reported by Theopompos ; see pag. 7.

‡ The ancient name for "season" was the word *ratu* itself, which is preserved in the corresponding Sanscrit *ritu* (the six seasons, as representatives of the Creator Prajâpati or Brahma, are often mentioned in the Vedic writings). But after the employment of this word in a more general sense, *yâre* conveyed their meaning. This is evidently indentical with "year."

§ This implies the name, and its epithet *areto—kerethana*, i. e. killer of enemies, by which animals of the bad creation, as frogs, lizards, serpents, are to be understood.

¶ In the first period heaven was created, in the second the waters, in the third the earth, in the fourth the trees, in the fifth the animals, and in the sixth man.

"who give abundance of all things, and chiefly of posterity," with Ardvi Sûra Anâhita (the heavenly water, see the Aban Yasht), the mountains, the angels Behram, Mithra, Râmanqâçtar (presiding over food), the ruler of the country, the Zarathustrôtema (supreme Highpriest, Destur-i-Desturân) etc.

After this general invitation of the genii of all orders to come to the meal prepared for them, the water, and Barsom (sacred twigs) are presented to them as a welcome (ch. 2). Several other invocations follow (ch. 3). The chief priest, who superintends the whole ceremony, the Zaota (called *Hota* in the Vedas), orders his subordinate priest, *Rathwi*, (now *Raspi*, *Adhvaryu* in the Vedas), to call the different orders of priests, representatives of all the three castes (priests, warriors, cultivators), the heads of houses, villages, towns, and districts, the ladies of houses, other respectable women, etc. Very likely all heads of the Iranian society of a whole district were, if possible, obliged to be present at the time of the celebration of the Gahânbars, for which Visparad seems to be particularly intended, and at which occasions it must be used even now.

This whole assembly praises now all good things (4), after which the chief priest (the Zaota) says, that he is the praiser and worshipper of Ahuramazda and the archangels, and that he is worshipping them in words and ceremonies (5.6.). Then the members of the congregation invoke several genii, as Sraosha, Mithra, etc. (7).

After these introductory prayers, the principal parts of the meal, Homa with a branch of a pomegranate tree, butter, fresh milk, bread, and fruits, flesh, are consecrated and presented to the "heads" of the whole creation (9-12). After the whole meal has been offered in a solemn way, the whole concludes with a series of prayers and invocations, in which, however, nothing remarkable can be found. Therefore I forego to translate some passages out of them.

## 12.—YASHTS.

By the name "Yasht" (*yêsti* i. e. worship by prayers and

sacrifices) there are 24 pieces extant, which have been collected and published for the first time in Westergaard's edition of the Zendavesta (pagg. 143-312). Their chief distinction from the prayers of the Yasna and Visparad is, that each of them is devoted to the praise and worship of one divine being only, or of a certain limited class of divine beings, as to that of Ahuramazda, the archangels (Amshashpants), the heavenly water Ardvi Sûra Anâhita, the sun (Mithra), the star Tistrya, the Fravashis etc., whereas in Yasna and Visparad all these beings are invoked promiscuously. The majority of these beings are called *Yazatas** (now Izad) or angels.

The devotee endeavours by enumeration of all the glorious, feats, achieved by the respective angel, and the miracles, wrought by him, to induce him to come and enjoy the meal, which is prepared for him, and then to bestow a similar blessing upon the present worshipper as had been bestowed by the angel upon his devotees in ancient times.

These praises are often highly poetical, and on a close enquiry we find them to contain really in several cases, metrical verses. They are to be traced to the songs of the Median bards, who are mentioned by Grecian historians, and the primary sources of the legends contained in the Shâhnâmah. For the legendary history of the ancient Iranians and chiefly for a critical inquiry into the celebrated Shâhnâmah, the Yashts are the most important pieces of the Zend Avesta.

I give in the following paragraphs a brief summary of them and add occasionally some extracts which may afford some interest.

## 13.—ORMUZD—YASHT.

Zarathustra asked Ahuramazda after the most effectual spell (mantra), to guard against the influence of evil spirits. He was answered by the Supreme Spirit, that the utterance of the different names of Ahuramazda, protects best from evil. Thereupon Zarathustra begged Ahuramazda, to communicate to him these

* It corresponds to the Vedic *Yajata* i. e. a being which deserves worship. The modern Persian *Yazdân*, "god," is the plural of this word *Yazata*.

names. He then enumerates twenty names. The first, for instance, is, *ahmi* i. e. I am ; the fourth *asha-vahista* i. e. the best purity (name of the archangel Ardibehesht), the sixth, " I am the wisdom," the eighth " I am the knowledge," the twelfth *ahura* i. e. living, the twentieth " I am who I am,* mazdâo" (*ahmi yat ahmi mazdâo*). Ahuramazda says then further : if you call me at day or at night by these names, I shall come to assist and help you, the angel Serosh will then come, to assist and help you, the genii of the waters and the trees, the spirits of the deceased pure men will come to assist you. For the utter defeat of the evil spirits, bad men, witches, Peris† (*pairika*) etc. a series of other Ahuramazda names are suggested to Zarathustra, such as, protector, guardian, spirit, the holiest, the best firepriest, etc.

## 14.—HAPTAN, ARDIBEHESHT, AND KHORDAD YASHTS.

In the *Haptan Yasht* i. e. the praise of the seven Supreme Spirits, Ahuramazda and the six archangels, who constitute the celestial council, are invoked. The main part of it offers no particular interest. At the end there is a short proper spell, such as we find, now and then, in the Zend Avesta. It is composed of short verses each consisting of 6—7 syllables in the following manner :—

| | | | | | |
|---|---|---|---|---|---|
| *Yâtu* | *zî* | *Zarathustra* | *vanat* | *daêvô* | *mashyô* |
| may he come | then | Zarathustra, | may he destroy | the devils | and bad men, |
| *Kô* | *nmânahê* | *badha* | *çpitama* | | *Zarathustra* |
| who (are) | in the house, | soon | Spitama | | Zarathustra |
| *Viçpa* | *Drukhs* | *jânâitê* | *Viçpa* | *drukhs* | *nâshâitê* |
| every | evil spirit | is slain | every | evil spirit | goes away |
| *Yatha* | *haonaoiti* | | *Aêshãm* | | *vachãm.* |
| when | he hears | | these | | words. |

* Compare the explanation of the name *Jehova*, as given in Exod. 3, 14. : *ehyeh asher ehyeh* I am who I am.

† The Peris i. e. fairies, so well known to the readers of modern Persian poetry, are evil spirits in the Zendavesta, because they seduce men by their beauty.

In the *Ardibehesht Yasht* Ahuramazda requests Zarathustra to protect and promote the "asha vahistas" (now Ardi-behesht) .e. the best truths, by praising, invoking, inviting (to sacrificial meals), worshipping, singing, etc. in order to keep up the splendour and light of the luminaries, which is indispensable for the growth of the good creation.

Zarathustra is ready to obey the divine command, but he first wants to know the appropriate words which might have the effect devised by Ahuramazda. The chief manthra for this purpose is the *Airyama ishyô* prayer (Yas. 54)* ; some spells follow, which are intended to remove diseases and evils of every kind, like those to be found in the Atbarvaveda, and those used up to this time by the wizards in Europe, as for instance: go away diseases! go away death! go away ye devils, etc.

Then the killing of the "serpent seed" (*ashi-chitra*), i. e. of all noxious animals, such as wolves, frogs, mice, ants, snakes, etc. which are believed to be the mere covers of evil spirits, is enjoined as meritorious and contributing largely towards the growth of nature, and preservation of light, which both are represented by the archangel Ardibehesht. The last sentences of this Yasht occur in Vend. 8,31 also.

The *Khordâd Yasht* is devoted to the archangel *Khordâd (Haurvatât* in Zend) which name signifies "completeness, wholesomeness." Ahuramazda says to Zarathustra, "I created the Haurvatâts for the religious men, and aids, that the archangels come to help them." As a chief means of preserving the Haurvatât or the same good condition, in which every being of the good creation has been created by Ahuramazda, the recital of manthras is recommended together with the Barashmon ceremony (described in Vend. 9; see the 26th paragraph). The manthra, which is intended to drive away the evil spirits, is hardly intelligible in a grammatical respect—the grammar of this and the two preceding Yashts being extremely bad. At the end Zarathustra is strictly ordered by Ahuramazda not to communicate this effective spell to any other man than to a son, or brother, or relative, or

* Addressed to *Airyama* an angel, who is a friend and assistant of pious men, and in possession of numerous helps.

to a priest of the three orders (*thrâyava* i. e. Herbads, Mobeds, and Desturs). Such interdictions of divulging manthras or spells are not unfrequent in the Yashts.

## 15.—ABAN YASHT.

This Yasht, which is of considerable length (30 small chapters containing 132 verses in all), is devoted to *Ardvi Sûra Anâhita* (now called Arduisur), the mighty goddess Anaitis of the ancient Persians, corresponding to the Mylitta of the Babylonians, and the Aphrodite (Venus) of the Greeks. Her name *Anâhid* is even now preserved in modern Persian and well known to the readers of Hafiz. In this Yasht she is always called by those three names, just mentioned, which are only epithets. *Ardvi* means "high, sublime," *çûra* "strong, excellent," and *anâhita* "spotless, pure, clean," which names refer to the celestial waters represented by her. The contents are as follows:

(1.) Ahuramazda calls upon Zarathustra to worship Anâhita who rolls under bridges, who gives salubrity, who defeats the devils, who professes the Ahura religion, who is to be worshipped and praised in this living world. She, as the giver of fertility, purifies the seeds of all males, and the wombs of all females, and provides the latter at the right time with milk. Coming from one of the summits of the mountain Alborz, she is as large as all other waters taken together, which spring out of this heavenly source. When she discharges herself into the lake *Vouru kasha,* then all its shores are widened. This heavenly fountain has a thousand springs, and a thousand canals, each of them a forty days' journey long. Thence a channel goes through all the seven keshvars or zones of the earth, conveying every where pure celestial water. She was created by Ahuramazda himself for the benefit of the house, the village, town, and country.

(3.) Her carriage is drawn by four white horses which defeat all the devils.

From the fifth section nearly up to the end all the praises which Anahita received and the rewards which she granted to her devotees, are enumerated.

(5.) Ahuramazda himself is said to have worshipped her in order to secure for him her assistance in inducing Zarathustra to become his prophet. She readily granted his request.

(6.) *Haoshyanha* (*Hosheng* in Shâhnâmah) sacrificed her a hundred horses, a thousand cows, and ten thousand sheep. She gave him strength to conquer all the devils and men, and to establish an empire.

(7.) *Yima Khshaêta* (Jemshid) asked the same blessing from her which she readily granted, whilst she refused to grant (8.) *Azhi dahâka's* (Zohak, the incarnation of the devil) prayer for strength to kill all men on the surface of the globe. But she assisted *Thraêtaona* (Feridun) who had worshipped her also, to destroy this tyrant. Besides these heroes, a good many others are mentioned as worshippers of Anâhita, such as *Kava Uç* (*Kai Kavus* in Shâhnâmah), *Kava Huçrava (Kai Khosroo* in Sh.) etc. The example set by Ahuramazda himself and the great heroes and sages of the Iranian antiquity, to worship Anâhita in order to obtain a blessing from her, was, of course, followed by Zarathustra, who and his royal disciple *Kava Vîstâçpa* (*Kai Gustasp* in Sh.) are always represented as having respected the ancient forms of worship.

In the sections 21 and 30, there are two smaller songs preserved, by the recital of which Anâhita was expected to appear. The first is ascribed to Ahuramazda himself. It commences as follows:

| | | |
|---|---|---|
| *âidhi* come | *paiti* before (me) | *ava-jaça* come down |
| *Ardvi çûra* Ardooisoor | | *Anâhitê* Anahita ! |
| *hacha* from | *avatbyô* yonder | *çtarebyô* stars |
| *avi zãm* on the earth | | *Ahuradâtãm* ; created by Ahuramazda |
| *Thwãm* Thee | *yazâoñtê* shall worship | *aurvâoṇhô* the handy |
| *ahurâoṇhô* mighty | | *dañhupatayô* rulers of the countries, |
| *puthrâoṇhô*† the sons | | *dañhupaitinãm* of the rulers of the countries. |

† It is nom. pl. From this passage one may clearly ascertain that *ahura* is not confined to the name of the Supreme Being, but can be applied to men also. The same is the case with the Hebrew word *elohîm* god, which is now and then used in the sense of 'judges,' Exod. 21,6. (according to the ancient Chaldaic translator Onkelos), and in that of kings (see Ps. 82,1.6.).

## 16.—KHURSHED AND MAH YASHTS.

The first Yasht is devoted to the sun, which is called in Zend *hvare kkshaêta* i. e. sun the king (preserved in the modern Persian *khor-shid* sun), the second to the moon, called *mâonh* (in the modern Persian *máh*).

The prayer addressed to the sun, commences as follows :—

" We worship the king sun, the immortal, brilliant. When he burns with his rays, then all the heavenly spirits rise by hundreds and by thousands to spread his splendour, to send it down to the earth, created by Ahuramazda, for protecting the cultivated fields *(gaêtháo)* and their bodies. * When the sun rises, then he purifies the earth, created by Ahuramazda, he purifies the flowing water as well as that of springs and lakes ; he purifies all the creatures of the white (holy) spirit. As long as the sun has not risen, all the devils are endeavouring to spread havoc throughout the seven zones of the earth, and none † of the heavenly spirits withstands and slays them, whilst all the living creation is drowned in sleep."

At the end, there is the conjunction of sun and moon particularly mentioned as the luckiest of all constellations. The word for 'conjunction' *hakhedhrem* is of a peculiar interest, because it is preserved in the modern Persian *akhtar* star, whose original meaning 'constellation' may still be seen from some phrases, such as, *akhtar-i-dânish* i. e. Jupiter and Mercury (literally the constellation, foreboding wisdom).

In the Mâh Yasht the moon is invoked by the epithets, *gaochithra* which means "cow-faced." All the immortal saints (angels) rise and spread the moonlight over the surface of the earth created

* In this passage, as well as in many others of the Yashts (and the Vendidad), are some interpolations added in later times, in order to illustrate phrases which were considered to be less intelligible. So, for instance, *hãm-bârayêiñti* (*anbâshtan* "to fill" in mod. Pers.) "to carry every where," is explained by *nipârayêiñti* i. e. make pass down (everywhere).

† This seems to be in contradiction with the Serosh Yasht, where Serosh is said to fight at night time against the evil spirits. But one has to bear in mind, that Serosh is none of the *Yazatas* or angels, but of a higher order ; he is the representative of the religion itself ; but for him the world would fall a prey to the devils during the night time.

by Ahuramazda, then the light of the moon shines through the tops of the yellow-coloured trees; and gold like it rises from the earth (i. e. it is reflected by her.)"* The new moon and the full moon are especially alluded to.

## 17.—TIR AND GOSH YASHTS.

The Tîr Yasht is devoted to the praise of the star *Tistrya* (Tashtar in Parsee, *tîr* in modern Pers.) i. e. Mercury. He is called the giver of wealth (*bakhta shôithrahê*) ; his lustre his red, and of great beauty. His most significant epithet is *afs-chithra* i. e. waterfaced (of one and the same nature with the water), because he brings the waters from the celestial ocean, Vouru kasha, down on the earth to fertilise the soil. He discharges this duty which is assigned to him with the utmost quickness, being "as swift as the river Tighris, which has the swiftness of an arrow, and is the swiftest of all Arian *rivers* when it falls from the *Khshaotha* mountain down to the *Qanvat* mountain." (Yt. 8, 6.)

He defeats and expels the fairies (*pairika*, *peri* in mod. Pers.) who "fall as star worms (i. e. glow worms) between earth and heaven into the sea Vouru-kasha (to prevent the waters from coming out)." But Tistrya enters this lake in the shape of a horse and in swelling it, makes overflow its borders and carries in such a way the waters as showers over the "seven zones of the earth."

His worship was compulsory at the time of a drought; because without the prayers of men being addressed to him, he was powerless to defeat the evil spirits, who kept back the waters in the lake. If men invoke him, says he, as they invoke other angels, then he proceeds from his magnificent palace to the Vouru kasha. He steps into the lake in the shape of a red horse with yellow ears. There the Deva *Apaosho* in the shape of a black horse with black ears, and tail, encounters him. Both are fighting for three days and nights; at length, he is defeated by the Deva. Tistrya then leaves the lake, crying aloud: "I am lost, the waters are lost, the trees are lost, the Mazdayasna religion is destroyed. Men do not worship me as they worship other angels. If they would

* The reflextion of moon light is called *paitidîti* i. e. that which looks against.

worship me, I would gain the srength of ten horses, ten camels, ten oxen, ten mountains, ten navigable rivers." When men then come to aid him by their prayers, and consequently his strength increases, he descends for a second time into the lake, attacks the Deva again and defeats him. After having conquered him, he proclaims the victory, gained by him, to the whole good creation. He makes then flow the waters of the lake over its borders, and fertilises the soil. In the midst of the lake, there is a mountain called *Hendva* (very likely the Hindu kush range of mountains is to be understood), over which the clouds are gathering together. Winds carry them rapidly off and they then discharge their watery load upon the thirsty and parched soil.

The GOSH-YASHT is devoted to a female genius, who is called here by the name *Drvâçpa* i. e. who keeps the horses in health. The name "gosh" (cow) which was given her in after times refers to *gêus urva*, the universal soul by which all living beings of the good creation are animated. From the terms, in which Drvâsp is spoken of in this Yasht, she was believed to preserve the life of the good animals. On heaven she represents the milky way, and in this respect is described as having many spies (eyes), having light of her own, having a far way, and a long constellation (*dareghô-hakhedhrayana*).

She was worshipped by the heroes of antiquity, such as *Haoshyanha Paradhâta* (Hosheng the Peshdadian in Shâhnâmah), *Yima* (Jemshid), *Thraêtaona* (Feridun), *Kava Viçtaspa*, *Zarathustra* himself, etc. and different favours asked of her, as to give strength to defeat the enemies, to rid the creation from evils, as heat, cold, to propogate the good religion, etc.

## 18.—MIHIR YASHT.

In this long Yasht, which comprises 35 sections (146 verses in West.), the angel presiding over, and directing the course of, the sun, who was called *Mithra* i. e. friend (*mihir* in Persian), is invoked and praised. His worship was widely spread not only in ancient Persia itself, but far beyond its frontiers in Asia Minor, and even in Greece and Rome.

In the first section of this Yasht, Ahuramazda says to Zarathustra Spitama : "I created Mithra who rules over large fields (*vouru-gaoyaoitis*) to be of the same rank and dignity (as far as worship is concerned) as I myself am. The wretch who belies Mithra,* spoils the whole country. Therefore break never a promise, neither that contracted with a fellow-religionist, nor that with an infidel. Mithra gives those who do not belie him, swift horses ; the fire, Ahuramazda's son, leads such men on the straightest way, the Frohars (Fravashis) give them children of superior qualities."

At the end of the first section there is a little song, by which Ahuramazda is said to call him. It consists of verses, each of which has about 8 syllables. It commences as follows :

*âcha nô jamyât avaṇhê* | *âcha nô jamyât ravaṇhê*
Hither to us may come to help | hither to us may come to face (before us)

*âcha nô jamyât rafnaṇhê*
hither to us may come to joy

*ughrô aiwithûrô yaçnyô* | *vahmyô anaiwidrukhtô*
the strong conqueror deserving worship | deserving praise not to be belied

*viçpem â aṇuhê açtvaitê*
all in the life endowed with bodies (i. e. in the creation)

*Mithrô yô vouru-gaoyaoitis*
mithra who rules over large fields.

" Mithra who speaks always the truth, has a thousand ears, ten thousand eyes, and is watching without falling asleep always over the welfare of creation."

" He first of the celestial spirits, crosses the mountain *Harô-berezaiti* (Alborj, the supposed centre of the world) on its eastern side, where the immortal sun with his swift horses is stationed ; he first, covered with gold, reaches the summits of that mountain, and thence overlooks the whole of Iran. Through him the rulers build their high fortresses, through him the high mountains, with their many pasturages, produce food for the animals, through him the deep wells have abundance in waters, through him the large navigable rivers run swiftly

* *Mithra* has several meanings, viz. angel of the sun, sun, friend, and promise, contract. Promise breaking, or lying, or not paying debts which are contracted, is called *Mithrô-drukhs* i. e. belieing Mithra.

through *Aiskata,** *Pourata* (Parthia, *Parthawa* in the cuneiform inscriptions), *Mouru* (Meru), *Harôyû* (Herat), *Gau Sughdha* (*Sogdiana*, Samarkand) and *Qâirizem* (Khowaresmia). He brings light to all the seven zones (the whole earth); victory resounds to the ears of those, who by their knowledge of the appropriate prayers and rites continuously worship him with sacrifices (Vss. 13-16)."

He protects those who do not break their promises from distress and misery; but inflicts severe punishments upon those who sin against him by lying, and promise breaking; he makes their arms and feet lame, their eyes blind, their ears deaf (verse 23). The same idea is embodied in the little song, which forms the 11th section (Vss. 47-49). The verses consist of 8 syllables. I shall give here a specimen.

*âat* *yat* *Mithrô* *fravazaiti* | *avi* *haênayâo* *khrvîshyêitîs*
Then when mithra drives | in the two armies ready for a battle

*avi* *hãm-yant* *araçmaoyo* | *añtare* *dañhupâperetânê*
against (each other) they encounter in two battle lines in order for the country to fight

*athra* *narãm* *mithro-drujãm* | *apãs* *gavô* *darezayêiti*
then of the men who break promise | away the hand he binds

*pairi* *daêma* *vârayêiti* etc.
round the face he covers etc.

i. e. At the time of a battle taking place between two hostile armies, and both being arrayed in battle lines against each other, in order to fight for a country, Mithra drives in his carriage to the battle field, and punishes all those who were formerly sinning against him by breaking promises; he causes the one to be made prisoners, and dooms others to loose their eyes, or their feet, or ears.

The residence of this mighty angel, the punisher of rascals and scoundrels, is on the mountain *Harô-berezaiti* (Alborj) where Ahuramazda himself has built a palace for him, where is "no night, no darkness, no cold winds, no heat, no smoke, no putrifaction, no fogs," which is the model of an Iranian paradise (Vers. 50).

All the devils (devas) flee from him when he, as the ruler of the whole earth, drives in his carriage on her right side. On his right side he is followed by *Sraosha*, the angel ruling over

* Not to be ascertained.

the whole of the divine service, and by *Rashnu rázista* (Rashnu rast), the angel of justice, and the spirits of the waters, trees etc. (100-101).

In verse 104 mention is made of the eastern and western Hindoos (*hiñdvô* = *sindhavas* i. e. the (seven) rivers in the Vedas, the ancient name of India).

Ahuramazda paid his respects to him. He drives out from paradise (*garôdemâna*) in a splendid carriage, drawn by four white horses. He carries with him weapons of all kinds for the destruction of the devas; among them is the *vazra** the most powerful.

## 19.—SEROSH HADOKHT AND RASHNU YASHTS.

The first, which is now particularly used at the time of initiating priests (chiefly of the lower grade, the Herbads) into their office, is dedicated to the angel Sraosha, of whom we have already given an account above (see pag. 170-172.). I forego, therefore, to give an analysis of this Yasht, affording no particular interest.

In the Rashnu Yasht the angel *Rashnu razista*, i. e. the rightest righteousness, who is believed to preside over the eternal laws of nature, as well of morality (he corresponds to the idea of the *Themis* among the ancient Greeks), is invoked and worshipped. He is everywhere, and represents, to a certain extent, the omnipresence of the divine being. He is particularly distinguished by firmity and the greatest hatred of disorder and immorality of any kind. His devotee, in paying his reverence to him by placing different sweet fruits and oil before the sacred fire, invokes and praises him wherever he may be, in one of the seven zones (*Karshvare*), or in the different places of the lake *Vouru Kasha* (the ocean surrounding the earth), either on the large tree, bearing all kinds of fruits at the same time which is planted in its middle, or on its borders, or in its depth. He is further praised, may he be on the ends of the earth, or on the celestial mountain *Harô-berezaiti* (Alborj),

* *Gurz* a club, battle axe in Pers. is identical with *vajra* i. e. thunderbolt in the Vedas, where it is Indra's weapon.

or on one of the stars, as Charles' wain (Ursa major) called *Haptôiriñg*,* or the water stars, or vegetation stars, or on the moon, or sun, or on the lights which were from beginning (*anaghra raochâo*), or in Paradise.

## 20.—FRAVARDIN YASHT.

This Yasht comprising 31 chapters, which are divided into 158 verses, is the largest of all. It is dedicated to the praise of the Frohars, *Fravashi* in Zend (best preserved in the name *Phraortes* which is *Fravartish* in the ancient Persian of the cuneiform inscriptions), which means "protector." These Frohars or protectors, who are numberless, are believed to be angels, stationed everywhere by Ahuramazda for keeping the good creation in order, preserving it, and guarding it against the constant attacks of fiendish powers. Each being of the good creation, which is living, or deceased, or still unborn, has its own Fravashi or guardian angel, who is from beginning. Hence they are a kind of prototypes, and may be best compared to Plato's "ideas," who supposed every thing to have a double existence, first in the idea, secondly in the reality.† Originally the Fravashis represented only the departed souls of the ancestors, comparable to the *pitaras* i. e. fathers of the Brahmans, and the *Manes* of the Romans.

* In modern Persian *haftwarang*. The word affords a high interest by its identity with the ancient Vedic and Grecian names of the same constellation. The original form in the Vedas is *riksha* i. e. bear (which is to be found only once in the songs of the Rigveda, 1, 24, 10.) = Greek *arktos*. According to an account in the Shatapatha brâhmana 2, 1, 2, 4. (second part of the white Yajurveda) this name was changed afterwards into that of "*Sapta rishayah*" i. e. the seven Rishis, by which name the stars of Ursa major are called in the later Vedic songs (see Rigveda 10. 82.2.. Atharvaveda 6, 40. 1.) and in the Classical Sanscrit writings. The sounds of *riksha* bear, and *rishi* seer. prophet, were so near to one another that at the time, when they commenced to deify those great founders of Brahmanism, nothing was more natural than to assign to them a place on the sky and make them one of the brightest and most beautiful constellations. In the Iranian languages, however, the old name 'the seven bears' was faithfully preserved.

† The ideas are the models (paradeigmata) of every thing existing; the reality (or according to Plato non-reality, because only the ideas have a real existence according to his doctrine) being only imitation thereof. The ideas are unborn, eternal, invisible, imperishable. but their imitation, the substances, are subject to all changes. See Parmenides pag 132, d. Steph., Timœus. 48, c. 52, a. According to Aristotle (Metaphysics 1,9,2.) Plato presumed as many "ideas" as things really existed. Such celestial or invisible prototypes of terrestrial things are mentioned in the Bible also. See Epist. to the Hebrews 9,23. Exod. 25,9. 40.

## EXTRACTS FROM THE FRAVARDIN YASHT.

(1-7.) Ahuramazda spoke to Zarathustra Spitama: To thee alone I shall tell the power and strength, beauty, usefulness and happiness of the good guardian angels, the strong victorious, righteous Zarathustra Spitama! how they come to help me [how they give me assistance]. By means of their splendour and beauty I uphold the sky which is shining so beautifully, and which touches and surrounds this earth* ; it resembles a bird which is ordered by God *to stand still there* ; it is high as a tree, wide stretched, iron bodied, having its own light in the three worlds (*thrisva*) ; on which (the sky) Ahuramazda together with Mithra, Rashnu and Spenta Armaiti puts a garment decked with stars, and made by God in such a way that nobody can see the ends of its parts.

By means of their splendour and beauty, I uphold the high strong Anâhitâ (the celestial water) with bridges, the salutary, who drives away the devils, who has the true belief, and is to be worshipped in the world, and to be praised in the world ; the good, who is furthering life, the good who is increasing wealth, the good, who is increasing property, the good, who makes thrive the fields, the good, who makes thrive the countries ; who purifies the seeds of all males, who purifies the wombs of all females to make them fit for conception, who makes all the pregnant females bearing fine offspring, who, at the right time, provides females with milk. The praised, far renowned, who is as large as all the waters which flow over the earth, who, with might, is running from celestial heights into the lake Vouru Kasha. All borders of it are then overflowing from its very centre, when those waters fall into it, when the high strong Anâhitâ is pouring them forth into their channels. She has a thousand springs, a thousand channels ; each of these springs

* *bavâva* would be according to Sanscrit the 1st pers. dual, but this meaning does not agree with the structure of the sentence ; it is evidently put for : *bavaiti va* 'it is for both.'

and each of these channels is of the circuit of a forty days' journey for a well-mounted messenger.

(11.) By means of their splendour and beauty, I uphold, Zarathustra! in the pregnant females the embryoes alive, to be formed out of a formless unanimated mass, to obtain a living soul, bones, form, consistency, growth of the faculty of walking and speaking. (12.) When the strong guardian angels of the good would not give me assistance, then cattle and men, the two best of the hundred classes of beings, would no longer exist for me; then would commence the devil's power, the devil's reign, the whole living creation would belong to the devil. (13.) Between earth and heaven may the devilish spirit take up his residence [between earth and heaven the devil may reside]; but he (the devil) will not be able to destroy entirely the *influence* of the holy spirit (Ahuramazda).

(14.) By means of their splendour and beauty, the waters are flowing straight forward in inexhaustible sources; by means of their splendour and beauty, trees grow out of the earth, by means of their splendour and beauty, the winds blow carrying with them vapours from inexhaustible sources.

(15.) By means of their splendour and beauty, the females are getting with children, by means of their splendour and beauty, they produce good offspring; by means of their splendour and beauty, there will be descendants.

(16.) By means of their splendour and beauty, that ingenuous man (Zarathustra), who spoke so good words, who was the source of wisdom, who, before Gotama* had such an intercourse *with God* (obtained revelation), was born. By means of their splendour and beauty, the sun goes on his paths; by means of their splendour and beauty, the moon goes on her paths; by means of their splendour and beauty, stars go on their paths.

(17.) These guardian angels of the good give great assistance in great battles (to be fought against the devilish empire). The

* *Gaotema* (in the original) is the proper name of Buddha, the founder of Buddhism. Its Sanscrit form is *gâutama*. That Buddhism was spread at Balkh is well known.

guardian angels of the good amongst the believers in the old religion (the Deva religion), or those of the prophets (*Soshyañto* Sosiosh) to come, for making perpetuation of life, are the strongest of all; then the guardian angels of the living good men are stronger than those of the dead.

(18.) When a man living, who is the ruler over all the estates of a country, supports well the guardian angels of the good, then each of his dominions will be well populated [who supports well your good friend (the sun *mithra*) with his far extended dominions and the probity which is protecting and sheltering estates].

(19.) Thus I tell thee, holy Spitama! the power, strength, beauty, support and delight of the strong victorious guardian angels of the good, how they come to assist me [how the strong guardian angels of the good bring me assistance].

(20.) Ahuramazda spoke to Zarathustra Spitama: When in this world, Zarathustra Spitama! thou hast to pass mischief bringing, bad, baneful ways and thy life is threatened, then shalt thou recite these words [then shalt thou speak these victorious words, Zarathustra!]:

(21.) I praise, invoke, and extol the good strong holy guardian angels of the good. We praise those who are in the houses, those who are in the villages, those who are in the towns, those who are in the countries, those who are in the Zoroastrian communities, those of the living good, those of the dead good men, those of the coming good men, all those invoked in countries where invocation is practised. (22.) Who uphold heaven, who uphold water, who uphold earth, who uphold nature, etc.

(49-53). We worship the religious men's good strong holy guardian angels who come to the village in the season, called Hamaspathmaêda. Then they roam there at large (haunt) during ten nights, wishing to learn, what assistance they might obtain, saying: who will praise us? who will worship *us*? who will adore *us*? who pray *to us*? who satisfies *us* with milk and clothes in his hand, with a prayer for purity? whom of us will he call here? whose soul is to worship you? To whom will he give that offering in order to enjoy imperishable food for ever? (quotation from Vend 2.)

Then who worships them with milk in his hand and with clothes and the prayer for purity, upon him the pleased (with this sacrifice), favourable, not-hurting, strong guardian angels of the religious men, bestow blessings. In this house (where they are worshipped in such a way), there will be abundance of cows and of men (posterity); there will be a quickly running horse and a well fastened carriage; there will be to be found a prudent man who will worship us *in future* with milk and clothes in his hand and with the prayer for purity.

(82-84.) We worship the good, strong, holy guardian angels of the good, those of the immortal saints (Amesha Speñtas), the rulers with their watchful eyes, the high powerful, swift, the living ones, of everlasting truth. All seven are of the same mind, speak the same words, perform the same actions [PAZEND: they have the same mind, the same words, the same action and the same master and ruler, the Creator Ahuramazda]. One looks into the soul of the other, considering about good thoughts, considering about good words, considering about good deeds, considering about the best life that the prayer may go up to their brightly shining paths.

(85.) We worship the good strong holy guardian angels, that of the blazing, holy, penetrating fire, and that of Sraosha, the true, swift, self-speaking, swiftly running, the living, and that of Nairyôçaṇha (an angel). (86.) That of the rightest righteousness (Rashnu razista), that of Mithra with his far extended dominions, that of the holy word (Manthra Spenta), that of the day, that of water, that of earth, that of the trees, that of nature, that of existence, that of the two pure worlds (visible and invisible, earthly and spiritual).

(87.) We worship the guardian angel of Gayô-marathan (Gayomard, Kayomors, the Adam or Manu of the Iranians), who first listened to Ahuramazda's thoughts and sayings; out of whose body he (Ahuramazda) formed the central mass (*nâfô* navel)* of the Arian countries, the surface of the Arian countries.

(88-94.) We worship the rule and the guardian angel of Zarathustra Spitama, who first thought good thoughts, who first spoke good words, who first performed good actions, who was the first priest, the first warrior, the first cultivator of soil, the first prophet, the first, who was inspired, the first, who has given to *mankind* nature and reality and word, and hearing of word, and wealth and all good things, created by Mazda which embellish reality (existence). Who first made turning the wheel among gods and men†, who first was praising the purity of the living creation, and destroying the idolatry, who confessed the Zarathustrian belief in Ahuramazda, the religion of the living god given against the devils. Who first spoke the word being directed against the devils‡, being the religion of the living God in the animated creation, who first promulgated the word being directed against the devas, being the religion of the living God in the animated creation; who first spoke the whole of what is given by the devas, and what is neither holy nor to be worshipped (it is profane), that is the strong blessed old belief of the countries (the ante Zoroastrian Deva-religion).§ Through whom the whole true and revealed word was heard, which is the life and guidance of the world, the praises of truth which is the greatest, best, and most excellent, the conversation consisting of different Chapters about the best religion. Whom all Amesha spentas together with the Sun worship with their sincere intellect in the mind, *instigated* by ardent devotion (that is, with all their heart) as the life and master of the world, as praiser of the greatest, best and most useful truth, as the promulgator of the best faith of the sincere men. Through his knowledge and speech the waters and trees become desirous of growing; through his knowledge and speech all beings, created

* Compare the Grecian appellation of Delphi: *Omphale gês*, navel of the earth i. e. centre.

† This is a Buddhistic expression, meaning "establish and propagate the good religion."

‡ That is to say: the whole Vendidad.

§ That means: Zarathustra is the originator of all religious thoughts of those current after, as well as of those current before his time.

by the holy Spirit, are uttering words of happiness. To our welfare the fire priest *(âthrava)* Zarathustra Spitama has been born, he brought for us sacrifices and was spreading the holy twigs. Thus comes forth from the waters (i. e. from its source) the good creed of the believers in Ahuramazda, spreading over the whole earth. (95.) There the friend of waters (sun), ruling over far extended dominions, produced all virtues of the countries by their means and makes them play when overflowing; then the son of waters, the strong fire, produced all virtues of countries and appeases them when overflowing.

We worship the virtue and the guardian angel of Maidhyô—mâonha, the disposer *of the good faith,* who first heard Zarathustra's speech and sayings.

(99.) We worship the guardian angel of Kavi Vîstâspa who speaks his own verses (such as made by him), the bold, attacker of *the devils,* the believer in Ahura who defiled,* for the benefit of the good creation, the face of the devil and the witches [who cleft the face of the devil and the witches, that is to say: who was the arm and support of the Zoroastrian belief in the living god]; who carried away from the Hunus† the standard [which was tied] and deposited it in the impregnable fortress Maidhyôishâdha, shielding cattle and fields [favourable to cattle and fields].

(104.) We worship the guardian angel of Huskyaothna, son of Frashaostra, that of Qâdaêna, son of Frashaostra, that of Hanghaurvat, son of Jâmâçpa, that of Vareshan, son of Hanghaurvat, that of Vohû-nemanh, son of Avâraostra, to ward off the mischief done by the nightmares, by the ghosts disguised as black-coloured animals, by the demons and by the witches.

(105.) We worship the guardian angel of Shimêzhi, the reciter of spells, the Harbad, who slew most of the Ushaghanas, who polluted the bodies and disturbed purity,

* The words from *yô druja* to *vaçtrahêcha* contain fragments of an old epic song in honor of Kavâ Viçtâspa with some interpolations. The meter is the Shloka.

† This nation is mentioned by the name *Hûnâs* in Indian writings also, see *Vishnu Purâna* translated by H. H. Wilson pag. 177. 194. They were hostile to the Iranians who seem to have often been engaged in war with them. They are the white Huns, who were once the terror of Europe.

who were irreligious, acknowledging neither the principle of life, nor its master, who were charmers, frustrating the help of the guardian angels to resist the hostilities which were crushing the good.

(129.) We worship the guardian angel of Açtvat-ereto who is called the victorious Soshyans. He is called Soshyans (Sosiosh), for he conduces(*çâvayat*) to the welfare of the whole animated creation. He is called Açvat-ereto, for he is keeping up the animated creation, guarding it against destruction, chiefly against the destruction, caused by the two legged demon Drukhs (personification of destruction), caused by the hatred of *the devils*, who annihilate the good things.

## 21.—BEHRAM AND RAM-YASHTS.

The Behram Yasht is devoted to the angel *Behram*. The original form of the name is *Verethraghna* which means "killer of enemies," i. e. conqueror, and is to be identified with Indra's name *Vritrahâ* to be found in the Vedas. He is the giver of victory, and appears personally before his devotee in different forms which he may like to assume. He appears in the shape of a wind, in that of a cow, in that of a horse, in that of a camel, in that of a boar *(varâza* = S. *varâha)*, in that of a boy aged 15 years, in that of a warrior, etc. Zarathustra worshipped him; he was rewarded by the angel with strength in his arms and firmity of his whole body.

Zarathustra, asking once Ahuramazda, in what way the angel Behram should be worshipped, is answered in the following manner : the Arian countries (i. e. their inhabitants, the Iranians, ancestors of the Parsees), shall consecrate water (called *Zaothra*), spread the sacred twigs, called Barsom, and kill an animal of a reddish or yellowish colour, the flesh of which is to be dressed. Of this Behram's meal, which is prepared up to this day occasionally, neither a criminal nor a whore, nor an infidel, who is an enemy of the Zoroastrian religion, is allowed to eat any thing. Should that happen, then the Arian countries will be visited by plagues and devastated by incursions of hostile armies.

The Râm-Yasht is devoted to the angel Râm, who is, however, never mentioned by this name in it, but called *vayus** *uparôkairyô* i. e. the wind whose business is above (in the sky), the celestial breath, or simply invoked by the names of *Apâ*, i. e. who is far, remote and *Bagha*† i. e. fortune. He is described as being everywhere (on all sides), and as primary cause (*Akhsti*) of the whole universe. From these remarks we may gather that he represents that very fine and sublime substance which is called *ether* and to the Indian philosophers known as *âkâça*.

He was worshipped by Ahuramazda and the great heroes and sages of antiquity, such as *Haoshyanh*, *Takhma (Takhmûras)*, *Yima*. Old maids beg him for a husband.

In the last (eleventh) section his manifold names are explained. *Vayus* is there traced to the root *vi* " to go," penetrate, and to *va* " both," and explained by " I go to both creatures, those of the white, and those of the black Spirit." By this and other names he is to be invoked at the time of worship. He has then the power of defeating hostile armies.

## 22.—DIN AND ASHI YASHTS.

In the Din Yasht the *daêna mâzdayaçnis* or the Zoroastrian religion is invoked like an angel. She was, of course, pre-eminently worshipped by Zarathustra. The way in which he invoked her, is described in a little song, commencing as follows :

> Rise from thy place ! go out from thy house ! thou wisdom ! created by Mazda, which is the rightest ; if thou art in the front (of the house), put up with me, if thou art behind it, return to me !

*Ashi* is a female angel whom the Desturs at present compare with *Lakshmi*, the Hindu goddess of wealth. But the Yasht, devoted to her, does not countenance this opinion. Her full name is *Ashis vaṇuhi* (now corrupted to Ashisheng), which means " the good truth." She is called a daughter of Ahuramazda, and

* There is, no doubt, the name seems to be connected with the Vedic god *vâyu*, the wind, the original long *â* having been shortened to *a*.

† See the first paragraph of the fourth Essay.

a sister of the Amesha Spentas or archangels. She makes continue the wisdom of all prophets and inspires them in their turn with the heavenly (lit. original) wisdom. She comes to help all that invoke her from far and nigh. The ancient heroes and sages, Yima, Thraêtaona, Zarathustra, Kavâ Vîstâspa, etc. worshipped her and to all she granted what they were praying for, such as wealth, victory, children.

## 23.—ASHTAD, ZEMYAD AND VANANT YASHTS.

The name *Ashtâd* which is to be traced to the Zend word *Arstât*, i. e. height, does not occur in the Yasht bearing this name. The brightness of the Arian countries, i. e. their riches and wealth in trees, cows, sheep, and all other things of the good creation, which are the most effective means for destroying the works of the devils, and for preserving every thing in its original purity, and the *Ashi vanuhi berezaiti*, i. e. the good high truth, are invoked here. The brightness (*qarenô*) being chiefly the subject of the Zemyâd-Yasht, and the Ashi Vanuhi that of the preceding Ashi-Yasht, we cannot ascribe any independent value to this Ashtâd Yasht, which is only an appendage to both these other Yashts. The name Ashtâd, by which the Desturs understand the height of mountains, was given to this short chapter only for distinguishing it by a separate name from the two other Yashts.

The name *Zamyâd* refers to the earth. She is not directly invoked in this Yasht which is chiefly devoted to the praise of the 'brightness' (*qarenô*) above mentioned. Its first section, which describes the origin of all mountains out of the heart of the central and primeval mountain Alborz (*Harô berezaiti*),* stands separate. Several names of mountains are particularly mentioned,† such as *Ushidhâo* (Creator of light), *Ushi-darenem*

* Here we find the peculiar form "*haraiti bares*" in which *haraiti* is an abstract noun, meaning "mountain range," and *bares*, *barez* (in the Vedas *brihas*) "elevated, high." Its heart (*zaredhô*) is here regarded as a separate mountain, surrounded by its vast mountain ranges.

† To express the word "mountain" we find here two words used: *gairi* and *paurvata* which both are to be found in Sanscrit also (*giri* and *parvata*).

(district of light) etc. The number of all mountains is said to be 2244.

In the following sections of this Yasht we find always invoked "the mighty brightness which was peculiar to the Kavis (the chiefs of the Iranian community in ancient times, chiefly before Zoroaster)." Ahuramazda produced it at the time of creating all that is good, bright, shining and propagates life. It attached itself generally to one of the great heroes of antiquity, such as Thraêtaona, Yima, etc. and enabled him to achieve great feats. This heavenly brightness is essential for causing the dead to rise at the end of the world. On this resurrection of the dead, which is a genuine Zoroastrian doctrine, we find in this Yasht two very interesting passages which are almost identical (19, 11. 12. and 89. 90. West.). I give here a translation of the second.

"This splendour attached itself to the hero *who is to rise out of the number* of prophets (called *Soshyanto*) and to his companions, in order to make the life everlasting, undecaying, imperishable, imputrescible, incorruptible, for ever existing, for ever vigorous, full of power, at the time, when the dead will rise again, and imperishableness of life will exist, making the life lasting by itself (without further support). All the world will remain for eternity in the state of purity; the devil will disappear from all those places whence he used to attack the religious men in order to kill (them); and all his brood and creatures will be doomed to destruction."

The *Vanant-Yasht* is a very small prayer addressed to the star *Vanant* by which the Desturs understand the milky way (*Kah-i-Keshân* in Persian), to kill all disturbers of the good creation. This star is said to stand in a straight line over Hell in order to frighten the devils*.

## 24.—TWO YASHT FRAGMENTS. AFRIN PAIGHAMBAR ZARTUSHT. VISTASP YASHT.

These four pieces conclude the collection of all the Yashts extant in Westergaard's edition.

* The Desturs are of opinion, that this star is the weapon (vazra) which is constantly aimed by Mithra at the head of the devas, as is stated in the Khurshid Yasht.

In the first, the praise of Ashem or truth, is recommended by Ahuramazda to Zarathustra as one of the most meritorious works. By this praise we can understand only the recital of the celebrated prayer: *Ashem vohu.* The larger or smaller amount of merit, resulting from repeating this prayer depends on the time and occasion when it is done. Thus, for instance, the merit is by far greater, if the praise is made at night than at day time.

The second fragment treats of the fate of the soul immediately after death. If a religious man dies, then his soul sits for three nights on the top of his head reciting the Gâtha ustavaiti (see above), which keeps the poor soul in the same condition as she was when living in her body. After the third night has passed away, at daybreak, the soul of the religious man is touched by an odorous wind waving over trees. This wind which comes from a southern direction, and whose scent and odour is superior to that of any other wind, blows upon her to carry her up. Then the own good thoughts of the religious man's soul assume the shape of a beautiful girl, of the age of fifteen years, who appears before him. The soul questioning her who she is, and whence she comes, is answered: I am the good mind, the good word and the good deed, thy own religion, which was in thy own body. The soul then is advised by her genius, appearing in the shape of that girl, to take rest beneath the trees of the beautiful grove (to which that wind had carried her up), to recite there the sacred prayers, to worship Ahuramazda, etc. After having been sitting there for some time, the soul begins to walk forward. The first step brings her to the paradise, called "good thought," the second to that of the "good word," the third to that of "the good deed," and the fourth to the "stars without beginning." Then having arrived before the throne of Ahuramazda, the soul is asked by him: whence dost thou come, and how didst thou come from the earthly to the spiritual life, from the perishableness to the imperishableness? The soul of the pure religious man and that of the pure religious woman enjoy then the most splendid meals which shine like gold.

The soul of the wicked, irreligious man, is sitting for three nights on her head also, and reciting the prayer: to what country shall I go, where shall I find shelter? (Ys. 46, 1. see pag. 155). After the third night, at daybreak, a wind which blows from a northern direction, and carries with it a bad smell, takes her off. She passes then through the same places as the soul of the religious man. After having passed them, she arrives at the region of the "darkness without beginning." Angrô mainyus, the devil, questions her about her way and announces her that she has to enjoy in future only poisoned meals. "This is the fate of the wicked man, and of the whore."

The *Aferin Paighambar-Zartusht* contains the blessing, by which the Highpriest (Zarathustra) of the Iranians used to bless a Governor or King. It is said to have been given by Zarathustra Spitama to his royal friend Kavi Vistaspa. The Highpriest wishes the King to have children, to be as victorious as the hero Feridun, as brilliant as Kai Kavus, as radiant as the sun, as shining as the moon, as just as the angel of Justice himself, as free from disease and death as Kai Khosru. Hereafter he (the blessed) may enjoy the happy life of the blessed in the land of light and splendour. The blessing concludes by the words "so it shall happen* as I bless you."

The *Vistasp Yasht*, the first chapter of which is identical with the preceding piece, is in grammatical respect so enormously corrupted that I refrain from giving here a statement of its contents which do not appear to afford any particular interest. The whole composition seems to be of a comparatively late date.

## 25.—SMALLER PIECES (NYAYISH, AFRIGANS, GAHS, SIROZAH).

These pieces, which are comparatively very small, contain the most common prayers used by the Parsees now-a-days; but offer, as to their contents, which all are taken from the other more genuine parts of the Zend-Avesta, chiefly from Yasna and

* *Atha Jamyât* in Zend; this phrase corresponds to our *amen* at the end of prayers and blessings.

the Yasht, no particular interest neither for the history of Zend literature, nor for the Parsee religion.

The five *Nyâyish* or praises, are devoted, to the Sun (Khurshed), and the angel of the sun (Mihir, Mithra), the Moon (*mâh*), Water (Abân), and Fire. The prayer addressed to the Sun and Mithra, are to be repeated thrice every day by every pious Parsee. Its neglect prevents the soul from passing the bridge *Chinvat* after death. Thrice every month the praise, addressed to the moon, is absolutely necessary. The repetition of the praise of the water or fire is meritorious, but not as indispensable as that of the three other Nyâyishs.

*Afrigâns* are blessings which are to be recited over a meal, consisting of wine, milk, bread, fruits, to which an angel or a deceased is invited, in whose honor the meal was prepared. After the consecration which only a priest can perform is over, the meal then is taken by those who are invited.

The performance of these Afrigans is required of every pious Parsee at certain fixed times during the year. These are the six Gahânbârs, each lasting for five days (the six seasons of the old year) ; for these the *Afrigân-Gahanbâr* is intended ; the five Gâtha days (the five last days of the year), during which the *Afrigân Gâtha* must be performed, and lastly, the third day (Ardibehesht) of the first month (Fravardin) in the year, at which the performance of the *Afrigân Rapithwin* devoted to the genius, presiding over the southern directions, who is the guardian of the paths to Paradise, is enjoined to every Parsee whose soul wants to pass the great bridge Chinvat after death.

The *five Gâhs* are the prayers which are devoted to the several angels, who preside over the five parts, into which day and night are divided (see their names and hours page 151). They must be recited every day at their respective times.

*Sirozah* i. e. 30 days, is extant in two forms. It is nothing but a calendar, an enumeration of the 30 divine beings, each of whom is supposed to preside over one of the thirty days of a month, and by whose names they are called. It is chiefly recited at the thirtieth day after the death of a man.

## 26.—VENDIDAD.

The Vendidad,* which is the code of the religious, civil and criminal laws of the ancient Iranians, consists in its present state, of twenty-two chapters, commonly called *Fargards* (exactly corresponding to the word *pericope*) i. e. sections. The style of its constituent parts is too different, as to admit of ascribing it to one author only. Some parts are evidently very old and might be traced to the first centuries subsequent to the prophet; but the larger bulk of the work contains (like the Talmud) too minute a description of certain ceremonies and observances as to induce a modern critic to trace it to the prophet or even to one of his disciples. The Vendidad as a whole (some of its parts seem to be lost, chiefly those containing the original texts, or the Avesta of the old laws), is apparently the joint work of the Zarathustras or Highpriests of the ancient Iranians during the period of several centuries. They started from old sayings and laws (Avesta), which partially must have descended from the prophet himself,† and interpreted them in various ways, often contradicting each other. These interpretations, the so called Zend, became in the course of time as authoritative as the Avesta or the original text of the scripture itself, and in many cases, seem to have superseded it. This Zend was then capable of further explanation, which was less authoritative and went by the name "Pâzend." That we can actually discover these three different stages in the present Vendidâd, the attentive reader will learn from a perusal of the following pages, where I endeavoured to separate them from each other as far as possible.

The Vendidad may as to its contents, be divided into three parts. The first (from Fargard 1 to 3) is only introductory, and formed very likely part of a very ancient historical or legendary work of a similar kind as the Shâhnâmah. It contains an enumeration of sixteen Arian countries, over which the Zoroastrian religion was spread (ch. 1.), the legends of King Yima (ch. 2.), and strong recommendations of agriculture as the most

* See the explanation of the name pag. 91.

† Compare for instance Vend 4 with Yas. 46, 5 (see pag. 155.)

useful and meritorious work (ch. 3.). The second part (from chap. 4-17), forming the groundwork of Vendidad, treats of laws, ceremonies and observances, without keeping to a strict order. The third part (from 18-22.) is apparently an appendix treating of various subjects.

Of the first or opening chapter of the Vendidad, I published formerly a translation and explanation which is translated into English and incorporated to the third volume of Bunsen's work " Egypt's place in Universal History." I shall notice here only one passage of it which is a striking proof of the existence of interpretations (Zend) of original texts to be found in the present Vendidad. In the 4th verse is said, that " there were ten months winter, and two months summer in Airyana Vâejô" (i. e. the pure Iran, the Iranian home, the Paradise). This was regarded in later times by some Highpriests as contradicting the perfect and good nature of the earthly paradise, and, therefore, changed as follows : " there are seven summer months and five winter months." This interpretation which upsets the original text (Avesta), was, in the course of time, added to the text, and forms now part of the original.

## (A) The Second Chapter of Vendidad.

### *(Yima, or Jamshid, the King of the Golden age.)*

### Avesta.

1. Zarathustra asked Ahuramazda :

Ahuramazda, thou holiest Spirit ! Creator of the estates with living beings therein, thou true ! with what other man didst thou, Ahuramazda ! converse first, besides me, who am Zarathustra (i. e. before me) ? [*Pázend* : whom didst thou teach the Ahurian Zoroastrian faith ?]

2. Then Ahuramazda told : with Yima, the happy, of great wealth, true Zarathustra ! with him I conversed first among men, I who am Ahuramazda, besides thee (i. e. before thee) Zarathustra, *Pázend :* [him I taught the Ahurian Zoroastrian faith].

Then I spoke unto him, Zarathustra ! I who am Ahuramazda : Be, O happy Yima Vivanghana ! my promulgator, and bearer of the faith (the Zoroastrian religion). Then he, Yima, the happy, answered me, Zarathustra: Neither am I fit nor known as promulgator and bearer of the faith.

4. Then I spoke unto him, Zarathustra! who am Ahuramazda: if thou Yima! shalt not be my promulgator and bearer of the faith, then wall in and fence my estates; then thou shalt be the conservator and the herdsman and the protector of my estates.

5. Then he, Yima, the happy, answered me, Zarathustra! I shall wall in thy estates; I shall fence thy estates; I shall be the conservator of thy estates and their herdsman and their protector; in my empire there shall not be cold winds nor heat, nor fogs, nor death.

6. ZEND: Speak that prayer which is against him [we worship the Fravashi of the true Yima vîvanha] who* counteracting men created immediately the Dêvas of the depths [thenceforward headless], through the evil words *spoken* by his own tongue; he sent that upon him Yima wherefrom he (Yima) became an evil-doer.

AVESTA.

7. Then I, who am Ahuramazda, brought forth instruments, a golden sword and a goad decorated with gold. Yima is to bear the royal dignity!

8. Tnen the sway was given to Yima for three hundred winters (i. e. years). Then the earth was to be filled with cattle, oxen, men, dogs, birds and red blazing fires. Not did find room therein cattle, oxen, and men.

9. Then I made known to Yima: Yima Vîvanhana, thou happy; the earth having fallen to thy lot, is to be filled with cattle, oxen, men, dogs, birds and red blazing fires.

10. Yima went up towards the stars when the sun was on his way at noon;† he touched the earth with his golden sword;

* Angrô mainyus, the devil. In this addition there is an allusion to the fall of Yima, the deprivation of his splendour known to the later legends.

† Zend: *rapithwa* means the time called *gâh rapithwan*, lasting from 10 A. M.—3 P. M.

he pierced her, speaking thus: Become wide, holy earth! increase and burst, O producer of cattle and oxen and men!

11. Then Yima made the earth extending herself and by one third larger, than she was beforehand; there the cattle and oxen and men walk according to their own pleasure [just so as it is their pleasure].

### ZEND.

12-15. Then the sway was given to Yima for six hundred winters. The following is a mere repetition of 8-11, from: then the earth was to be filled till "Yima made the earth extending herself;" where is added "by two parts larger" than she was beforehand.

16-19. Then the sway was given to Yima for nine hundred years. The following is a mere repetition of 8-11; after "Yima made the earth extending herself" is added "by three thirds larger" than she was beforehand.

20. Then Yima established truth during the first thousand years* for such long a time as the creation of celestial spirits remained pure.

### AVESTA.

21. An assembly was held by Ahuramazda, the creator, with the celestial spirits, by him, the renowned in Airyana-vêjô of good qualities.

### ZEND.

An assembly was held by Yima the king, of great wealth, with the best men, by him, the renowned in Airyana-vejo of good qualities. To this assembly came Ahuramazda, the creator, with the celestial spirits, he, the renowned in Airyana-vejo of good qualities.

### AVESTA.

To this assembly came Yima, the king of great wealth, with

* According to the Zend lore developed, after the text of Avesta was fixed, the world is to last for 12,000 years; the original number being only 4,000: in the first thousand or in the first three thousand there was the golden age; King Yima was the ruler.

the best men, he, the renowned in Airyana-vejô of good qualities.

(22.) Ahuramazda spoke unto Yima : O happy Yima Vivanhana ! upon the world of animated beings the evils of winter will come and consequently a strong deadly frost.

ZEND.

Upon the world of animated beings the evils of winter will come ; consequently much snow and ice will fall on the highest mountains, on the summit of the heights.

(23.) From three places, Yima ! go the cows away, from the most baneful place (desert) and from the tops of mountains, and from the chaps of valleys, into the well fastened cottages.

AVESTA.

(24.) Before this winter the country was bearing pasturages ; water overflowed them, after the ice had melted and tanks were formed. There Yima considered about the world of animated beings to descry a place for cattle, goats, and sheep.

(25.) Then make this district of the length of one day's journey ; bring thither the seeds of cattle, oxen, and men, and dogs and red-blazing fires.

ZEND.

Then make this district of the length of one day's journey on all the four sides, to be a dwelling place of men, of the length of one day's journey on all the four sides, to be a pasturage for the cows.

AVESTA.

(26.) There first make the water flowing down the way of the size of a Hathra ; there fix marks on a gold-coloured spot *provided* with imperishable food ; there build houses composed of mattes and poles and walls and fences.

ZEND.

(27.) Thither bring the seeds of all males and females who are the greatest, best, and finest on this earth. Thither bring the seeds of all kinds of cattle which are the greatest, best, and finest on this earth.

(28.) Thither bring the seeds of all trees which are the highest and most odoriferous. Thither bring the seeds of all kinds of food which are the most eatable and odoriferous. Make in the whole of the district imperishableness, because these men live in these districts.

### AVESTA.

(29.) There shall not be overbearance nor low-spiritedness, neither stupidity, nor violence, neither poverty nor deceit, neither puniness nor deformation, neither too large teeth nor bodies beyond the usual measure. Nor shall there be one of the other signs through which men use to become defiled by the evil spirit.

(30.) In the uppermost part of the country make nine bridges, in the middle six, in the undermost three. To the bridges in the uppermost part bring the seeds of a thousand men and women, to those of the middle part, those of six hundred, and to those of the undermost part, those of three hundred. And round about these districts make golden pillars and furnish the whole on its frontier with a shinning door, having its own light from inside.

(31.) Then Yima considered: how shall I make the district ordered by Ahuramazda? Then Ahuramazda spoke unto Yima: Thou happy Yima Vîvanhana! with thy heels extend this earth, with thy hands, make her asunder like as men now extend the earth in cultivating.

(33-38.) Then Yima made the district (25-30 repeated).

### ZEND.

(39.) Creator of the fenced estates with living beings threin! which then are those lights, O true Ahuramazda! which shine there in those districts which Yima has made?

(40.) Then Ahuramazda answered: Self-created lights and created ones [PAZEND: all unbegotten lights shine from outside, all begotten ones from inside]; once *a year* one sees there stars, moon and sun rising and setting.

(41.) And they think a day what is a year. Every forty years a couple gives birth to two men [Pazend: a pair, male and female]. The same is the case with the cattle. Those men enjoy the greatest happiness in those districts which Yima has made.

(42.) Creator of the fenced estates with the living beings therein: who was propagating there in these districts which Yima made, the belief in Ahuramazda? Then Ahuramazda answered: The bird Karsipta, O Zarathustra Spitama.

(43.) Creator of the fenced estates with the living beings therein: who is their nourisher and master? Then Ahuramazda answered: Urvatat-narô and thou, who art Zarathustra.

## (B) THE THIRD FARGARD.

*(The Holiness of Agriculture Vend.* 3, 24-33.)

(24.) This earth is not a place which is to lie long uncultivated. She is to be ploughed by the ploughman, that she becomes for them (men) a quarter of every good thing. Then (if cultivated) becomes pregnant the beautiful woman (earth), who was not getting with child for a long time. Then all good things will be produced for them.

(25.) ZEND: If one cultivates this earth, Zarathustra Spitama! with the left arm and the right, and with the right arm and the left, then she bears fruit likewise as if *a woman* on a bed for cohabitation [Paz: lying on a place*] sets forth a son [or fruit.]

(26.) If one cultivates this earth, Zarathustra Spitama! with the left arm and the right, with the right and the left, then says this earth: O man who cultivatest me with the left and the right, with the right hand and the left: I shall, indeed, make thrive the countries here; I shall come to bear all *sorts* of nourishments [the fields produce plenty of them as wheat and so on].

(28.) If one does not cultivate this earth, Zarathustra, Spitama! with the left arm and the right, with the right arm and the left, then says this earth: O thou man, who dost not cultivate me

* The words: *gâtus çayamnô* are an explanation of the older phrase: *vantavê çtareta*; *gâtus*, place, being that of *vantavê* and *çtareta* "stretched" corresponding to *çayamnô*.

with the left arm and the right, with the right arm and the left ;
29 there thou standst before another man's door going for food [amongst those who beg for it] ; sitting outside, food is brought to thee only by drops (in very small quantities). [Paz : they are brought to others who have abundance of goods.]

(30.) O, Creator : How is the Mâzdayaçna religion to be made growing ? Then Ahuramazda replied : Chiefly by cultivation of barley, O Zarathustra Spitama !

(31.) Who cultivates barley, he cultivates purity ; [he is furthering the Mâzdayaçna religion] ; he makes this Mâzdayaçna religion increase by hundred victorious combats *against the devils*, by thousand offerings, by ten thousand prayer-readings.*

AVESTA.

(32.) When barley there is,†
Then the devils whistle ;
When barley is thrashed,
Then the devils whine ;
When barley is ground,
Then the devils roar ;
When flour is produced,
Then the devils perish.

ZEND.

There the devils are driven out from the place [Paz : in the house where this flour is kept] ; their jaw-bones are then burnt by it ; many of them disappear entirely, when barley grows in large quantity.

(33.) Then may he recite the following verses :

AVESTA.

There is no strength in those who do not eat ;
Neither for keeping up a strong life,
Nor for hard agricultural works,
Nor for begetting strong children.

* Cultivation of barley, wheat, is equivalent as far as the destruction of the bad Creation, the duty of every Zoroastrian, is concerned, to 100, 1000, and 10,000 other meritorious works.

† The original contains metrical verses, which show even a rhyme.

[Pâzend: By eating only all living beings exist; without eating they must die].

## (C) THE FOURTH FARGARD.

### *(Civil and Criminal Laws.)*

### AVESTA.

(1.) Who does not return any property to the owner of the property, is a thief of it, taking it with force, even if he seize for his own only a small fraction of their (*who have deposited it*) property, which has been agreed upon there, at day, or at night.

### ZEND.

(2.) Creator of the living beings, thou pure! How many such agreements (*Mithra*) are there? Then Ahuramuzda answered: Six, true Zarathustra! The first *is made* by word; the second by offering the hand *as a pledge*; the third by depositing the value of a sheep; the fourth by depositing the value of an ox, the fifth by depositing the value of a man (slave), the sixth by depositing the value of a country [Pazend: a well thriving, fenced in, walled in, well arranged, prosperous *country*].

3. The word makes the first agreement (promise). After that, the offering of the hand as *a pledge* is marked [PAZEND: the offering of the hand *as a pledge* takes place after that among friends]; after that, that of a sheep's value is marked [that agreement of a sheep's value takes place among friends]; after that, that of an ox's value is marked [that agreement of an ox's value takes place among friends]; after that, that of a man's value is marked [that agreement of a man's value takes place among friends]; after that, that of a land's value is marked. [that agreement of a land's value takes place among friends].

(5.) Creator of the animated beings, thou true! What punishment has the breaker of an agreement, made by a word, to undergo? Then Ahuramazda answered: he has to pay a fine of three hundred pieces *of money* to the kinsmen *of the offended.*

(The fine varies from 300 to 1000; breaking of the second class of agreements is fined by 600, that of the third by 700, that of the fourth by 800, that of the fifth by 900, that of the sixth by 1000 pieces of atonement money).

### Pazend.

(11.) Creator of the animated beings, thou true! Who violates an agreement made by a word *only*, what is his punishment? Then Ahuramazda answered: one may give him three hundred blows with a rod [three hundred with a whip].

(According to Pazend the number of blows varies from 300 to 1000, exactly in the same order as above).

### Avesta.

(17.) When a man rises to murder, that is attempt *at murder*; when he attacks, that is violence; when he seizes him with an evil intention, that is consummation of murder; at the fifth time, that he consummates *the evil intention*, he is guilty of death.

What follows from vss. 18—42, is Pazend, which is, as to its character, completely in accordance with the Pazend of 11-16. The Zend, or the old explanation of this criminal law, is lost. From this Pâzend may be seen, that the distinctions, made regarding the degree of guilt in attempted, or accomplished murder, have become in course of time much more numerous. In the old text or Avesta, as quoted above (4,17), there are only three degrees distinguished: *âyereptem* or attempt; *avaoiristem* or attack; *aredus* or consummation of action. In its Zend or Commentary, there were probably more distinctions made and the different degrees of punishment mentioned, as we may infer from the Zend given to 4,1. In this Avesta only the capital punishment is ordered, when the "aredus" has been committed five times. In the Pazend or second commentary there is a detailed list of punishments to be found consisting of blows with a rod or a whip varying from 5 to 200.

Towards the end of the 4th Fargard (from 44 to 54 West.) we have only Avesta, without Zend or Commentary. This Avesta, which is certainly very old, and apparently of various contents, is, as to its style, very dark and obscure, and is the most difficult passage of the whole Vendidad. In its beginning, there is an ancient law, enjoining the greatest friendship and equality among the members of the Zoroastrian Community. It runs, as follows: "If men, who profess the same (Mazdayasna) religion, brothers or friends, should be desirous of obtaining a field, or of marrying a woman, or of acquiring wisdom (knowledge), then shall those who aspire after a field, get offered this field (to own it), and those who aspire after a woman, they shall get offered her in marriage, and those who aspire after wisdom, they shall be taught the sacred word."

## (D) THE FARGARDS 5—18.

From the fifth to the eighth Fargard, we find very minute and detailed precepts for the treatment of a dead body, the constructing of Dakhmas, or towers of silence, the purification of men or things brought into contact with a corpse. The idea, pervading the whole, is the utter impurity of a dead body, and the utmost purity and sacredness of earth, fire, and water. The most impure thing can, therefore, not be thrown upon one of these elements, because it would spoil the good creation by increasing the power and influence of the daêvas or devils, who take possession of a body as soon as a man is dead. It is, therefore, to be carried on the barren top of a mountain or hill, placed on stones (or iron plates), and exposed to dogs and vultures to benefit in this way the animals of the good creation. A man, who touches a dead body, the contagious impurity of which has not been previously checked by holding towards the corpse a peculiar kind of dog,* is at once visited by a spectre, representing death itself. This is called *drukhs naçus* i. e. the destructive corruption. To get rid of this annoyance, he is to be sprinkled with water on the different parts of his body, which is described with the greatest minuteness in the eighth Fargard.

In the same Fargard (vss. 73-96) there is the preparation of the sacred fire described. Fires from sixteen different places are

* He is called "the four-eyed dog," a yellow spot on both his eyelids being considered as eyes. He has yellow ears, and the colour on the other part of his body is divided between yellow and white. To his eyes a kind of magnetic influence is ascribed.

requried, which, after having been purified by praying over them, must be brought to one and the same hearth (called *dâityô-gâtus*, now *Dâdgah*). Indispensable is the fire, by which a dead body is being burnt. Though it be the most impure of all,* it is believed to have absorbed the fire (electricity) which is in the animal body. It is called *naçupâka* ; its obtaining and purifying by placing it into a certain number of holes, called *hañdaresa*, (in modern Persian *andâzah*, a measure), which requiries great trouble, is more minutely described than that of the other fires (those of dyers, potters, glassworkmen, steelsmiths, bricklayers, etc). The collective fire obtained in this way, represents the essence of nature, the fluid, pervading the whole earth, the cause of all growth, vigour and splendour. Therefore it is regarded with such a high reverence by the Parsees.

In the 9th Fargard there is a very detailed description of the great purification ceremony, called *Barashnom of* 9 *nights* which lasts for nine days (or rather nights). It is intended for the removal of any uncleanliness whatever, and chiefly undergone by priests. The person, who will undergo the ceremony, must drink the urine of a cow, sit on stones within the compass of certain magic circles, and, while moving from one heap of stones to another, rub the body with cow urine, then with sand, and, lastly, wash it with water. This custom has descended from the most ancient times, where a purifying and healing influence was ascribed to the urine, proceeding from such a sacred animal, as the cow was to the ancient Arians.

In the tenth and eleventh Fargards, there are chiefly prayers enumerated, which were believed to have the power of removing the impurity caused by the touch of a dead body. All theseprayers are to be found in the old Yasna.

The 12th Fargard treats of the duration of mourning for the different degrees of relationship and the head of a famity. If one dies as a pious righteous man by the law of nature (these

* To burn a dead body, is, according to the spirit of the Zoroastrian law, one of the greatest crimes.

are called *dahmas*), then only half as much time is required as is wanted for those who die by their own hands or are executed (these are called *tanu-perethas*).

The 13th and 14th Fargards treat of dogs and water dogs (*udra*, otter) which are not to be badly treated, wounded, mutilated, starved or killed. Should a man be found guilty of such charges, he is to be severely punished. As a horrible crime is chiefly the killing of an otter regarded, which animal is believed to contain the souls of a thousand male and a thousand female dogs. A man, who commits this crime, has to receive ten thousand blows with a horsewhip according to the later interpretation ; or, he must kill ten thousand animals of the bad creation, as snakes, mice, lizards, frogs, etc. and carry ten thousand loads of wood to the fire etc.

In the 15th Fargard various topics are treated : the sins, called Pesho-tanus (i. e. such actions which by themselves not being considered as hurtful or injurious, may under certain circumstances cause damage or injury) ; the crime of killing an illegitimate child ;* the treatment of pregnant dogs.

The whole 16th fargard is devoted to the treatment of women at the time of their menses.

In the 17th there are precepts given, how to treat nails and hairs which have been cut. The devils must be prevented from using them for doing injury to the good creation.

The contents of the 18th fargard are of a various kind and are not connected with each other. In its first part (1-6), Ahuramazda informs Zarathustra as to what qualities are required to be a true fire-priest (he is called *âthrava*), and how to distinguish him from mere pretenders to the priestly dignity. All those who wear only the garb of a priest and carry with them the sacerdotal implements, such as the cloth, covering the mouth, the sacred twigs, (Barsom), the instrument for killing bad animals (called *khrafçtraghna*), without studying hard day

* To kill such a poor creature is prohibited. Should it be done, the man, the girl and the nurse, are equally guilty of the murder.

and night the sacred books, and sending up constantly their prayers to the Almighty for their community and themselves, to make them after death pass safely that great bridge, which leads from this to the other life, are called by Ahuramazda false priests who do not deserve this name. Then follow some questions put by Zarathustra to Ahuramazda on different topics, the profanation of the sacred bread or meat (*myazda*), the services rendered by the cock (*Parô-dars*), which bird is attached to the great angel Serosh, and awakens men from sleep (which was considered to be the work of the devils), exhorting them to feed the fire, to pray, to wash, to dress etc. Between these questions we find inserted a conversation which was said to have taken place between the angel Serosh and the she devil called *Devi-Drukhs* (30-59), regarding her different husbands. Men get married to her by certain impure actions.

## (E) THE NINETEENTH FARGARD.

### FRAGMENT OF AN OLD EPIC SONG :

(*The devil's attempts to frustrate Zarathustra's doings* 4.6-9.)

The verses 1-3 are introductory to the ancient song, and evidently composed to make better understood the contents of this ancient piece. Here in the introduction is described, how Drukhs, one of the evil spirits in Ahriman's service, came forth from the northern regions at her master's command, to destroy Zarathustra. The prophet frustrated all those attempts to ruin him simply by repeating the holiest prayer : *Yathâ ahuvairyô.* Drukhs, having been thus defeated, told the chief of the evil spirits, Angrômainyus, that it was impossible to do any mischief to the prophet.

Zarathustra perceived these snares laid to him and thought about escaping them. This is described with the very verses of an old song, undoubtedly current in the mouth of the Iranian people. The song is composed in the heroic meter of the ancient

Arians, the Anustubh, which has given rise to the common Shloka*

(1.) From the northern country (Paz. : from the northern countries), Angrô mainyus, the death-darting, the devil of the devils, broke forth. Thus spoke the evil knowing Angrô mainyus the death-darting : Drukhs (devil of destruction and father of lies), break forth and kill the pious Zarathustra. Then the Drukhs broke forth, the devil Bûiti, the destroyer with the intention of killing *him*.

(2.) Zarathustra recited the prayer Ahuna vairya ; he invoked the good waters of good qualities, he confessed the Mazdayaçna faith (belief in Ahuramazda). Drukhs was slain ; the devil Bûiti, the destroyer, intending to kill *him*, ran away.

(3.) Drukhs then spoke to Angrô-mainyus : Impostor Angrô mainyus ! I do not think about doing any harm to Zarathustra

* I subjoin here the original ballad in its metrical form. The translation is given above.

(4)

*Uçchistat Zarathustrô | açaretô aka mananiha*<br>
*khruzhdyâi tbaêshô-parstanãm | açânô zaçta drazhimnô*

DEFECTIVE.

(6)

*Paiti ahmâi adavata | duzhdâmô Angrô mainyus*<br>
*Mâ mê dãma merechanuha | ashâum Zarathustra.*<br>
*Têm ahi Pourushâçpahê | puthrô barethryat hacha*<br>
*Zâvisi apa-çtavanuha | vanuhîm daênãm mâzdayaçnîm*<br>
*Vindâi yânem yatha vindat | Vadhaghanô danhupaitis.*

(7)

*Paiti ahmâi avashata | yô çpitâmô Zarathustro*<br>
*Nôit hê apaçtvânê | vanuhîm daênãm mazdayaçnîm*<br>
*Nôit açta nôit ustânem | nôit baodhaçcha urviçyât*

(8)

*Paiti ahmâi adavata | duzhdâmô Angro mainyus*<br>
*Kahê vacha vanâhi | kahê vacha apayaçâhi*<br>
*Kana zaya hukeretâonhô | mana dãma Angro mainyus.*

(9)

*Paiti ahmâi avashata | yô çpitâmô Zarathustrô.*<br>
*Hâvanacha tastacha Haomacha vacha mazdô-fraokhta*<br>
*Mana Zaya açti vahistem | ana vacha vanâni*<br>
*Ana vacha apa yaçâni | ana zaya hukeretâonhô*<br>
*âi duzhda Angro mainyô | dathat çpentô mainyus*<br>
*Dothat Zruni akaranê | fradathen ameshâo çpenta*<br>
*Hukhshathrâ hudâonhô.*

Spitama [the brilliant pure Zarathustra]. Zarathustra perceived by his mind that the evil doing spirits are laying snares to him.

SONG.

(4). There arose Zarathustra [Zarathustra went forward] to annihilate all those hostile intentions *of the evil spirits*, holding a shepherd's hook with nine knots in his hand [Z : which are as large as a cottage.] The pious Zarathustra was praying to Ahuramazda the creator : Wherever thou touchest this wide round far extended earth, recite efficacious prayers to protect from ruin Pourushâspa's house.

(5). Zarathustra informed Angro mainyus ; evil doing Angro-mainyus ; I shall slay the creation produced by the devils, I shall slay the death, I shall slay the Pairika *Khnãthaiti** for whose *destruction* Sosiosh will be born out of the water Kaçoya from the eastern country [from the eastern countries].

(6). To him spoke Angrô mainyus the creator of evils : Do not destroy my creations, pious Zarathustra ! Thou art Pourushâspa's son, so art thou called by thy mother. Curse the good belief in Ahuramazda, then thou shalt obtain as much fortune as Vadhaghanô, the king.

(7.) To him replied Zarathustra Spitama : I shall not curse the good belief in Ahuramazda, even not, if my life *would perish*, and my body and soul then become separated.

(8.) To him spoke Angro mainyus the creator of evils : With whose words wilt thou destroy my creations ? with whose words wilt thou pollute my creations, what weapons are so well made as to be used against my creations, those of Angro-mainyus ?

(9.) To him replied Zarathustra Spitama : the Haoma and its mortar and dish, and the words pronounced by Ahuramazda are my best weapons ; with these words shall I destroy, with these words shall I pollute thy *creations*. These good weapons, evil-knowing Angrô mainyus ! were made by Ahuramazda in the boundless time, the immortal holy spirits, the rulers and masters of the good creation, assisted him in *making them*.

* Probably an idol worshipper in Kandahar or thereabout.

## VSS. 27—32.

### *The fate of the soul after death.*

27. Creator of the fenced estates with living beings, thou true! What events will be [*Pazend*: what events will happen? what events will take place? what events will be met with?] when a man gives up his soul in this world of existence?

28. Then Ahuramazda replied: when a man is dead [Paz. when a man has departed this life, when the running evil doing devils make destruction *of his life*], then, after the third night, at daybreak [when aurora is shining], he reaches Mithra, rising above the mountains resplendent of their own spotless lustre [Paz.: when sun is rising].

29. The devil Vîzareshô by name, O Zarathustra Spitama! carries the soul tied towards the country of the worshippers of the running devas.* It goes on the old paths, the soul of the good man as well as that of the bad, to the bridge of the gatherer, the good, created by Ahuramazda, where they ask for her conduct *whilst living* in the fenced estates, i. e. world [for what was achieved in the world of existence.]

(30.) He, the happy, well formed, swift, tall Serosh, comes thither with the dog, with the nine knotted hook, with cattle, with the twigs of *Barsom*†. He dismisses the sinful soul of the bad into darkness, i. e. Hell! He meets the souls of the good when crossing the *celestial mountain* Harô berezaiti (Alborz), and guides them over the bridge of the gatherer [the bridge of the heavenly spirits].

31. The *arch angel* Bah-man (Vohu-manô) rises from his golden throne; Bah-man speaks *thus to the soul*: how happy that you have come here to us from the mortality to the immortality!

(32.) The souls of the good go joyfully to Ahuramazda, to the immortal saints, to the golden throne, to paradise [the residence of Ahuramazda, of the immortal saints, and of other good spirits].

* The country of the deva worshippers is India.

† These things are considered to be efficacious means for guarding against infernal influences. The dog is requisite to be looked at by a man at the last gasp; the nine knotted shepherd's hook (called generally *açânô*) is essential in certain ceremonies and Zarathustra himself is said to have used it, when attacked by the evil spirit.

*(Fragment not connected with the preceding contents.)*

(33.) The good man is to be made pure after his death; the devils *then* run together and frighten the soul like as a sheep is frightened by a wolf.

(34.) The good assemble, Nairyô-çanha assembles. Say: Ahuramazda's weapon is Nairyô-çanha; invoke thyself Zarathustra! this creation of Ahuramazda.

(35.) Zarathustra said unto me that word: I praise the beings, created by Ahuramazda; I praise the earth, created by Ahuramazda, the water, created by Ahuramazda, the good trees; I praise the sea Vouru Kasha (i. e. having distant shores, wide, large); I praise the brightly shining sky, I praise the unbegotten lights (fixed stars), self created.

(36.) I praise the best life (paradise) of the good, every where resplendent of its own brilliancy; I praise the house of songs (*gerôdemâna*, equivalent to *Beheseht* or paradise), the residence of Ahuramazda, the residence of the immortal saints, the residence of the other good; I praise the bridge Chinvat (bridge of the gatherer), created by Ahuramazda, in the self-created intermediate world (between heaven and hell).

(37.) I praise the good flame widely shining; I praise the strong guardian angels of the good, all created by Ahuramazda for the benefit *of the good creation*; I praise Behram, the bearer of splendour created by Ahuramazda; I praise the shining beautiful star Tîr (Tistrya, Mercury), who has the body of a cow and golden hoofs.

(38.) I praise the holy songs (the five Gâthâs), ruling over the *five* parts of the day, the good ones. I praise the Ahunavaiti Gâtha; I praise the Ustavaiti Gâtha; I praise the Spentômainyus Gâtha; I praise the Vohû-khshathra Gâtha; I praise the Vahistôistis Gâtha.

(39.) I praise the zone (Karshvare, Keshvar) Arezahi and Savahi; I praise the zone Fradadafshu *and* Vîdadafshu; I praise the zone Vouru-baresti and Vourn-jaresti; I praise the zone Qanirathem, the splendid Hêtumat (Hilmend), the brightly shining, the beautiful. I praise the good nature; I praise the good science, I praise the rightest science. I praise the beauty of the Arian countries, I praise the beauty which obtained Yima of great wealth.

The three last fargards of the Vendidad (20-22) seem to have belonged originally to a medical book. They contain spells for curing diseases, which resemble very much the mantras which are intended for the same purpose in the Atharvaveda. *Thrita* is said to have been the first physician who relieved mankind from the distress and misery caused by diseases. The angel, presiding over the medical art is called *Airyaman* to whom even Ahuramazda despatches his messenger *Nairyó çanha* (Neriosengh).

## 27.—BRIEF SURVEY OF ZEND LITERATURE.

Having characterised and illustrated by select specimens in this long chapter, the various branches of the sacred literature of the Parsees, I confine myself here at the end, to a brief summary and survey of the whole only.

At the head of the literature there are undoubtedly the FIVE GATHAS, which we must regard as the work of Zarathustra Spitama himself, and his disciples, as every one will easily convince himself from a careful perusal of the numerous passages, translated above from these collections, and comparing them with those communicated from the other parts of the Zend Avesta. Besides the internal evidence, which is strong and convincing enough, there may be some external reasons alleged to corroborate the opinion, that these Gâthas contain the undoubted teaching and sayings of the celebrated Zoroaster himself. While the other parts are nowhere said to be the work of Zarathustra Spitama himself, he is in the Serosh Yasht distinctly and expressly mentioned as the author of these ancient and sacred songs (see pag. 133). Whereas in the other works of the Zend Avesta Zarathustra is spoken of in the third person, and even occasionally invoked like a divine being, in the Gâthas he speaks of himself in the first person, and acts throughout as a man who is commissioned by God to perform a great task. We find him placed among men, surrounded by his friends, Kava Vistâspa, Jâmâspa and Frashostra, preaching to his countrymen a new and more pure religion, exhorting them to leave idolatry and to worship the living God only.

The Gâtha literature was, in ancient times, certainly not confined to these scanty fragments which are now only extant. There existed, no doubt, a much larger collection of the songs and sayings of Zarathustra Spitama and his disciples, including those of the ancient prophets called *Soshyanto*, which are now and then alluded to in Yasna. Out of this larger collection those verses were selected, which were believed to be most efficacious for putting down evil enfluences from the part of the hostile devas and their priests (the Brahmans), and for increasing the welfare of the Zoroastrians; and these only have been preserved. The collection of the Gâthas extant now-a-days, may be well compared with the Sâmaveda, which contains detached verses, selected from the Rigveda, intended only for being sung at the celebration of the great Soma sacrifices. While the Brahmans completely preserved their Rigveda, i. e. the large collection entire songs, irrespective of their liturgical application, the ancestors of the Parsees, who were apparently more careless of their sacred literature, than their Brahmanic brothers, lost it entirely.

Next to the Gâthas in rank stands the "YASNA OF SEVEN CHAPTERS" (see page 161-163). From reasons pointed out above, we cannot regard it as a genuine work of Zarathustra Spitama himself. It appears to be the work of one of the earliest successors of the prophet, called in ancient times *Zarathustra* or *Zarathustrôtema* (see the 3rd paragraph in the 4th Essay), who, deviating somewhat from the high and pure monotheistic principle of Spitama, made some concessions to the adherents to the ante-Zoroastrian religion by addressing prayers to other beings than Ahuramazda.

The first part of the Yasna, styled by me above the YOUNGER YASNA is certainly of a far later date than even the "Yasna of seven chapters." The High-priests seem to have tried to conciliate the men of the old party (called *poiryô-tkaêshô*, i. e. of the old creed), who were unwilling to leave the ancient polytheistic religion, and their time-hallowed rites and ceremonies. The old sacrifices were reformed, and adapted to the more civilized mode of life of the Iranians. The intoxicating Soma beverage was replaced by a more wholesome and invigorating drink, prepared from another plant than the original Soma plant, together with the branches of the pomegranate tree, and without any process of fermentation (simply water is poured over them); but the name in the Iranian form "Homa" remained, and some of the ceremonies also, as we shall see in the 4th Essay; the solemn sacrificial cakes of the Brahmans (*purô-daça*) were superseded by the sacred bread, called afterwards "Daruṇ." New invocations, addressed to those divine beings, who were occupying the places of the ancient devas or Gods, branded by Zarathustra Spitama as the originators of all evil and sin, were composed and adapted for the reformed Soma sacrifice (Homa ceremony). These new prayers form the substance of the younger Yasna which was to represent the formulas of the Brahmanic Yajurveda.

If we compare this younger Yasna with the Gâthas, we find as to contents (irrespective of the difference of dialect), such a vast difference, that it is quite impossible for a conscientious critic to assign them to one author. While in the Gâthas we never find mentioned neither Homa, Barsom, nor gods, like Mithra, Anâhita, nor even the general name for the heavenly councillors, Amesha spenta (Amshashpand), we meet with them nearly on every page of the younger Yasna. Here naturally the question arises, why has the author of the Gâthas, in propounding his new religious doctrines, entirely overlooked those things, which were considered in after times as most indispensable implements of the divine service, and disregarded those gods and divine beings whose neglect was held afterwards very punishable? The only answer is, that he neither believed in them, nor thought them to be an essential part of the religion.

On the same line with the younger Yasna, stands VISPARAD, on which see pag. 172-74. It is made by one of the later High-priests for the celebration of the Gahanbars.

Whilst Yasna and Visparad represent the Vedas of the Parsees, their VENDIDAD corresponds exactly to the *Smritis* or collections of customs, observances laws, penalties, and fines which form the groundwork of the so-called Dharma Shâstra. I noticed above its different constituent parts, from which every thinking man will convince himself of the impossibility to ascribe the whole to Zarathustra Spitama himself. The book pretends only to give the conversations, which Zarathustra was unanimously (even in the Gâthas) said, to have held with God himself, and that there in very ancient times a work, purporting to contain these conversations, must have existed, follows undoubtedly from the notice of such a work to be found in Visparad and the Vendidad itself (see pag. 135.).

If we compare Zarathustra's conversations with Ahuramazda, as contained in the Gâthas, with those, which are reported in the Vendidâd, we find a considerable difference between both. In the Gâthas, there is never an allusion made to the numerous ceremonies and observances, which were deemed absolutely necessary for a pious Ormuzd worshipper. Thus, for instance, among the questions, put by Zarathustra Spitama to Ahuramazda in Yasna 44. (see page 149—53.), on the true religion, and its keeping, there is not a single one which refers to the treatment of the dead body, one of the most important things in times of the Vendidad, or to the great purification ceremony (see pag. 211), deemed so essential for the welfare of the Iranian Community. Very likely Zarathustra Spitama himself never gave any direct precepts about the customs and usages which might have existed already at his time. Had he done so, we should expect him to allude to them chiefly in those verses where he mentions the means of checking the evil influence exercised by the devas (devils) ; but all he knows, is : the splendour of the fire, the mighty words, revealed to him by Ahuramazda, and the cultivation of the soil, and purity in thought, word and deed. From his never mentioning those ceremonies undoubtedly follows, that, though he might know them, he did not attach much weight to keeping and observing them.

Only in one point we find the laws given in the Vendidad corroborated by the Gâthas. These are those which refer to the sacredness of a promise or contract, called *Mithra*, as one may learn from comparing Vend. 4 (see pag. 208) with Yas. 46,5 (see pag. 155.). These seem to have originated from Zarathustra Spitama himself, when he called into existence a new religious community to be founded on the principle of inviolable faith and truth.

In careful consideration of these and other circumstances which are pointed out above (pag. 200), we cannot regard the Vendidad as a work of Zarathustra Spitama himself, but as the joint work of his successors, the Supreme High-priests of the Iranian community. That the Chief High-priests together with the Kings were believed to stand in direct communication with Ahuramazda himself and to receive from him answers to their questions, we may see distinctly from Visp. 1,30. (quoted above). The Chief High-priest is there called *Zarathustrôtemô* which word literally means (*tema* is the superlative suffix see pag. 89) : the greatest Zarathustra i. e. High-priest. His communications are held sacred in this passage, and placed on one line with the Gâthâs. From this circumstance we may distinctly gather, that works of the Zarathustrôtemas, were held in ancient times about equally sacred with those of Zarathustra Spitama himself. If we then consider the Vendidad as their joint work, compiled during several successive centuries, it is not to be wondered at finding it so highly revered by the Zoroastrians up to the present day.

Of the three stages, which we can discover in the present Vendidad, the Avesta, no doubt, is very old and partially perhaps traceable to oral sayings descended from the prophet himself. Even the Zend, which makes up by far the larger portion of the present Vendidad, belongs to a very early age and seems to be at least as old as the younger Yasna. The Pazend is the comparatively youngest, and seems to be more of a literary and learned character, than of practical consequence.

On the Yashts which correspond partially to the Puranic literature of the Brahmans, see above page. 174—198. One may distinguish in them chiefly two classes of works, firstly songs, secondly conversations with Ahuramazda.

The metrical pieces or songs represent the fragments of the ancient epic poetry of the Iranians as living in the mouth of their bards, and are not only to be found in the properly so-called Yashts, but are scattered through the whole Zend Avesta (see Yas. 9.10. Vend. 19.). In the present form, the Yashts are evidently, together with those smaller prayers, such as Afrigans, Gâhs, etc. (see pag. 199.) the most modern pieces of the Zend Avesta, and have not the slightest claim to have been composed by Zarathustra, or even his earliest successors. This kind of literature grew up at a time, when the Zoroastrian religion had already very much degenerated, and its original monotheism partially given way to the old gods, who had been stigmatised and banished by Zarathustra Spitama, but were afterwards transformed into angels. The songs of the bards, which we find made use of in the Yashts, may be old and genuine, but, strictly speaking, they concern very little the Zoroastrian religion. The Zoroastrian conversations with Ahuramazda, with which we meet often in the Yashts, may be the work of later High-priests; but they seem to be entirely strange to all that we know of Spitama.

The tendency of the authors of these Yashts was, to raise the dignity of the angels, such as Mithra, Tistrya, Anâhita, etc. to that of Ahuramazda, with whom they are said even to have equal rank (see Yt. 10,1.). Therefore Ahuramazda himself is called, now and then, their worshipper. Zarathustra is reported to have paid them high reverence also, but of all this not the slightest trace can be discovered in his own Gâthâs. This kind of literature has, no doubt, largely contributed towards the deterioration of the religion founded by Zarathustra Spitama, and partially reestablished what the prophet had endeavoured to destroy.

As to its age, there is happily a certain historical hint to be found in the Fravardin Yasht, where mention is made, of *Gautama* (*Buddha*), the founder of the Buddhism, (see page 188.). That Buddhism was spread in Bactria at a very early time, we know from other sources. Buddha entered Nirvâna (died) in 543 B. C. Before his lore could spread in Bactria, at least 100-200 years must have elapsed since the master's death. Thus we arrive for the Fravardin Yasht (in language and ideas, there is no difference between it, and the others) at about 350-450 B. C. A later date, than this, cannot be reasonably assigned to the majority of the Yashts, because the language began to die out already before the commencement of the Christian era, and most of the Yashts are written in a comparatively good language, without too many grammatical errors in which some parts of the Vendidad so abound. There is another reason besides, for assigning to the principal Yashts the 5th century before the Christian era. At that time, as we may learn from two inscriptions of the King Artaxerxes Mnemon,* the worship of Mithra and Anahita was spreading through all the dominions of the Persian Empire, which was not the case at the time of Darius Hystaspes, who never mentions these deities in his numerous inscriptions. This new form of worship called a new appropriate sacred literature forthwith into existence, which is partially preserved in the Yashts.

As to the age of the other older parts of the Zend Avesta, the decision of this question is closely connected with that about the time at which Zarathustra Spitama himself lived. As we shall see in the 4th Essay, we cannot place his era at a much later date than 1,200 B. C. If we assign this date to the Gâthas as the work of Zarathustra Spitama and his disciples, then we must fix the age of the larger portion of the Vendidad at about 900 or 1,000 and of the younger Yasna at about 7—800. The Pazend portion of the Vendidad is very likely not older, than 500 B. C. and at the same time the collection of its different parts might have taken place.

If we date the commencement of the sacred literature of the Parsees from 1,200 B. C. and place its close at 400 B. C., we obtain a space of about 800 years, which is, in comparison with other sacred literature as that of the Jews and Brahmans rather too short, than too long.

* See Benfeiy; Persische Kelinsehriften pag. 67; Norris, memoir on the Scythic version of the Behisten incription pag. 159.

# IV.

# THE ZOROASTRIAN RELIGION

AS TO ITS

# ORIGIN AND DEVELOPMENT.

---

In this Essay I intend to state my views on the origin of the Zoroastrian religion,* its general character and development as far as it is to be ascertained from the original Zend texts. Having furnished the reader in the previous Essay with a translation of a good many passages referring particularly to the subject, I can, in reference to them, condense the matter here into a few paragraphs only.

## 1.—THE RELATIONSHIP BETWEEN THE BRAHMANIC AND ZOROASTRIAN RELIGIONS.

Before we can discuss properly the question as to the origin of the Zoroastrian religion and the time, when its founder flourished, certain traces of an originally close connection, which the attentive reader of both, the Vedas and the Zend Avesta, will readily perceive to exist between the Brahmanic and Zoroastrian religions, customs and observances, must be pointed out.

### (a) NAMES OF DIVINE BEINGS.

The most striking feature, in this respect, is the use which we find made in both, the Vedas and the Zend Avesta, of the names,

* This subject has been already briefly treated in my pamphlet: Lecture on the origin of the Parsee religion, delivered on the first of March 1861, at the United Service Institution, and more fully in the Essay appended to my German work on the Gâthâs (see vol. II, pag. 231-59).

*deva* and *asura* (*ahura* in Zend). *Deva* is in all the Vedas and in the whole Brahmanic literature the name of the divine beings, the gods who are the objects of worship form the part of the Hindoos up to the present day. In the Zend Avesta, from its earliest down to its latest parts, and even in the modern Persian literature, *deva* (modern Pers. *div*) is the general name of an evil spirit, a fiend or devil, who is inimical to all that comes from God and is good. In the confession of faith, as recited even up to this day, the Zoroastrian religion is distinctly said to be *vî-daêvô* i. e. against the Devas, opposed to them (see Yasna 12 pag. 164.), and one of their most sacred books is called *vî-daêvô-dâta* (now corrupted to *Vendidâd*) i. e. what is given against, or for the removal of, the devas. The devas are the originators of all that is bad, of every impurity, of death, and are constantly thinking of putting to destruction the fields, trees, and the houses of religious men. The spots, most liked by them, are, according to the Zoroastrian notion, those filled most with dirt and filth, chiefly the cemeteries which places are, therefore, objects of the greatest abomination for a true Ormuzd worshipper.

*Asura* is, in the form *Ahura*, the first part of AHURAMAZDA (Hormuzd), the name of God among the Parsees, and the Zoroastrian religion is distinctly called the Ahura religion (see Yasna 12 pag. 164.), in its strict opposition to the Deva religion. But among the Hindus it has assumed a bad meaning, and is applied to the bitterest enemies of their devas (gods), with whom they are constantly waging war, and as even Hindu legends acknowledge, not always without success. This is the case throughout the whole Purânic literature, and goes up as far as the later parts of the Vedas; but, in the earliest parts of hte Rigveda Samhitâ, we find this word "*Asura*" used in as good and high a sense as we find it in the Zend Avesta. The highest gods, such as Indra (Rigveda 1,54,3.),* Varuna, (1,24,14), Agni (4,2,5. 7,2,3), Savitar (1,35,7), Rudra or Shiva (5,42,11.),

* In my quotations from the Rigveda, the first number means the Mandala (book, there are ten), the second the song, and the third the verse.

etc. are honoured with the epithet "Asura" which means "living, spiritual," signifying the divine, in its opposition to the human nature. In the plural, it is even, now and then, used as a name of all the gods, as, for instance, Rv. 1,108,6. : This Soma is to be distributed as an offering among the "Asuras," by which word the Rishi means his own gods whom he was worshipping. Often we find particularly one Asura mentioned, who is called "Asura of heaven" (5,41,3., the heaven itself is called by this name 1,131,1.), "our father, who pours down the waters" (5,83,6.) ; Agni, the fire god, is born out of his womb (3,29,14.) ; his sons support heaven.

In a bad sense we find Asura used only twice in the earlier parts of Rigveda (2, 32,4. 7,99,5.), in which passages the defeat of the "sons or men of the Asura" is ordered or spoken of; but more frequently we find the word in such a sense in the last book of Rigveda (being only an appendix, made at later times to the whole), and in the Atharvaveda, where the Rishis are said to have frustrated the tricks of the Asuras (4,23,5.), and to have the power of putting them down (6,7,2.).

In the Brâhmanas, or sacrificial books, belonging to each of the Vedas, we find the Devas always fighting with the Asuras.* The latter are the constant enemies of the Hindu gods, and make always attacks upon the sacrifices, brought by their devotees. To defeat them, all the craft and cunning of the Devas was required; the means of checking them was generally found in a new sacrificial rite. Thus the Asuras are said to have given rise to a good many sacrificial customs, and in this way they largely contributed towards making the Brahmanic sacrifices so complicated and full of particular rites and ceremonies. To give the reader an idea, in what way the battles between the Devas and Asuras are said to have been fought, I give here a translation of a passage

* In the Purâns the *Asuras* are fighting not with the Devas, but with the *Suras*. The latter word is a mere fiction of later times, and not to be found in the Vedas. A false etymology has called into existence this new class of gods. The bad sense, attached to Asura, was thought to lie in the *A* (the negative prefix), and therefore their opponents must appear without it, in the shape of "Sura."

taken from the *Aitareya Brâhmana* (1,23.)* which belongs to the Rigveda.

"The Devas and Asuras waged war in these worlds. The Asuras made these worlds fortified places (*pur i. e.* polis, town) and them as strong and impregnable as possible; they made the earth of iron, the air of silver, and the heaven of gold. Thus they transformed these worlds into fortified places (castles). The Devas said: These Asuras have made these worlds fortified places; let us thus build other worlds in opposition to these (now occupied solely by them); they then made out of her (the earth) a seat, out of the air a fire-hearth, and out of heaven two repositories for sacrificial food (these are called *Havirdhâna*). The gods said: "let us bring the *Upasads*;† by means of the Upasads one may conquer a large town." When they performed the first Upasad, then they drove them (the Asura) out from this world (the earth); when they performed the second, then they drove them out from the air, and when they performed the third, they drove them out from heaven. Thus they drove them out from these worlds. The Asuras, thus driven out of these worlds, repaired to the Ritus (seasons). The gods said: let us perform Upasad. The Upasads being three, they performed each twice (that makes six in all, corresponding with the number of the seasons, viz. six). Then they drove them (the Asuras) out from the Ritus. The Asuras repaired now to the months. The Devas made twelve Upasads, and drove them out from the months. After having been

* An edition and translation of this whole work (in two volumes) is at present being prepared by me and already in print. I shall give there a full information on the Brahmanic sacrifices, which are as yet little known (which is scarcely possible without oral information to be obtained from professional sacrificial priests) to European Sanscrit Scholars. But they are too essential a part of the Vedic religion (now chiefly preserved by the so-called *Agnohotris*) as tobe overlooked by those who are inquiring into the Brahmanic religion and its history.

† This is a particular ceremony which is to take place immediately after the great *Pravargya* ceremony, during which the priests make to the sacrificer *(yajamâna)* a golden celestial body with which alone he is permitted by the gods to enter heaven. If in this way the sacrificer is new born, he is to receive the nourishment, appropriate for an infant body, and this is milk. The chief part of the Upasad ceremony is, that one of the priests (the *Adhvaryu*) presents to him milk, in a large wooden spoon, which he must drink. Formerly it was to be drunk from the nipples of the cow which was to be milked by the Adhvaryu. But this custom has now fallen into disuse.

defeated here also, they repaired to the half months. The Devas performed twenty-four Upasads and drove the Asuras out of the half months. After having been defeated again, the Asuras repaired to day and night, the Devas performed the Upasads and drove them out. Therefore, the first Upasad ceremony is to be performed in the first part of the day and the other in the second part of the day. He (the sacrificer) leaves thus only so much space to the enemy as exists between the conjunction of day and night (that is the time of twilight in morning and evening)."

That the Asura of the Brahmanic literature are the Supreme Beings of the Parsees (Ahuramazda with his archangels) is, according to these statements, hardly to be doubted. But I have to notice a perhaps still more convincing proof. Among the metres, used in the Yajurveda, we find seven, which are marked by the epithet *ásurí*, such as *Gáyatrí ásurí*, *Ushnih ásurí*, *Pankti ásurí*.* These Asura metres, which are strange to the whole Rigveda, are actually to be found in the Gâtha literature of the Zend Avesta which professedly exhibits the doctrines of the Ahura (Asura) religion. The *Gáyatrí ásurí* consists of 15 syllables, which metre we discover in the Gâtha Ahunavaiti (see pag. 136.), chiefly if we bear in mind, that the number of 16 syllables, of which it generally consists, is often reduced to 15 only (compare, for instance, Yas. 31,6. and the two first lines of 31,4.). The *Ushnih ásurí*, consisting of 14 syllables, is completely extant in the Gâtha Vohu Khshathrem (Yas. 51), each verse of which comprises 14 syllables. The *Pankti ásurí* consists of 11 syllables, just as many as we found (pag. 137.) in the Gâtha ustavaiti, and Spenta-mainyus. This coincidence can certainly not be merely fortuitous. It shows clearly, that the old Gâtha literature of the Zend Avesta was perfectly known to the Rishis, who compiled the Yajurveda.

Of a great importance, for the original close relationship between the Brahmanic and Parsee religions, is, that several of

* See the White Yajurveda, edited by A. Weber, vol. I. pag. LX.

the Indian gods are actually to be found by their very names in the Zend Avesta, some as devils, others as angels.

*Indra*, the Chief god of the Brahmans in the Vedic times, the thunderer, the god of light, and god of war, for whom pre-eminently the Rishis, the ancient founders of Brahmanism, squeezed, and drank the intoxicating Soma beverage, is expressly mentioned in the list of the devas or devils, which we find in Vend. 19,43. He is there second only to *Angrô-mainyus* (Ahriman), the arch fiend of all that is god, who is very commonly designated as "*dêvanãm dêvô*" i. e. god of the gods, but in the Zoroastrian language devil of the devils.

Next to him stands *çâurva daêva* whom we discover in one of Shiva's names *Sharva* (*çarva*, see the white Yajurveda 16,28). In the *Nâoṇhaithya daêva* we readily recognize the *Nâsatyas* of the Vedic songs, which name is there given to the two Ashvins, the Dioskuri of the Indian mythology.

Some names of the Vedic Devas, are, however, used in a good sense, and are transformed into Yazatas (Izeds) i. e. angels in the Zend Avesta. The most noticeable is *Mithra*, the Sanscrit form being *Mitra*. In the Vedic hymns, he is generally invoked together with *Varuna* (identical with the god *Uranos* of the Greeks), the ruler of heaven, and master of Universe,* but in the Zend Avesta, he was throughout separated from his ancient companion. However there is one song to be found in the Rigveda (3,59. *mitrô janân yâtagati*), in which Mitra (as the sun) alone is addressed in the following way :—

"Mitra calls men to their work ; Mitra is keeping earth and heaven ; Mitra looks upon the nations always without shutting his eyes. To Mitra bring the offering with ghee !

"O Mitra ! that man who troubles himself to keep thy order (rule), O son of eternity (âditya) ! shall have abundance ; he, protected by thee, shall neither be slain nor defeated ; no distress befalls him, neither from nigh, nor from far."

In comparing these verses with the extracts given above from

* In later times he was believed to preside over waters only : but in the Vedic songs he occupied a much higher position. The whole Universe is subject to his laws.

the Mihir Yasht, one may easily be convinced of the entire identity of the Vedic Mitra, and the Persian Mithra.

Another Vedic deity, *Aryaman*, who is generally associated with Mitra and Varuna (Rv. 1,136,2.), is at once recognized in the genius *Airyaman* of the Zend Avesta. Aryaman has in both scriptures a double meaning, (a) a friend, associate (in the Gâthas it chiefly means a client); (b) a deity or genius, who particularly seems to preside over marriages, at which occasion he is invoked both by Brahmans and Parsees (see pag. 134.). He seems to be either another name of the sun, like Mitra, Savitar, Pûshan, etc., or his constant associate and representative. In the Bhagavad Gîta (10,29.), he is mentioned as the head of the *pitaras* i. e. manes.

*Bhaga*, another deity of the Vedas, belonging to the same class as Mitra and Aryaman (to the so-called *Adityas*), is to be recognised in the word *baga* of the Zend Avesta, which word is, however, there not employed as a name of a particular divine being, but conveys the general sense "god, destiny"* (lit. portion). That the Vedic god *Bhaga* (compare the adjective *bagô-bakhta* ordained by fate, which is to be found in both the Veda and the Zend Avesta), was believed to be a deity, presiding over the destiny and fortune of men, may clearly be seen from some passages in the Rigveda, of which I quote here one (7,41,2). "Let us invoke the victor in the morning (i. e. the sunlight after having defeated the darkness of night), the strong Bhaga, the son of Aditi (imperishableness, eternity), who disposes all things (for during night time all seemed to be lost). The poor and the sick as well as the king pray, full of trust, to him, saying: give us our portion."

*Aramati*, a female genius in the Vedas, meaning (a) devotion, piety (Rv. 7,1,6. 34,21) (b) earth (10,92,4.5.), is apparently identical with the archangel *Armaitii*, which word has, as the reader will have learnt from the 3rd Essay, exactly the same two

* This word is to be found in the Slavonian languages (Russian, Polish, etc.) in the form *bog* as the common name for 'god.' The ancient Slavonian mythology knew a *Biel bog* i. e. white god, and a *czerny bog* i. e. black god.

meanings in the Zend Avesta. In the Vedas she is, however, of rare occurrence, and to be found in some hymns of the Rigveda only.* She is called a Virgin who comes with butter offerings at morning and evening to Agni (Rv. 7,1,6.), a eclestial woman (*gná* see pag. 161.), who is brought by Agni (Rv. 5,43,6).

*Narâçansa* (see Yâskas Nirukti 8,6.), an epithet of several Vedic gods, such as Agni, Pûshan, Brahmanaspati (but chiefly of Agni), is identical with *Nairyô-çaṇha* (Nerio Singh), the name of an angel in the Zend Avesta, who serves Ahuramazda as a messenger (see Vend. 22.) in which capacity we find *Agni* and *Pûshan* in the Vedic songs also. The word means " one praised by men" i. e. renowned.

The Vedic god *Vâyu* (wind, chiefly the morning wind) " who first drinks the Soma at the morning sacrifice" is to be recognised in the genius *Vayu* of the Zend Avesta, who is supposed to be roaming everywhere (see the Ram Yasht pag. 194.). He is the only Vedic deity who is, by its very name *(vayû)*, mentioned in the Gâthas (Yas. 53,6.), but, of course, not called a *deva*, which word is always of a bad meaning in the Zend Avesta.

*Vritrahâ* i. e. killer of Vritra (a demon) one of the most frequent epithets of *Indra* in the Vedic books, is to be recognised in the genius Verethraghna (Bahram see the Bahram Yasht pag. 193.). It looks rather strange at the first glance, that we find one and the same Vedic god, Indra, in his proper name " Indra" entered into the list of devils, but by his epithet " Vritrahâ" worshipped as a very high angel. But the problem is very easily to be solved, if one bears in mind, that *Vritrahâ* is applied in the songs of Rigveda not exclusively to " Indra", but to another deity, *Trita*, who occupied in the most ancient times the place of Indra as thunderer and killer of the demons of the air (Rv. 1,18,71.). That this Trita is identical with Thraêtaona (Feridoon) in the Iranian legends, we shall see soon.

A very remarkable coincidence, as to the number of divine beings worshipped, is to be found between the statements of the

* See about *Aramati* and *Armaiti* my article in the journal of the German Oriental Society vol. VIII. (1854) page 769-71.

Vedas and the Zend Avesta. In the Vedas, chiefly in the Atharvaveda, and the Brâhmanas, the gods number thirty-three (*trayas-triñçad devâh*) in all. Although the passages do not vary as to the number, they do not throughout agree, as to the names of the individual gods, by which the number is made up. In the Aitareya Brâhmanam (3,22 pag. 69. of my edition), they are enumerated in the following order : 8 *Vasavas*, 11 *Rudras*, 12 *Adityas*, 1 *Prajâpati*, and 1 *Vashatkâra.** Instead of the two last, we find in the Shatapatha-Brâhmanam (it forms part of the white Yajurveda) 4,5,7,2. *Dyâvâ-Prithivî* (heaven and earth) enumerated. In another passage (11,6,3,5.) of the same work, we find Indra and Prajâpati as the two last. In the Râmâyana (3,2,15.) the two Ashvins are mentioned instead of them.† In the Atharvaveda (10,7,13.22.27.) all thirty-three gods are said to be contained in Prajâpati (Brahma) as his limbs.‡

To these thirty-three devas of the Vedas, the "thirty-three *ratus* i. e. heads, for keeping prevailing the best truths, as they are instituted by Mazda, and promulgated by Zarathustra (Yas. 1,10)" may well be compared. From their not being expressly enumerated according to their several classes, as the 33 devas in the Vedas, we may gather with a certain reason, that it was a time hallowed formula only to count the divine things, its bearing and import being not more understood at all by the Iranians after their separation from the Brahmans.

* This is a personification of the formula *Vaushat* (he—Agni—may carry it up !) which is pronounced with a very much lengthened sound by the sacrificial priest, when throwing the offering into the fire. If personified, the efficacy of the sacrifice is to be underttood.

† The later tradition, as laid down in the Purânas, has increased the Vedic number of 33 deities to 33 Kotis i. e. 330 millions. This fact is a striking instance, how unscrupulously and ridiculously the statements of the Vedas have been expanded and exaggerated in later times, which contributed towards bringing Hinduism into that deplorable state in which we find it now.

‡ This tendency towards establishing a kind of monotheism is now and then to be discovered in the ancient Vedic Songs. Compare, for instance, the celebrated passage Rigveda 1,164,46. where is said that "the wise men understand by the different gods only one being."

## (b) NAMES AND LEGENDS OF HEROES.

There is not only a great similarity between, and identity of, names of divine beings in both, the Veda and Zend Avesta, but it extends even to legends on heroic feats, reported in both scriptures. But, at the very outset, we may discover, notwithstanding all traces of a similarity existing, a striking difference between the Iranian and Brahmanic notions, as regards these legends. The Brahmans attribute them generally to gods, the Iranians partially to great heroes, partially to angels. I enumerate here some of the most striking resemblances.

*Yima Khshuêta (Jamshid)* and *Yama râjâ*. The names and epithets are the same; *Yima* is identical with *Yama*, and *Khshaêta* means the same as *râjâ* king. The family name of both is the same: *Vîvanhâo* i. e. son of *Vîvanghvat* in the Zend Avesta (see the second chapter of the Vendidâd), and *Vaivasvata* i. e. son of *Vivasvat*, in the Veda. In the Zend Avesta he gathers round him men and animals in flocks, and fills with them the earth; and after the evils of winter (see the 2nd fargard pag. 204.) had come over his territories, he leads a select number of the beings of the good creation to a secluded spot, where they enjoy an uninterrupted happiness. According to the songs of the Rigveda, " Yama, the king, the gatherer of the people, has descried for many, a path which leads from the depths to the heights; he first found out a resting place from which no body can turn out the occupants; on the way the forefathers are gone, the sons will follow them (Rigveda 10,14,1,2.)" Yama is here the progenitor of mankind; as the first mortal man, he first experienced death, and first went up from the low valley of this earth to the heights of heaven, where he gathers round him all his descendants who must follow his tracks by the law of nature, and rules over all who have entered his dominions which are full of bliss and happiness. This happy ruler of the blessed in Paradise was in the modern Hindu mythology transformed into the fearful god of death, the inexorable judge of men's doings, and the punisher of the wicked. In the legends of the Iranians, as extant in the Zend Avesta and Shâhnâmah, he was the king of the golden age and the happy ruler of the Iranian tribes.

*Thrita, Thraêtona (Feridûn)* and *Trita, Trâitana.* Thrita, one of the Sâma family (of which the great hero Rustem was an offspring), is in the Zend Avesta (see pag. 218.) the first physician, the curer of the diseases created by Ahriman, an idea which we find attached to *Trita* in the Vedas also. He is said in the Atharvaveda (6,113,1.) to extinguish the illness in men, as the gods have extinguished it in him; he must sleep for the gods (19,56,4). He grants a long life (Taittirîya Samhitâ—Black Yajurveda—1,8,10,2.). Any evil thing is to be sent to him, to be appeased by him (Rigveda 8,47,13.). This circumstance is hinted at in the Zend Avesta by the surname *Sâma* which means "appeaser." He is further said to have been once thrown into a well whence Brihaspati rescued him (Rigv. 1,105,17.). The Indian tradition makes him a Rishi, and ascribes several songs of Rigveda to him (as for instance the 105th of the first book). There are some traits to be discovered in the ancient hymns which make him appear rather like a god than a mortal man. He drinks Soma, like Indra, for obtaining strength to kill the demon Vritra (1,187,1), and, like him, cleaves with his iron club the rocky hole where the cows (the celestial waters) are concealed (1,52,5.).

*Thraêtona* (*Feridûn*) is completely to be recognized in the Vedic *Traitana* who is said to have severed the head of a giant from his shoulders (Rigv. 1,158,3). His father is called *Athwyô* which corresponds exactly with the frequent surname of *Trita* in the Vedas, viz. *Aptya.* Both Trita and Trâitana, seem to have been confounded in the Veda, whereas they originally were utterly distinct from one another. Trita was the name of a celebrated physician, and Traitana that of the conqueror of a giant or tyrant; the first belonged to the family of the *Sâmas*, the latter to the *Aptyas.* In the Zend Avesta the original form of the legend is better preserved (see about *Thraêtaona* pag. 167.).

*Kava Us (Kaikavus* in Shâhnâmah) and *Kâyva Uçana.*

He is one of the great heroes of the Iranians, and believed to have been a ruler over Iran. In the later Indian literature, he is identified with *Shukra*, the planet Venus, and said to have been during his life time the Guru (prophet, teacher) of the Daityas or Asuras, the enemies of the gods. But he is not viewed in this light in the ancient Vedic songs. There he is associated with the god Indra, who calls himself, Kâvya Uçana (Rigv. 4,26,1.), and is invoked by the name " *Kavi Uçana*" (Rv. 1,130,9.). This Kâvya Uçanâ (it means : *Uçanâ*, son of *Kavi*) has installed Agni as a High-priest for mankind (8,23,17.) ; he led the heavenly cows (the clouds) to pasturage (1,83,5.), made Indra's iron club, by which the god killed his enemy Vritra. In the Bhagavad Gîta (10,27.) he is considered as the first of the poets, wherefore Krishna, who calls himself the first in every particular branch, identifies himself with Uçanas. According to the Mahâbhârata (1,2544), he has four sons, who bring sacrifice for the Asuras. In the Iranian legend he does not appear as blameless ; he is said to have been so proud and selfconceited, as to the endeavour to fly up to heaven for which arrogance he was then severely punished.

The name *Dânava* is in both the Vedas and Zend Avesta given to enemies with whom wars are to be waged. Compare Yt 5,73. and Atharva Veda 4,24,2. In the Rigveda it is often a name of the archdemon Vritra, with whom Indra is fighting.

In the legend on Tistrya (see pag. 181) some of the particulars, relating to *Indra* and *Brihaspati* in the Vedas may be recognized. Tistrya cannot bring the rain from the lake Vouru Kasha over the earth, if not assisted by the prayers of men. In the same way Indra cannot release the celestial cows (the clouds) from the rocky hole, whither they are carried by demons, without the assistance of *Brihaspati*, who is the representative of the prayers sent up by men to the gods, and the personification of their devotion and meditation.

## (c) SACRIFICIAL RITES.

Although sacrifices are reduced to a few rites in the Parsee religion now-a-days, we may discover, in comparing them with the sacrificial customs of the* Brahmans, a great similarity and even identity of both.

I point out here some of the most striking similarities.

At the very outset the attentive reader of the Vedas and the Zend Avesta will observe the identity of a good many terms referring to priestly functions. The very name for "priest" in the Zend Avesta, *âthrava*, is to be recognized in the *atharvan* of the Vedas, by which word a Fire, and Soma priest there is meant. The Vedic words *ishti* (a series of invocations of several deities, accompanied by the offering of the sacrificial cakes, the so called Purodaça) and *âhuti* (the invocation of one deity with the offering, within the limits of the *ishti*) are to be recognized in *isti* and *âzûiti* of the Zend Avesta, where the original peculiar meaning is lost and only the general "gift" and "invocation, praise" has remained. The particular names of several officiating priests at the time of performing a solemn ceremony are the same. The *Hotar* i. e. the reciter of the mantras of Rigveda, is identical with the *Zaota* priest, while the *Adhvaryu* or managing priest, who is to prepare all for the Hotar, is the same with the *Rathwi* (now called Raspi), who is only the servant of the Zaota or chief priest. In the *çraoshôvâreza*, who represents the angel Serosh, the *Pratiprasthâta* of the Brahmanic sacrifices may be discovered; because this priest is holding in his hand a wooden sword during the time of sacrifice to drive away the evil spirits, which weapon is constantly ascribed to Serosh for the same purpose (see pag. 171.). In the *Atarevakshô* i. e. who has charge of the pot in

* Most of the Vedic sacrifices are still in use.

Those Brahmans, who perform all the sacrifices, required for going to heaven, according to the Vedic system, are called *Agnihotris*. Their number was very large at the time of the Peishwas and is even now considerable in some of the native states, as, for instance, in the dominions of the Gaicwar at Baroda. The performance of the manifold sacrifices enjoined to the Agnihotris or the strict followers of the Vedic religion, entails too much expenses upon an individual, as to be performed by many without public support. The Peishwas used to support them. Among all the Agnihotris (about 12-15) who presented themselves at the late Dakshina meeting at Poona (between the 15th November and 15th December 1861), I found only one (he was from Sattara) who had performed all the numerous sacrifices some of which require from 6 to 12 days for their performance and an outlay of many thouands of Rupees.

which thefire is, we find the *Agnídhra* (who holds the fire) of the Brahmans.

The Izeshne ceremony, as performed by the Parsee priests now-a-days (see pag. 132), contains all the elements, of which the different parts (4 or 7) of the *Jyotishtoma* cycle of sacrifices, the prototype of all the Soma sacrifices, is composed. The Agnishtoma (i. e. praise of Agni, the fire), which is the opening sacrifice of this cycle, and indispensable for every Agnihotri, to gain the object wished for, viz. heaven, bears particularly a resemblance to the performance of Izeshne. Of course, the whole ceremony is much shortened and the rites changed in accordance with the more enlightened and humane spirit of the Zoroastrian religion. In the Agnishtoma four goats must be killed and their flesh is partly offered to the gods by throwing it into Agni, the fire, who is the mediator between gods and men, partly to be eaten by the sacrificer and the priests. During the Izeshne ceremony no animal is to be killed; only hair of an ox is to be placed in a small vessel and together with the other things to be shown to the fire. This is now-a-days the only remainder of the animals sacrificed at this occasion; formerly they used a piece of meat besides. This *Purôdaça* of the Brahmans, or the solemn sacrificial cakes, which must be offered to different deities in a certain order, under the recital of two mantras for each diety, is changed into a flat kind of bread (similar to a cake), called *Darun*. The fresh milk, required at the time of performing the Upasad ceremony (see pag. 228.), is to be recognized in the *gâus jîvya* (see pag. 132). Ghee, butter, etc. required for less important ceremonies at the time of Agnishtoma (when making the so called *Prayâjas* for the 6 seasons) are represented by the *gâus-hudhâo* (see pag. 132). The *Zaothrâ* or consecrated water is required at the commencement of the Brahmanic sacrifices also, where it is called *udaka çânta*.

The chief part of the offerings in both the Jyotishtoma sacrifices and the Izeshne ceremony, is the juice of the Soma plant. In both the plant itself (the Brahmans use the stalks of the Pûtika, which is the substitute for the original Soma, the Parsees the branches of a particular tree) in its natural state is brought to the sacred spot, where the ceremony is to take place, and there the juice extracted under the recital of prayers. The contrivances used for obtaining the juice as well as the vessels required, are somewhat different, but, on a closer enquiry, an original identity may be recognized. The Brahmans beat the stalks of the plant which are placed on a large flat stone with another smaller stone till they form one lump; this is then put into a vessel and water poured over it. After some time, this water which has extracted the greenish juice, is poured through a cloth, which serves as a strainer, into another vessel. The Parsee priests use instead of stones an iron mortar with a beater, where the branches of the Homa plant together with one of the pomegranate tree are bruised, and pour then water over them to obtain the juice which is strained by means of a flat vessel with nine holes. This juice (Parahaoma) has a yellow colour, and only very little of it is drunk by one of the two priests (the *Zota*) who must be present, whereas all the Brahmanic priests (16 in number), whose services are required at the Jyotishtoma, must drink, and some of the chief priests (such as the Adhvaryu and Hotar) even a very large quantity. The Parsee priests never throw any thing of the juice into the fire, but the Brahmans must first offer a certain quantity of the intoxicating juice to different deities, by throwing it from variously shaped wooden vessels into the fire, before they are allowed to taste "the sweet liquor." The Parsee priests show it only to the fire, and then drink it. Afterwards the juice is prepared for a second time by the Chief priest (Zota) and then thrown into a well. These two preparations of the Homa juice correspond to the morning libation (*prâtah Savana*) and midday libation (*madhyandina Savana*) of the Brahmans; for the third, or evening libation, there was no room in the Parsee ritual, because no sacrificial rites are allowed to be performed at evening or night time.

The Barsom (*Bareçma*) or the bundle of twigs, which is indispensable at the time of reciting Izeshne, is to be traced to one of the sacrificial rites at the great Soma sacrifices. It has as yet erroneously been identified with the *Barhis* or sacred grass (Kusha grass is taken) of the Brahmans, which they spread at their sacrifices as a seat for the gods who are expected to come. But its close connection with the Izeshne ceremony, and the circumstance, that wood (branches of a particular tree) and no grass, is taken, and that these branches are laid on a stand, not spread on the floor, lead to the conclusion, that it does not represent the seat for the divine beings, as the Kusha grass does. It refers, in all likelihood, to a peculiar rite at the great Soma sacrifices, which is as yet not known, but on which I had an opportunity of obtaining oral information. At the time of the Soma libation (called *Savana*) which is to be performed three times on the same day from 8-12 A. M. (morning libation), 1-5 P. M. (midday libation), 6-11 P. M. (evening libation), the three Sâmaveda priests, the Udgâtar, the Prastotar, and the Pratihartar, require a certain number of wooden sticks to be placed into a certain order when chanting the sacred Sâmans (verses of the Sâmaveda). They use for this purpose the wood of the Udumbara tree and call them *kusha* which name is generally given to the sacred grass. In Agnishtoma 15 such sticks are required at the morning libation, 17 at noon, and 21 at evening; in other sacrifices, as Aptoryâma, even a much larger number of such sticks is required. Those three singers must chant then successively, one by one, in a very solemn manner, the five parts,* into which every Sâman, or verse adapted for singing, is divided at certain sacrifices whilst putting some of the sticks into a proper order. This ceremony is considered to be most essential, and without observing it, or performing it properly, all effect of the Sâmans which are believed to carry up the sacrificer to heaven (the most important of all is called *Rathantaram*, i. e. carriage), is lost.

At the same time, there is another peculiar custom to be

* Such Sâmans are called *panchabhaktika* i. e. divided into the five parts, viz: *Prastâva* (prelude), *Udgîtha* (the principal part, to be chanted by the Udgâtar), *Pratihâra* (response), *Upadrava* (little finale) and *Nidhana* (great finale, to be chanted by all three). I shall treat more fully of the subject in the second volume of my edition of the Aitareya Brahmanam.

observed, which may be traced in the Yasna also. As soon as the singers have chanted their verse, one of the Hotars must repeat a series of mantras (not in the usual way of repetition, but in one approaching the recital of the Yajurvada), from the Rigveda, to praise and extol the Sâman, which ceremony is called *Shastram.* At the end of the different Hâs of the Yasna, chiefly its Gatha portion, verses of these songs are often invoked like divine beings, and in page 169 (Yas. 19, 6.), we have seen, that it is considered very meritorious to worship the Ahuna vairya prayer, after having repeated it.

In regard to the division of the *Sâmans* into five parts, I may remark that the Ahuna vairya prayer, which is for the Parsees of a similar importance, as the Rathantaram Sâman was for the Vedic Brâhmans, was divided into five parts also (see pag. 169).

In the Afrigân ceremony of the Parsees (see pag. 199) there may be discovered a recollection of the Brahmanic Apri ceremony (see Aitareya Brahmana 2, 4. pag. 28 of my edition), which is preparatory to the killing and offering of the sacrificial goats. The name is the same : *â-prî* in Sanscrit, *â-frî* in Zend (the formula used is *âfrînâmi*), which literally means " to invite," by which invitation always the name of the being, or beings, in whose honour the ceremony is being performed, must be mentioned. The Parsees mention the name of a deceased, or of an angel, the Brahmans the names of different deities* (there are eleven invocations), who are expected to come and relish in the meal prepared for them. These solemn invitations being accompanied with a blessing, the Parsees understand by this ceremony a benediction, which form it seems to have assumed at a very early time.

The *Darça pûrnama ishti* (new and full moon sacrifice) seems to correspond with the *Darûn* ceremony of the Parsees. Both are very simple ; the Brahmans use chiefly the Purodasha, or sacrificial cakes, the Parsees the sacred bread (Darun) which corresponds to the Purodasha.

* See Yâska's Nirukta 8,4—21, and Max Müller, History of Ancient Sanscrit Literature pag. 463—67.

The *Châturmâsya ishti*, or the sacrifice, brought to four months, or two seasons, corresponds to the Gahânbar ceremony of the Parsees which is celebrated six times a year. Sacrificing of animals was essential for the proper performance of them among the Parsees until late; so it is with the Brahmans also. But as to animal sacrifice, there is always a great difference between the Brahmanic and Zoroastrian rites. The Brahmans must throw some parts of the slaughtered animal, as the *vapá* (the peritoneum), into the fire, while the Parsees simply consecrate the flesh and eat it as a solemn meal, without throwing anything into the fire. At such an occasion even the Brahmans now-a-days eat some flesh also.

## (d) RELIGIOUS OBSERVANCES, DOMESTIC RITES, COSMOGRAPHICAL OPINIONS.

Although there are a good many similarities to be discovered in respect to observances, domestic rites, etc., I must refrain here from giving a full account of all particulars to avoid unnecessary diffuseness. A few striking points of coincidence may suffice.

With the great purification ceremony (see pag. 211) by means of cow-urine, called *gomez*, as practised by the Parsees up to this day, a similar observance of the Brahmans is to be compared. They use, in order to remove all impurity from the interior body, the so called *Panchagavyam* i. e. five things proceeding from the most sacred animal, the cow, one of which is her urine. This custom comes from the most ancient times, where this liquid was regarded as a very effective remedy against any disorder of the bodily organs. Such means as cow dung, and cow urine are applied also on the continent in Europe by peasant physicians up to our time.

To the Parsees, as well as to the Brahmans, the investiture with the sacred thread (called *kosti* by the Parsees, *aiwyâoṇhanem* in the Zend Avesta) is enjoined as a religious duty. As long as this ceremony has not been performed one is no real member of either the Brahmanic or Zoroastrian Community. The time for performing it goes among the Brahmans from the 8th to 16th year (see Yâjnavalkya 1,14,37.); the Parsees are invested with the Kosti in the seventh year.

In regard to the funeral rites of both, some similarities may be pointed out. After the death of a man, Brahmans as well as Parsees must pray to raise the soul of the deceased up to heaven, which is the so called third day's ceremony of the Parsees. On the tenth day after the death, the Parsees perform a certain ceremony (Izeshne is read), and the Brahmans make the important ceremony of *Kákasparça*, that is, they expose a ball of rice to be taken by a crow.

As to cosmographical opinions the Brahmans divide the whole world into seven *Dvípas*, the Parsees into seven *Kishvars* (*Karshvare* in Zend) i. e. Zones. Both acknowledge a central mountain, which called by the former *Meru*, by the latter *Alborj* (*Harô berezaiti* in Zend).

## 2.—ORIGIN OF THE ZOROASTRIAN RELIGION. ZARATHUSTRA SPITIMA. HIS PROBABLE AGE.

After having established in the preceding paragraph the fact of a close and intimate connection having once existed between the religion of the Parsees and that of the Brahmans, I proceed to trace the origin of the Zoroastrian religion and characterize the period at which it must have arisen.

### (*a*) TRACES TO BE FOUND IN BOTH THE VEDAS AND ZEND AVESTA.

In the Vedas, as well as in the earlier portions of the Zend Avesta (see the Gâthas), there are sufficient traces to be discovered, that the Zoroastrian religion arose out of a vital struggle against that form of the Brahmanic religion, which it had assumed at a certain early period. Both creeds are known as diametrically opposed to one another in both scriptures. One is called the belief of the Asuras (Ahura in Zend), the other that of the Devas. This circumstance cannot be merely fortuitous, the less, as we find used the word *Asura* in the earliest Vedic hymns (see pag. 226.), in a perfectly good sense, and as name of the several Devas themselves, which fact clearly shows, that there must have been once a vital struggle between the professors of the Deva and those of the Ahura-religion, in consequence of which the originally good meaning of Asura was subsequently changed to a bad one.

If it is, therefore, impossible to deny the existence of the original close connection between the Deva and Asura religions, some might, however, be inclined to doubt, whether the adherents of the Deva religion actually have been the direct ancestors of the present Brahmans. It is true, the words *deva** and the cognate word *dyâus*, are found in most of the Arian languages in the meaning of "heaven," or "divine being," and the Deva worshippers, combatted by the Zoroastrians, might be another kindred tribe of the Arian stock, different from the Brahmans. But the fact, that several of the Brahmanic devas, are mentioned by their very names in the Zend Avesta, leaves no doubt whatever, that the opponents of the Ahura religion actually were the ancient Brahmans; for the names of the devas, mentioned in the Zend Avesta, such as Indra, Sharva, Nâsatya, are purely Brahmanic and unknown to any other nation of the Arian stock.

We have seen above that not all names of Indian gods were entered into the list of the Zoorastrian devas or devils, but some of them retained their old dignity by being transformed, in accordance with the new spirit of the Zoroastrian religion, from gods into angels (Yázatas). Their very names are also identical with those of some Vedic deities, such as Aryaman, Mitra, Aramati, etc.

Some of the ancient gods occur by one name in the list of angels, by another in that of the devils. So is, for instance, the Zoroastrian devil, *Indra*, under his other name, Verethraghna (Vritrahâ), one of the mightiest angels, as has been shown above (pag. 193.)

* It is best preserved in the Litthuanian *diewas*, god, and in Latin *deus*. The cognate *dyâus* "heaven," is extant in the Grecian *Zeus*, gen. *Dios*, and the name of an ancient Teutonic god *Tius* preserved in the word "Tuesday" (in Anglo-saxon: *Tives Dæg*).

These facts throw some light upon the age, at which that grand religious combat was fought, the consequence of which was the entire separation of the ancient Iranians from the Brahmans, and the foundation of the Zoroastrian religion. It must have taken place at the time when Indra was the chief god of the Brahmans. This was the case at that early period to which we must assign the composition of the majority of the Vedic hymns, before the Brahmans had immigrated into Hindostan Proper. In the post-Vedic period, whose events called into existence the great epic poems Mahâbhârata and Râmâyana, we find his place at the head of the gods occupied by the Trimûrti: Brahma, Vishnu, Shiva, which idea is utterly strange to the Vedic hymns. The Trimûrti never being alluded to in the Zend Avesta, we must assign to the religious struggle a much earlier date.

Before I proceed to fix the probable age of the origin of the Zoroastrian religion, I must adduce some facts to be derived from passages of the Vedas and the Gâthas, which throw much light upon this difficult subject.

The priests and prophets of the Devas are mentioned by the names *Kavi*, *Karapan* and *Uçikhs* in the Gâthas (see Yas. 32,14; 46,11; 44,20; 48,10; 51,14.). The first is of very frequent occurrence in the Vedic songs, the third is there occasionally to be met with also, and of the second name, the verb (*kalpayati*)* and noun (*kalpa*) are very frequently employed. *Kavi* which means in the classical Sanscrit "poet," is in the Vedic songs the name of seers and priests (Rigv. 1,128,8.142,8.188,1.); by drinking the "delicious," but intoxicating, Soma juice, the power of Kavi is attainable (1,91,14.); the word, therefore, is applied to the Soma priest (9,37,6.72,6.); these Kavis or seers being believed to be in possession of divine revelation and secret wisdom, they were consulted as prophets (1,164,6. 7,86,3.). The gods themselves, chiefly Agni, are called by this name (2,23,1. 3,14,1.), which circumstance clearly shows, that it was

* The sound *l*, being completely unknown to the Zend language, is there always represented by *r*.

a high title, which could be given only to the heads and spiritual guides of the ancient Brahmanic community.

Synonymous with this name is *Uçij*, which exactly corresponds to *uçikhs* (nom. Yas. 44,20.) in the Gâthas. It means a wise intelligent man, as one may see from such passages as Rigv. 2,21,5. 10,46,2. and Shânkhâyana's Grihya Sûtra 6,12,19. where it changes place with "Kavi," as is the case in Yas. 44,20 also.

By *Karapanô*, who are mentioned together with the *Kâvayas* in the Gâthas, we must understand chiefly the sacrificial priests, the performers of the sacrifices, those men who are known now-a-days to the Brahmans by the name of Shrotriyas. As to its grammatical formation, this word is derived from a root *karap*, which wholly corresponds to the Sanscrit root *kalp*, "to perform a ceremony," whence the word *kalpa* i. e. the ritual, the doctrine of the ceremonies, is derived. *Karapanô*, therefore, means really 'performer of sacrificial rites.'

Those two names, *Kavi* and *Karapan*, designate in the fullest sense all the spiritual guides of the professors of the Deva religion, who tried to put down the worshippers of the Ahuramazda religion, and we necessarily find, therefore, a bad meaning attached to them in the Gâthas. This appears the more strange, as the word *kavi* itself forms part of highly celebrated personages of the Iranian antiquity, such as Kavi Husrava (Kai Khosru), Kavi Kavâta (Kai Kobâd), Kavi Vistâspa (Kai Gustâsp) etc., and has become, in its derived adjectival form "Kayanian," the name of a whole lineage of the ancient Bactrian rulers.

Here naturally the question arises, how could a word, which marked the bitterest enemies of the Zoroastrian religion, be applied to kings, who were like Kavi Vistâspa, believed to be its staunchest friends and protectors? The only answer to be given, is, that before the outbreak of the schism, when the Iranians and Brahmans lived peacefully together, the Kavis were at the head of both communities, and that on account of their violent opposition to the religions and social reforms, which were adopted by some of the Arian tribes, the Iranians, their very name was branded and became a word of abomination with the

Zoroastrians. But the word having been already too closely connected with their ancient history, and having become the constant epithet of some of their greatest heroes and kings, it was difficult, nay impossible, to expunge it in its good and high sense entirely from the language. The adversaries of the Kavis, therefore, must rest satisfied with a slight change of the hateful word, when it was to be applied in the good meaning. Thus we find actually in the old passages this word, if forming part of the names of the great Iranian heroes and kings, changed from its only true and original form *Kavi* into *Kavâ*, as, for instance, *Kavâ Vistâspa*, instead of *Kavi Vistâspa.**

Now this word *Kavâ* became a party name, denoting the opponents of the Deva religion. And in this sense we find it unmistakeably employed in the ancient Vedic songs. *Kavâsakha* or *Kavâri* or *Kavatnu*, which all mean "followers of Kavâ or adherents to Kava," are names, given to the enemies of Indra and the despisers of his sacred drink (Soma). In one passage (Rigv. 5,34,3.) this *Kavâ sakha* is even called a *maghavâ*, by which name the disciples and earliest followers of Zarathustra are denoted (see pag. 160.) in the Gâthas. Indra is said there to turn out the Maghava, who follows the Kava party, from his possession, which refers to the settlements (*gaêthas*) of the Iranians.

That Zarathustra's attacks were really directed against the Soma sacrifices of the Brahmans, undeniably follows from several passages of the Gâthas (32,3.48,10. see above). This is not to be wondered at, if we bear in mind, that the Indian tribes as described in the ancient songs of the Vedas, never engaged themselves in their frequent predatory excursions for robbing cows, horses, sheep, etc. without having previously secured the assistance of Indra by preparing for him a solemn Soma feast. The Karapans dressed it in the due manner, and the Kavis composed or applied those verses, which were best calculated to induce Indra to accept the invitation. The Kavis were believed to

* See all the particulars in my work on the Gâthas I. pag. 179,80. and II. pag. 238—41.

recognize by certain marks the arrival of the god. After he had enjoyed the sweet beverage, the delicious honey, and was supposed to be totally inebriated, then the Kavis promised victory. The inroads were undertaken, headed by those Kavis who had previously intoxicated themselves, and they appear to have been in most cases successful. The Iranian settlers, who had to suffer so much from these attacks (see pag. 164.), ascribed the success to those Soma sacrifices, which, therefore, must have been an object of abomination and horror to them. But the belief in the great efficacy of such a ceremony, as the solemn squeezing and preparing of the Soma juice, being too deeply rooted in the minds of the Iranians, as well as in those of the ancient Indians, the Iranians left only the old Arian fashion of preparing the sacred drink, and invented one of their own, which was more in accordance with the spirit of their new religion (see pag. 239.) As we have seen, Zarathustra Spitama himself never mentions this reformed Homa (Soma) ceremony in the Gâthas; it is doubtful, therefore, whether it existed at his time, or, if so, whether he approved of it. It is true, legends were afterwards circulated, that he himself had given his sanction to this ceremony, as the reader will have learnt from the Homa Yasht (see pag. 166—68).

Having established now beyond any doubt, as I think, the fact, that the Zoroastrian religion arose in consequence of a serious conflict of the Iranians with those Arian brother tribes which immigrated into Hindustan Proper, and whose leaders became in later times the founders of Brahmanism, the questions as to the causes of this religious schism, the leader of the succeeding party, and the time at which this great event happened, are to be decided.

## (*b*) CAUSES OF THE SCHISM.

The causes, which led to the schism, may readily be learnt from the more ancient pieces of the Zend Avesta, chiefly from the Gâthas. They were both of social and political, and religious nature. The Arian tribes, after they had left their original home, which was in all likelihood a cold country (see the reports on it in the first and second Fargards of the Vendidad), led mainly a pastoral life, and cultivated only occasionally some patches of land for their own support. In this state we find the ancient Arian society throughout the earlier Vedic period, and the Brahmanic tribes were given to the nomadic life, as long as they occupied the upper part of the Punjâb, whence they then immigrated into Hindustan Proper. Some of these tribes, whom we may style the proper Iranians, became soon weary of these constant wanderings, and after having reached such places between the Oxus and Yaxartes rivers, and the highland of Bactria, as were deemed fit for permanent settlements, they left the pastoral life of their ancestors and their brother tribes, and became agriculturists. In consequence of this change, the Iranians estranged themselves from the other Arian tribes, which still clung to the ancestoral occupation, and allured by the hope of making booty, regarded those settlements as the best fitted objects for their excursions and warfages. How frequent these attacks upon the property of the Mazdayasnas from the part of the Deva worshippers must have been, the reader might have learnt from the formula, by which the Deva worshippers left their religion, and entered the community of the Iranians (see pag. 163 165), and from some verses of the Gâthas (chiefly Yas. 32 and 46).

The success of the attacking Deva worshippers was, as we have seen, mainly ascribed to spells (mantras), and sacrificial skill. Their religion, therefore, must become an object of hatred in the eyes of the Iranians, though they were well aware, that it was closely related to their own, or even to a certain extent identical with it. The religion, therefore, was to be totally changed, in order to break up all communication whatever with the devastators of their settlements. The Deva religion was branded as the source of all mischief and wickedness, and instead of it, the Ahura religion of agriculture was instituted, which separated them thenceforth for ever from their Brahmanic brothers.

If we ask, as to who instituted this Ahura religion, we can hardly believe, that it is the work of a single man only, though it is not to be denied that the peculiar form which it assumed is mainly due to one great personage, viz.

## (c) ZARATHUSTRA SPITAMA.

In the Gâthas we find Zarathustra alluding to old revelations (Yas 46,6.), and praising the wisdom of the *Soshyantos*, i. e. fire priests (46,3. 48,12). He exhorts his party to respect and revere the *Angra* (43,15.) i. e. the *Angiras* of the Vedic songs, who formed one of the most ancient and celebrated priestly families of the ancient Arians, and who seem to be more closely connected with the ante Zoroastrian form of the Parsee religion, than any other of the later Brahmanic families. These Angiras are often mentioned together with the Atharvans or fire priests, which word (in the form *âthrava*) is the general name given to the priest caste in the Zend Avesta, and are regarded in the Vedic literature as the authors of the Atharva Veda which is directly called the Veda of the Atharvângiras, or Atharvana, or Angirasa veda, i. e. Veda of the Atharvans or Angiras.* This work was for a long time not acknowledged as a proper Veda by the Brahmans, because its contents, which chiefly consist in spells, charms, curses, mantras for killing enemies etc., were mostly strange to the three other Vedas, which alone originally were required for sacrifices. In comparing its contents with some passages of the Yashts and the Vendidâd, we may discover a great similarity.

Although a closer connection between the ante Zoroastrian and the Atharvana and Angirasa religion is hardly to be doubted, yet this relationship refers only to the magical part which was believed by the ancient Greeks to be the very substance and nature of the Zoroastrian religion.

In all likelihood, as the names " Atharvana and Angirasa" i. e. firepriests indicates, the fireworship was a characteristic feature of this ancient religion.

* See Max Müller, History of Ancient Sancrit literature pag. 448.

The Soshyantôs or firepriests, who seem to be identical with the Atharvans, are to be regarded as the real predecessors of Zarathustra Spitama, who paved the way for the grand religious reform, carried out by the latter. It is distinctly said (Yas. 53,2.), that the good Ahura religion was revealed to them, and that they professed it in opposition to the Deva religion, like Zarathustra himself and his disciples (Yas. 12,7. see pag. 164). These ancient sages, therefore, we must regard as the founders of the Ahura religion who first introduced agriculture and made it a religious duty, and commenced war against the Deva religion.

The struggle might have heen lasting even for several centuries, before Zarathustra Spitama, ordered by a divine command, to strike a death blow on idolatry and banish it for ever from his native soil, appeared in Iran. But the decisive step of separating the contending parties completely from one another, and establishing a new community, governed by new laws, was made by Zarathustra Spitama. He, therefore, has at least claims to be regarded as the founder of the proper Mazdayasna or Parsee religion, which absorbed the old Ahura religion of the ancient fire-priests. He himself was one of the Soshyantos or firepriests, because we find him, when standing before the sacred fire, deliver his speeches and receiving answers from Ahuramazda out of the sacred flames.

As to his life, almost all is enshrouded in darkness, to dispel which will be for ever a work of impossibility, should no authentical historical records be discovered in Bactria, his home. The reports regarding him, given by the Greeks and Romans (see the first Essay and my Lecture on the origin of the Parsee religion pag. 5), are as unhistorical and legendary as those to be found in the majority of the Zend books themselves. In the Vendidad and the Yashts (see pag. 191.), he is represented to us not as a historical, but as a dogmatical personality, stripped nearly of every thing that is peculiar to human nature, and vested with a supernatural and wholly divine power, standing next to God himself and being even elevated above the archangels. The temptations of the devil, whose whole empire was threatened by the great prophet, formed a favourite subject of the traditional reports and legends. He was the abyss of all wisdom and truth and the master and head of the whole living creation (see pag. 191.92.).

The only source, whence to derive something like very scanty historical facts, is the old Yasna. In this part of the scripture only, he appears before our eyes as a real man, acting a great and prominent part in the history of his country, and even in the history of the whole human race in general. He was a member of the Spitama family, which name is given to the *Hechatâspas* also (Yas. 46,15.), who seem, therefore, to have been his nearest relations. His father's name was according to the younger Yasna and Vendidad *Pourushâspa*. Of his children only his daughter *Pouruchista* (Yas. 53,3.) is mentioned by the two names : *Hechataçpâna Spitâmî*, which can be interpreted only as "belonging to the Spitama family of the Hêchatâspa lineage." He was distinguished by the surname *Zarathustra*, which the Greeks corrupted to "Zarastrades, Zoroastres," the Romans to "Zoroaster," by which name alone he is known to the Europeans, while the Persians and Parsees changed it to "Zerdosht." Although the original meaning of this name is uncertain,* yet it can hardly be doubted, that it was not the mere proper name of the founder of the Parsee religion, but denoted a certain high dignity, that of the Highpriest of a country. This follows clearly from Yas. 19 (see pag. 170), where the "Zarathustra" is mentioned as the fifth head, in those countries, where there are four others of an inferior order, and as the fourth, where are only three others below him, and from the name *Zarathustrôtemô*. This word must mean according to grammar (*tema* is the superlative suffix) "the greatest or highest Zarathustra," which denomination has only then a sense, when we assume

* See my work on the Gâthas II. pag. 245.4.6. note 1. where the different explanations given hitherto of the name are mentioned and refuted. The most probable meaning of "Zarathustra" is not "the most excellent poet" as I explained formerly, but 'Senior, Chief' (in the spiritual sense) to be traced to the Sanscrit *jarat*, which means in compositions "old ;" *ustra* then is *uttara*, best, excellent.

several contemporaneous Zarathustras, at whose head he was placed. The name "Zarathustra," therefore, must have conveyed in ancient times about the same sense, as the word Destur now-a-days, meaning the spiritual guide and head of a whole district, or even province. The *Zarathustrôtemô* then is to be compared with the Destur-i-Desturân or Chief Highpriest. Even according to the notions of the modern Parsees, a Destur occupies a very high rank among them; he is a *ratu* or head in the living creation, and in his praise and honor even ceremonies may be performed.

A clear proof, that the word "Zarathustra" itself was not deemed sufficient to distinguish once for all the prophet from other men, is, that generally his family name "Spitama" is added, if he is spoken of. This circumstance implies distinctly, that there were other Zarathustras besides that one, who was distinguished by the name 'Spitama,' and who alone was regarded as the real founder of the Mazdayasna religion.

His home seems to have been Bactria, which is called "*berekhdha Armaiti*" in the Gâthas, and *Bâkhdhi* (a corruption of the former) in the Vendidad. In his own works he calls himself a *manthran* i. e. a reciter of mantras, a *dûta* i. e. messenger, sent by Ahuramazda, a speaker *(maretan)*; he listens to the oracles given by the spirit of nature *(gêus urva)*, and sacred words are revealed to him by Ahuramazda through the flames.

His doings being best to be learnt from the extracts of the Gâthas which I have given above, I refrain here from expatiating on them and confine myself to a few remarks on his age only.

## (*d*) ZARATHUSTRA'S AGE.

The accounts given of the time, when he is said to have flourished, differ so widely from one another, that it is impossible to fix exactly the era when he was living. The Greeks and Romans make him very ancient. Xanthos of Lydia (470 B. C.), the earliest Grecian writer, who mentions Zoroaster, says, that he lived about 600 years before the Trojan war (about 1800 B. C.). Aristotle and Eudoxus place his era even at 6000 years before Plato, others 5000 years before the Trojan war (see Pliny Historia Naturalis XXX. 1-3.). Berosos, the Babylonian historian, makes him a King of the Babylonians, and the founder of a dynasty, which reigned between 2200 and 2000 B. C. over Babylon.

The Parsees believe, that their prophet lived at the time of Darius' father, Hystaspes, whom they identify with *Kava Vistaspa* of the Zend Avesta or Kai Gustasp of the Shâhnâmah, and place his era accordingly at 550 B. C. But how groundless this supposition is, I have shown in my lecture on the origin of the Parsee religion (pag. 17.18.) to which I refer the reader. That even the ancient Persians were quite uncertain as to who this Hystaspes has been, one may clearly see from the passage of Agathias communicated above (pag. 8.9.). Darius' father, Hystaspes (Vîstâspa), and the Kava Vîstâspa of the Zend Avesta, who is known in the Shâhnâmah as Kai Gustasp, are two utterly distinct persons, who have nothing in common but the name, which is entirely fortuitous.

In comparing the accounts of the Greeks about the early era of Zoroaster, with the researches into the original texts of the Parsee scripture, we must believe them to be much more trustworthy and reliable than the opinions held by the modern Parsees. There can be no doubt whatever, that Zarathustra Spitama, the founder of the Parsee religion, lived at a very early period, because the grand religious movement, of which he was the chief leader, is even alluded to in the earlier portions of the Vedas. Of his high antiquity at least two significant traces may even be discovered in the present Zend Avesta. Firstly, as we have seen in the 27th paragraph of the 3d Essay, he stands at the head of the extensive Zend literature, which required centuries for its growth, and which was already complete about 400 B. C. Secondly, he is expressly called " the celebrated in *Airyana vaêjô*" (Yas. 9,14.), that means, " the celebrated in the Arian home" whence the Iranians and

Indians emigrated in times immemorial. This title certainly had not been given to him, had his followers not believed him living at that early time. Under no circumstances, we can assign to him a later date than 1000 B. C., and I am even not disinclined to place his era much earlier and make him a contemporary of Moses. Pliny, who compares both, Moses and Zoroaster, whom he calls inventors of two different kinds of magic rites, goes much farther in stating, that Zoroaster lived several thousand years before Moses (Historia Naturalis XXX. 2). The confusion of opinions regarding his age, was, no doubt, mainly caused by the appellative name "Zarathustra" i. e. Highpriest, which was taken afterwards as the only proper name of the prophet. The assertion, that he was born at *Ragha* (*Rai* near Teheran) is owing to the circumstance, that according to Yasna 19 (see pag. 170.) this large town seems to have been governed by the Zarathustras themselves; it was therefore, pre-eminently the Zoroastrian country.

## 3.—ZARATHUSTRA SPITAMA'S THEOLOGY AND PHILOSOPHY AND THEIR INFLUENCE ON THE DEVELOPMENT OF THE PARSEE RELIGION.

Having shown in the preceding paragraph the historical origin of the Zoroastrian religion, I proceed to point out the new thoughts, theological and philosophical, which he introduced into the world, and in consequence of which he may be said to have become the founder of a new religion, and exercised a lasting influence on the history of the human mind.

His real doctrines, untouched by the speculations of later ages, can be learnt only from the old Yasna, chiefly from the Gâthas. The leading idea of his theology was *Monotheism*, i. e. that there are not many gods, but only one, and the principle of his speculative philosophy *Dualism*, i. e. the supposition of two primeval causes of the real world and of the intellectual, while his moral philosophy was moving in the *Triad* of thought, word, and deed. In respect to the early period, at which he must have lived, long before the Greeks were acquainted with any thing like philosophical speculation, we cannot expect him to have established a complete and developed system of philosophical thoughts, which can even not be said of Plato; but those few ideas, which may be discovered in his sayings, show, that he was a great and deep thinker, who stood far above his contemporaries, and even the most enlightened men of many subsequent centuries. The great fame he enjoyed even with the ancient Greeks and Romans, who were so proud of their own learning and wisdom, is a sufficient proof of the high and pre-eminent position, he must have occupied once in the history of the human mind.

## (a) ZARATHUSTRA'S MONOTHEISM.

That his theology was mainly based on monotheism, one may easily ascertain from the Gâthas chiefly from the second (see pag. 146-158). His predecessors, the Soshyanto seem to have been worshipping a plurality of good spirits, whom they called *Ahuras*, i. e. the living ones who were opposed to the Devas. Spitama, not satisfied with this indistinct expression of the Divine Being, reduced this plurality to an unity. The new name, by which he called the Supreme Being, was *Ahurô mazdâo* which means "that Ahura who is called Mazdâo." *Mazdâo* which has been compared with the Vedic *medhâs* i. e, wise (applied to priests: skilful, who are able to make every thing) means either "joint Creator," or "Creator of all" (see the note to pag. 100.). Those Ahuras, who were regarded as creative powers, might have been called by the name *mazdâo* (we find the plural: *mazdâonhô* Yas. 45,1.) already by the Soshyantôs. But they had no clear conception of the nature and working of this creative power. Although Spitama combined both names, which were formerly quite loose, and not intimately connected with each other, to one: *Ahurômazdâo*, yet they were not considered as a compound, because we find both its constituent parts subject to inflection (e. g. *ahurâi mazdâi* dative, not: *Ahura-mazdâi*); one of them *Mazdâo*, was the chief name, the other *ahura* the adjectival epithet. But in consequence of their being jointly employed to express the name of the Supreme Being, they were then afterwards made a compound, as we may distinctly see from the cuneiform inscriptions of the Achemenidian Kings, where he is generally called *Auramazda*, only the latter part of the word being subject to inflection, while both words only in a few instances are inflected. In the Sassanian times the name was changed to *Ahurmazd*, and in modern Persian to *Hormazd* or *Ormazd*, which form is used by the Parsees now-a-days. In the Gâthas we find both words frequently separated, and promiscuously employed to express the name "god;" but no difference of meaning is attached to either. In translating then *Ahura* may best be rendered by "living" and *mazdâo* by "wise" or "Creator of universe."

Zarathustra Spitama's conception of Ahuramazda as the Supreme Being is perfectly identical with the notion of *Elohîm* (god) or *Jehovah*, which we find in the books of the Old Testament, Ahuramazda is called by him "the Creator of the earthly and spiritual life, the Lord of the whole universe at whose hands are all the Creatures." He is the light and the source of light; he is the wisdom and intellect. He is in possession of all good things, spiritual and worldly, such as the good mind (*Vohu manô*), immortality (*ameretât*), wholesomeness (*haurvatât*), the best truth (*asha vahista*), devotion and piety (*Armaiti*) and abundance of every earthly good* (*Khshathra vairya*). All these gifts he grants to the righteous pious man, who is pure in thoughts, words, and deeds. But he, as the ruler of the whole universe, does not only reward the good, but he is a punisher of the wicked at the same time (see Yas. 43,5). All that is created, good or evil, fortune or misfortune, is his work (Yas. 48,4. pag. 159.51,6 pag. 160). A separate evil spirit of equal power with Ahuramazda, and always opposed to him is entirely strange to Zarathustra's theology, though the existence of such an opinion among the ancient Zoroastrians can be gathered from some later books, such as the Vendidad.

* See chiefly Yas. 47,1. (pag. 159).

33

## (b) ZARATHUSTRA'S TWO PRIMEVAL PRINCIPLES.

The opinion, so generelly believed now, that Zarathustra was preaching Dualism, that is to say, the supposition of two original independent spirits, a good and a bad one, utterly distinct from each other, and one counteracting the creation of the other, is owing to a confusion of his philosophy with his theology. Having arrived at the grand idea of the unity, and indivisibility of the Supreme Being, he undertook to solve the great problem, on which so many a wise man of antiquity and even of modern times was engaged, viz. how are the imperfections discoverable in the world, the various kinds of evils, wickedness and baseness, compatible with the goodness, holiness and justice of God? The great thinker of so remote an antiquity solved the difficult question *philosophically* by the supposition of two primeval causes, which, though different, were united, and produced the world of the material things, as well as that of the spirit, which doctrine may best be learnt from Yas. 30 (see pag. 141-43).

The one, who produced the reality (*gaya*), is called *vohu manô* i. e. good mind, the other, through whom the non-reality (*ajyâiti*) originated, bears the name *akem manô* i. e. naught mind. All good, true, and perfect things, which fall under the category of " reality," are the productions of the " good mind," while all that is bad and delusive, belonging to the sphere of " non-reality," is traced to the " naught mind." They are the two moving causes in the universe, united from beginning, and, therefore, called " twins" (*yêma-yama*, twin, in Sanscrit). They are spread everywhere, in Ahuramazda, as well as in men.

These two primeval principles, if supposed to be united in Ahuramazda himself, are not called *vohu-manô* and *akem manô*, but *çpentô mainyus* i. e. white or holy spirit, and *angrô mainyus*, i. e. dark spirit. That Angrô mainyus is no separate being opposed to Ahuramazda, is unmistakeably to be gathered from Yas. 19,9. (see pag. 170), where Ahuramazda is mentioning his " two spirits," who are inherent to his own nature, and in other passages (Yas. 57. see pag. 170) distinctly called the " two Creators" " the two masters" (*pâyû*). And, indeed, we never find mentioned in the Gâthas, Angrô mainyus as a constant opponent to Ahuramazda, as is the case in later writings. The evil, against which Ahuramazda and all good men are fighting, is called: *drukhs*, i. e. "destruction" and "lie," which is nothing but a personification of the *devas*. The same expression for "the evil," spread in the world, we find in the Persian cuneiform inscriptions, where, moreover, Angromainyus as the opponent of Ahuramazda is never mentioned. God (Ahuramazda) is in the rock records of King Darius only one, as Jehovah in the Old Testament, having no adversary whomsoever.

Spentomainyus was regarded as the author of all that is bright and shining, of all that is good and useful in nature, while Angromainyus called into existence all that is dark, and apparently noxious. Both are as inseparable, as day and night, and though opposed to each other, are indispensable for the preservation of creation. The bright spirit appears in the blazing flame, the presence of the dark is marked by the wood converted into charcoal. Spentomainyus has created the light of the day, and Angromainyus the darkness of the night, the former awakens men to their duties, the latter lulls them into sleep. Life is produced by Spentomainyus, but extinguished by Angromainyus, whose hands, by releasing the soul from the fetters of the body, enables her to go up to immortality and everlasting life.

## (c) DEVELOPMENT OF ZARATHUSTRA'S DOCTRINES OF THE SUPREME BEING. THE TWO SUPREME COUNCILS. SEROSH. THE TIME WITHOUT BOUNDS.

Such is the original Zoroastrian notion of the two creative spirits, who form only two sides of the Divine Being. But in the course of time, this doctrine of the great founder was, in consequence of misunderstandings, and false interpretations, changed and corrupted. Spentomainyus was taken as a name of Ahuramazda himself; then, of course Angromainyus, by becoming entirely separated from Ahuramazda, was regarded as the constant adversary of Ahuramazda, and thus the Dualism,

God and Devil, was called forth. Either was an independent ruler, one endeavouring to destroy the creation of the other, and thus both waging constantly war. This Dualism is best to be perceived from the first chapter of the Vendidad. After the sovereignty and independence of both supreme rulers was once acknowledged by some of the most influential leaders of the congregation, founded by Zarathustra Spitama, either was then supposed to have, like terrestrial rulers, his own council and court. The number of councillors was fixed at six, who were regarded as the actual governors of the whole universe, each ruling over a separate province, assigned to him by the respective head. To Ahuramazda or Spentomainyus no other power was left but to preside over the celestial council. We find him even often included in the number of the celestial councillors, who are then called "the seven Amesha spentas" (now corrupted to Amshashpand) i. e. immortal saints.

The several names, by which we find called the Amesha spentas : Vohu manô, Asha vahista, Khshathra vairya, Spenta Armaiti, Haurvatât and Ameretât, are frequently mentioned in the Gâthas, but they are, as the reader may clearly see, from the passages (Yas. 47,1.) as well as from etymology, nothing but abstract nouns and ideas, representing all the gifts which Ahuramazda, as the only Lord, grants to those who worship him with a sincere heart, by speaking always truth, and performing good actions. In the eyes of the prophet they were no personages, which opinion was interpreted into the sayings of the great master by some of his successors.

Vohu-mano (Bahman) is regarded as the vital faculty in all living beings of the good creation. Originally he is nothing but the term for the good principle, as emanating from Ahuramazda, who is, therefore, called the father of Vohu-manô, and penetrating the whole living good creation. All good thoughts, words and deeds of men are wrought by him.

Asha vahista (Ardibehesht) represents the blazing flame of fire, the light in luminaries, and brightness and splendour of any kind whatever, wherever it may be spread. The first part of the name *asha* (plur. of *ashem*) has various meanings, such as "truth, growth, purity," and its epithet *vahista* means originally 'most splendid, beautiful,' but was afterwards used in the more general sense of "best." Light being the nature of Ahuramazda, and this fluid being believed to penetrate the whole good creation, Asha Vahishta represents the omnipresence of the Divine Being. Light keeping up the vitality of the whole creation, animated and inanimated, and being the cause of all growth, Asha vahista is the preserver of all life, and all that is good. He represents, in this respect, God's Providence.

KSHATHRA VAIRYA (Shahravar) presides over metals and is the giver of wealth. His name means simply : possession, wealth, afterwards it was applied to metal, and money. Wealth is considered as a gift from Ahuramazda.

SPENTA ARMAITI (Isfandarmat) i. e. the white or holy Armaiti, represents the earth. The original meaning, as we have seen above (see pag. 231.32.), however, is : devotion, obedience. She represents the pious and obedient heart of the true Ahuramazda worshipper, who serves only God with his body and soul. If the name is applied to the earth, it means that she is the servant of men who, if well treated (i. e. cultivated) yields abundance in food.

HAURVATAT and AMERETAT (Khordâd and Amerdât) preside over vegetation, and produce all kinds of fruits ; but this is very likely not the original meaning. As the names indicate (*Haurvatât* means wholesomeness, integrity, and *Ameretât* immortality), they represent the preservation of the original uncorrupted state of the good creation, its remaining in the same condition, in which it was created by God. Both are generally mentioned together, and express therefore one idea only.

Quite separate from the celestial council stands SRAOSHA (Serosh), who is, however, regarded as an archangel vested with very high powers. While the Amesha Spentas in Zarathustra's eyes represent nothing but the qualities and gifts of Ahuramazda, Sraosha seems to have been considered by him as a personality.

He is the angel who stands between God and man, the great teacher of the good religion who instructed the prophet in it. He shows the way to heaven and pronounces judgment of the human actions after death (for further information see the Serosh Yasht pag. 170-172.). Originally his name means "hearing" (from the root *çru* to hear), which, taken in a religious sense, is the sacred tradition. In this respect we may best compare the word with the Sanscrit *Shruti*, by which name the Brahmans understand the sacred tradition, as laid down in the various parts of the Vedas, chiefly that one, which treats of sacrificial rites. With this meaning of his name, all that is said of him in the Serosh Yasht, wholly agrees. We must, therefore, regard him only as the personification of the whole divine service, including the prayers as well as the sacrificial rites. If he is said to be the guardian of the whole creation, and that without his protection the world would fall a prey to the devils, then these expressions mean, that men must offer up prayers to God and worship him; should they fail doing so, the good mind (Vohu-manô) in them becomes powerless, and the bad mind (akô-manô) takes entire possession of them, instigating them to commit sins and crimes, in consequence of which they will become utterly distressed in this life and in that to come. He fights mainly against the Devas. This means, that the Zoroastrian divine service is destined to counterbalance the mischief, which the Indian Devas were supposed to be doing against the good creation.

Likewise as Ahuramazda, his adversary Angrômainyus was in later times surrounded also by a council. This idea is completely strange to older pieces, and evidently only a counterfeit of the celestial council. The number of the councillors of the infernal kingdom was likewise fixed at six (not in the Zend texts, but in the Bundehesh only) who were called pre-eminently *Devas* and headed by Angromainyus, who, for this reason, was called *Devañam Devô* i. e. arch devil. The first in rank after Angromainyus is AKO MANO, which means: naught mind, and is nothing but Zarathustra's philosophical term of the second principle, the "non-reality." He produces all bad thoughts in men, makes them utter bad words and commit sins. His influence is checked by Vohumanô, the good mind. The second seat in the infernal council is occupied by the King of the Vedic gods, INDRA; the third place is assigned to SHAURVA, the Shiva of the Hindus. Fourth in rank is NAONHAITYA, the collective name of the Indian Ashvins (Dioscuri); the fifth and sixth places are occupied by two personifications: DARKNESS and POISON (see Bundehesh, edited by Westergword, page 5).

There are a good many other names of Devas to be found in the Zend Avesta; but almost all are nothing but personifications of vices and evils. Thus for instance, *aêshema* means "rapine, attack," *driwis* is poverty, *daivis* deceit, etc. While the celestial council is always taking measures for promoting life, and spreading truth, the infernal councillors are constantly plotting designs for the distruction of life and endeavouring to spread lie and falsehood every where. The Zoroastrian idea of the Devil and the infernal Kingdom coincides entirely with the Christian. The Devil is a murderer and father of lies according to both the Bible and the Zend Avesta.

In consequence of this entire separation of the two sides of Ahuramazda and the substitution of two independent rulers, governing the universe, the unity and oneness of the Supreme Being was lost, Monotheism was superseded by Dualism. But this deviation from, and entire change of, the prophet's doctrine could not satisfy the minds of all the divines and philosophers in ancient Persia. It very likely was only the innovation of an influential party or sect, probably that one which is called *Zendik*, i. e. followers of the interpretation (Zend), and which was opposed by that of the *Magi* (see pag. 11). That Dualism was actually the doctrine of the Zendiks, we best learn from the commencement of the Bundehesh, which book purports to expound the lore of this party. The Magi seem still to have clung to the prophet's doctrine of the oneness of the Supreme Being. But to refute the heretical opinions of the Zendiks, which were founded on interpretations of passages from the sacred texts, a new and fresh proof of the Unity of the Supreme

Being was required. This was found in the term "*Zarvan-akarana*" i. e. time without bounds, which we meet occasionally in the Zend Avesta. The chief passage, no doubt, was Vend. 19,9. (see pag. 20-21 and 215); but the interpretation for proving that *Zarvan akarana* means the Supreme Being, out of whom Ahuramazda and Angromainyus are said to have sprung up, rests on a grammatical misunderstanding, as we have seen above (pag. 21). This interpretation, however, must be very old; for all the present Desturs believe in it as an incontrovertible fact.

That this doctrine of Zaruan akarana, was commonly believed in Persia during the times of the Sassanids, one may distinctly see from the reports, quoted above (pag. 10-11). The true meaning of the expression, that "Ahuramazda created in the boundless time," is, that God (Ahuramazda) is from eternity, self-existing, neither born nor created. Only an eternal being can be independent of the bounds of time to which all mortals are subject.

## (*d*) THE TWO INTELLECTS; TWO LIVES; HEAVEN AND HELL. RESURRECTION, PALINGENESIS.

In the Gâthas we frequently find "two intellects" (*khratu*), and "two lives" (*ahu*) spoken of. These notions, therefore, formed undoubtedly part of Zarathustra Spitama's speculation. The two intellects are distinguished as the "first," and "last." From the passages, where they are mentioned (Yas. 44,19. 48,4.), their meaning is not with certainty to be ascertained. But happily we find them mentioned in later Zend writings (see Yt. 2,1.) by more expressive names; one is called *âçnô khratu*, i. e. the original intellect or wisdom, which we best identify with the "first" in the Gâthas; the other is styled, *gaoshô-çrûtô khratu*, i. e. the wisdom, perceived by the ear, which corresponds to the "last." Another name of the "first" is: *mainyu khratu (mînô khirad)* i. e. spiritual, heavenly wisdom. Now we cannot be mistaken as to the meaning of these two intellects. The "first intellect" is not from this earth, but from heaven, not human, but divine. The "last intellect" represents what man has heard, and learnt by experience. The wisdom gained in this way, is of course inferior to the heavenly. Only the latter can instruct man (as we see from a later book, called "Mîno-khirad, which is written in Parsee or Pazend) in the higher matters of life.

The "two lives" are distinguished as a bodily, called *açtvat* or *parâhu* (prior life), and as a mental, called *manahya* or *daibitya* "(the second)" (see Yas. 28,3.43,3.). Their meaning is clear enough, and requires no further comment; they express our idea "body and soul." To be distinguished from these "two lives," are the "first" and the "last lives," which means this life, and that hereafter.

The idea of a future life, and immortality of the soul is expressed very distinctly already in the Gâthas, and pervades the whole later Zend literature. The belief in a life to come, is one of the chief dogmas of the Zend Avesta. See the passages about the fate of the soul after death translated in the 3rd Essay pag. 197,216.

Closely connected with this idea, is the belief in HEAVEN and HELL which already Zarathustra Spitama himself clearly pronounced in his Gâthas. The name for Heaven is *Garô-demâna* (*Gorotman* in Persian) i. e. house of hymns, because the angels are believed to sing there hymns (Yas. 28,10.34,2.), which description agrees entirely with the Christian idea as founded on the prophet Isaiah (ch. 6), and the Revelation of St. John. Garô demâna is the residence of Ahuramazda, and the most blessed men (Yas. 51,15). Another more general name for Heaven, is *ahu vahista*, i. e. the best life, afterwards shortened to *vahista* only, which is still extant in the modern Persian "*Behesht*" i. e. Paradise.

Hell is called *Drûjô demâna*, i. e. house of destruction, in the Gâthas. It is chiefly the residence of the poets and priests of the Deva religion, i. e. the Rishis of the Brahmans (Yas. 46,11.). The later name is *Duzhaka*, which is preserved in the modern Persian *Duzak* (Hell).

34

Between Heaven and Hell is CHINVAT PERETU (*Chinvat púl*) i. e the bridge of the gatherer, or the bridge of the judge (*Chinvat* can have both meanings), which the soul of the pious alone can pass, while the wicked fall from it down to Hell. It is mentioned as we have seen, already in the Gâthas (Yas. 46,10.11.).

The belief in the RESURRECTION of the body at the time of the last judgment forms also one of the Zoroastrian dogmas as the reader will have learnt from passages, communicated above (pag. 196). In consequence of Burnouf's inquiries into the phrase *yavaécha yavatâtaécha*, which had been translated by Anquetil "till resurrection," but which means nothing but "for ever," the existence of such a doctrine in the Zend Avesta was lately doubted. But that there is not the slightest reason for doubting it, every one may convince himself from the passage communicated above (pag. 196), where it is clearly stated, that the dead shall rise again. That the resurrection of the dead body was a common belief of the Magi, long before the commencement of our era, one may learn from the statement of Theopompos (see pag. 6). Now the question arises, has already Zarathustra Spitama pronounced this doctrine, which is one of the chief dogmas of Christianity (and the Jewish and Mahommedan religions), or is it of later, perhaps foreign origin ?

Though in the Gâthas there is no particular statement made of the resurrection of the dead, yet we find a phrase used which was after wards always applied to signify the time of resurrection and the restitution of all life that was during the duration of creation lost. This is the expression *frashem kerenaon ahûm* (Yas. 30,9.* see above143.) "they make the life lasting," i. e. they perpetuate the life. Out of this phrase the substantive *frashô-kereti*, i. e. perpetuation of life, was formed, by which, in all the later Zend books, the whole period of resurrection and palingenesis at the end of time is to be understood. The resurrection forms only a part of it. That this event was really included in the term of *frashô-kereti*, one may distinctly infer from Vend. 18,51., where Spenta Armaiti (earth) is invoked to restore "at the happy time

* A full explanation of it is to be found in my work on the Gâthas vol. I, pag. 109-112.

of perpetuation of life, the seeds lost and make of them a pious Zoroastrian who knows the Gâthas, the Yasna, and the divine conversations."

According to these statements, there can be no doubt, that this important doctrine is a genuine Zoroastrian dogma, which developed itself naturally from Zarathustra Spitama's sayings. There is not the slightest trace of its being borrowed from a foreign source.

Besides these direct proofs we have of its forming a genuine and original part of Zoroastrian theology, it agrees wholly with the spirit and tendency of the Parsee religion. All life of the good creation, chiefly that of man, the bodily as well as the spiritual, is a sacred pawn entrusted by God to man who must keep clean the body from impurity, and the soul from sin. If death destroys the body, (in its natural course),* it is not the fault of man who falls to an inexorable fate; but it is considered as the duty of God, who is the perserver of all life, to restore all life that has fallen to the prey of death, to destroy this arch fiend of human life and make the life then everlasting. This is to be done at the time of the grand act of resurrection.

A detailed description of the resurrection and the last judgment is contained in the 31st chapter of the Bundehesh (see pag. 70-77 Westerg.), which is, no doubt, founded on original Zend sources which are now lost. In it there is an old song embodied, the purport of which is to show, that, though it appears to the short-sighted mortals impossible, how the body, if once dissolved into its elements, and its parts being scattered everywhere, could be restored again, yet nothing is impossible for the hand of the Almighty, who created heaven and earth, endows the trees with sap, gives life to the embryoes in the womb, etc.

For awakening the dead bodies, restoring all life destroyed by death, and holding the last judgment, the great prophet *Sosiosh*

* Suicide is according to the Zoroastrian religion one of the most horrible crimes, belonging to the class of the *Margerzans* or "deadly sins." To the same class belongs "adultery." The committal of such sins leads straight down to Hell whence no Izeshne can release the soul.

(*Soskyans* in Zend) will appear by the order of Ahuramazda. This idea is already to be found in the Zend texts, only with the difference, that sometimes several (pag. 196.),sometimes only one Sosiosh is mentioned (see pag. 215.). The later Parsee legend distinguishes three great prophets who will appear before the end of the world. These are the " men who perpetuate the life" (who make *frashô-kereti)*, men of the same stamp as the ancient prophets and fire priests, and bearing the same name, viz. Soshyantô. They will be commissioned to check the influence of the devil, which increases at the time when this world is verging towards its end, by restoring truth and faith and the good Zoroastrian religion. Their names are poetical and imply a simile: the dark period of wretchedness and sin, in which they appear, being compared to the night; and the era of eternal bliss they are endeavouring to bring about, to the bright day. The first is called *Hukhshathra Mâo* (Oshadarmâ) i. e. the moon of happy rule, the second is *Hukhshathra Bâmya* (Oshadar bâmî) i. e. aurora of happy rule, and the third and greatest is then called *Soskyans* (Sosiosh). He is believed to be a son of Zarathustra Spitama, begotten in a supernatural way. This means, that likewise as Zarathustra Spitama was the greatest prophet and priest in ancient times, Sosiosh will be the greatest of those to come. Therefore he alone brings with him a new Nosk of the Zend Avesta which was unknown hitherto, to reveal it to mankind.

---

# ZEND ALPHABET.

## VOWELS.

*a*, *â*, *ã*; *i*, *î*; *u*, *û*; *e*, *ē*, *ê*; *o*, *ô*; *ai*, *âi*; *au*, *ao*; *âu*, *âo*; *eu*; *ôi*, *aê*.

## CONSONANTS.

a, Gutturals : *k*, *kh*, *q*; *g*, *gh*; *h*.

b, Palatals : *ch*; *j*.

c, Dentals : *t*, (at the end of words) *t*, *th*; *d*, *dh*.

d, Labials : *p*, *f*, *b*.

e, Semivowels : *y*, *r*, *v*, *w*.

f, Sibilants : *ç*, (ss), *sh*, *s*; *z*, *zh*.

g, Nasals : *m*, *n*, *ṅ*, *ṇ*, *ñ*.

## SPECIMEN OF READING.

(The *Yathâ Ahû vairyô* prayer)

To be read from right to left.

*t î ch t â sh a s u t a r â th a ô y r i a v û h a â th a y*

*â ch a h*

*m ã n a thn oa y k s ô h ṇa n a m â zd a d s u ē h ṇ a v*

*i â d z a m s u ē h ṇ a*

*ô y bu g e r d m i y â i â r u h a â ch m e r th a sh kh*

*.m e r â t ç â v t â d a d*

## SUBSCRIPTION LIST.

| Names of Subscribers. | Number of Copies. |
|---|---|
| His Excellency the Earl Canning | 5 |
| His Excellency Sir George Russell Clerk, K.C.B. | 2 |
| His Excellency Sir Hugh Rose, G. C.B. | 1 |
| The Hon'ble Sir H. B. E. Frere, K.C.B. | 1 |
| The Hon'ble C. J. Erskine, C. S. | 1 |
| His Excellency Sir Wm. Mansfield, K.C.B. | 2 |
| Colonel Marriott | 1 |
| G. Inverarity, Esq., C. S. | 1 |
| Sir Jamsetjee Jejeebhoy, Bart. | 30 |
| Rustomjee Jamsetjee Jejeebhoy, Esq. | 25 |
| The Director of Public Instruction, Bombay | 50 |
| Sir Alex. Grant, Bart. | 10 |
| E. I. Howard, Esq., M. A. | 20 |
| T. C. Hope, Esq., C.S. | 1 |
| The Hon. W. B. Tristram | 1 |
| Ardaseer Framjee, Esq. | 1 |
| Alexander Garden Fraser, Esq. | 3 |
| Byramjee Nasserwanjee, Esq. | 10 |
| Byramjee Jejeebhoy and Nanabhoy Byramjee, Esqs. | 10 |
| Cowasjee Jehangeerjee, Esq. | 20 |
| Cursetjee Nasserwanjee Cama, Esq. | 20 |
| Cursetjee Rustomjee Cama, Esq. | 10 |
| Nowrojee Furdoonjee, Esq. | 1 |
| S. Shapoorjee, Esq. | 2 |
| Sorabjee Framjee, Esq. | 2 |
| Merwanjee Framjee, Esq, | 2 |
| Nowrojee Rustomjee Motabhoy, Esq. | 5 |
| Bomanjee Hormuzjee, Esq. | 5 |
| H. Framjee, Esq. | 3 |
| Shapoorjee Dorabjee, Suclatwalla, Esq. | 1 |
| Framjee Sorabjee Bhroocha, Esq. | 2 |
| Nowrojee Byramjee Suntok, Esq. | 1 |
| For the Mechanics' Institution | 1 |
| Nasserwanjee Manockjee Pitty, Esq. | 5 |
| Dossabhoy Framjee Karaka, Esq. | 1 |
| Pestonjee Framjee Camajee, Esq. | 5 |
| Bomanjee Framjee Camajee, Esq. | 5 |
| Dhunjeebhoy Cursetjee Shroff, Esq. | 1 |
| Merwanjee Framjee Panday, Esq. | 2 |
| Cursetjee Furdoonjee, Esq. | 7 |
| Bomanjee Jejeebhoy, Esq. | 2 |
| Limjee Manockjee, Esq. | |
| K. R. Kolah, Esq. | 1 |
| Walter R. Cassels, Esq. | 1 |
| Professor Candy | 1 |
| A. D. Robertson, Esq., C. S. | 1 |
| Framjee Banajee | 1 |
| Nanabhoy Framjee Banajee | 1 |

†

| Names of Subscribers. | Number of Copies. |
|---|---|
| Dinsha Maneckjee, Esq. ... ... ... ... ... ... | 5 |
| Pestonjee Hormusjee Camajee, Esq. ... ... ... ... ... | 5 |
| Dossabhoy Hormusjee Camajee, Esq. ... ... ... ... | 5 |
| Heerjeebhoy Merwanjee Wadia, Esq. ... ... ... ... | 1 |
| N. Cursetjee Dady, Esq. ... ... ... ... .. ... | 3 |
| Jehangir Nowrojee Wadia. Esq. ... ... ... ... ... | 1 |
| Jamsetjee Dhunjeebhoy Wadia, Esq. ... ... ... ... | 1 |
| Sorabjee Nowrojee, Wadia, Esq. ... ... ... ... ... | 1 |
| Dhunjeebhoy Framjee, Esq. ... .. ... ... ... ... | 1 |
| Merwanjee Nusserwanjee, Esq. .. ... ... ... ... | 1 |
| A. Cursetjee Dady, Esq. ... ... ... ... ... ... | 1 |
| Nowrojee Dorabjee, Esq. ... ... ... ... ... ... | 1 |
| Rustumjee Bomanjee, Esq. ... ... ... ... ... ... | 1 |
| Dinshaw Nowrojee, Esq. ... ... ... ... ... ... | 1 |
| Eduljee Framjee Curranee, Esq. ... ... ... ... ... | 1 |
| Pestonjee Hormusjee and Sons ... ... ... ... ... | 1 |
| Muncherjee Pestonjee Wadia, Esq. ... ... ... ... ... | 1 |
| Pallunjee Hormusjee Capurdia, Esq. ... ... ... ... | 2 |
| Merwanjee Nasserwanjee, Esq. ... ... ... ... ... | 1 |
| Nusserwanjee Ruttonjee. Tatta, Esq. ... ... ... ... | 1 |
| Bhikajee Ardaseer Chinoy, Esq. ... ... ... ... ... | 1 |
| Sorabjee Vachaghandhi's Sons ... ... ... ... ... | 1 |
| Heerjeebhoy Hormusjee Sett, Esq. ... ... ... ... ... | 1 |
| Hormusjee Eduljee Madon, Esq. ... ... ... ... ... | 1 |
| Hormusjee Pestonjee Battlewalla, Esq. ... ... ... ... | 2 |
| Jamsetjee Hormusjee, Esq. ... ... ... ... ... ... | 1 |
| Muncherjee Bomanjee Punthkey ... ... ... ... ... | 5 |
| Dossabhoy Merwanjee. Esq. ... ... ... ... ... ... | 1 |
| Framjee Cowasjee Mehta, Esq. ... ... ... ... ... | 1 |
| Hormusjee Cursetjee Cowasjee, Esq.... ... ... ... ... | 1 |
| Dinshaw Dadabhoy Ghandy, Esq. ... ... ... ... ... | 1 |
| Manockjee Bomanjee, Esq. ... ... ... ... ... ... | 1 |
| Manockjee Shapoorjee, Esq. ... ... ... ... ... ... | 1 |
| Dosabhoy Cursetjee Wadia, Esq. ... ... ... ... ... | 1 |
| C. Cowasjee Maneckjee, Esq. ... ... ... ... ... ... | 5 |
| Dadabhoy Pestonjee Patel, Esq. ... ... ... ... ... | 1 |
| Ruttonjee Eduljee, Esq. ... ... ... ... ... ... | 2 |
| Dadabhoy Cowasjee, Esq. ... ... ... ... ... ... | 1 |
| Ruttonjee Bomanjee Doobash, Esq. ... ... ... ... ... | 1 |
| Framjee Hormusjee, Esq. ... ... ... ... ... ... | 1 |
| Hormusjee Byramjee Moos, Esq. ... ... ... ... ... | 1 |
| Cowasjee Framjee's Sons ... ... ... ... ... ... | 1 |
| Sorabjee Jamsetjee Jejeebhoy, Esq. ... ... ... ... ... | 21 |
| Eduljee Cowasjee Bisnee, Esq. ... ... ... ... ... | 1 |
| Karsondass Madhuvudass, Esq. ... ... ... ... ... | 1 |
| Cowasjee Eduljee Kanga, Esq. ... ... ... ... ... | 1 |
| Jamsetjee Rustomjee Erany, Esq. ... ... ... ... ... | 5 |
| Sorabjee Dhunjeebhoy Setna, Esq. ... ... ... ... ... | 1 |
| Dossabhoy Dhunjeebhoy Soorty, Esq. ... ... ... ... | 1 |
| Eduljee Rustomjee, Esq. ... ... ... ... ... ... | 1 |
| Jeewajee Ruttonjee's Sons ... ... ... ... ... ... | 1 |
| M. R. Westropp, Esq... ... ... ... ... ... ... | 2 |
| Muncherjee Pestonjee, Esq. ... ... ... ... ... ... | 1 |

| Names of Subscribers. | Number of Copies. |
|---|---|
| Ruttonjee Bomonjee, Esq. ... ... ... ... ... ... | 1 |
| Dhunjeebhoy Sorabjee Malegamwalla, Esq. ... ... ... ... | 1 |
| J. S. White, Esq. ... ... ... ... ... ... ... | 1 |
| Pestonjee Jeewanjee, Esq. ... ... ... ... ... ... | 1 |
| J. P. Hughlings, Esq. ... ... ... ... ... ... | 1 |
| R. W. Lodwick, Esq., C.S. ... ... ... ... ... ... | 1 |
| T. C. Anstey, Esq, ... ... ... ... ... ... ... | 1 |
| W. Wordsworth, Esq. ... ... ... ... ... ... ... | 2 |
| The Rev Dr. John Wilson. ... ... ... ... ... ... | 3 |
| Dr. R. S. Sinclair ... ... ... ... ... ... ... | 2 |
| Lieut. R. C. Lockett ... ... ... ... ... ... ... | 1 |
| Nusserwanjee Chandabhoy, Esq., Assistant Engineer ... ... | 1 |
| Muncherjee Rustomjee Heeramanicknah, Esq. ... ... ... | 1 |
| **POONA.** | |
| Bishop of Bombay. ... ... ... ... ... ... ... | 2 |
| Dustoor N. Jamaspjee, High Priest of the Parsees ... ... | 3 |
| Major Candy ... ... ... ... ... ... ... ... | 1 |
| Dorabjee Pestonjee Heerabagh, Esq ... ... ... ... ... | 15 |
| Dorabjee Eduljee Colabawala, Esq. ... ... ... ... ... | 1 |
| Hormusjee Muncherjee Sopareewalla ... ... ... ... | 1 |
| Dorabjee Pestonjee, Esq., Government Contractor ... ... ... | 3 |
| Dinshaw Ruttonjee, Esq. ... ... ... ... ... ... | 1 |
| Pestonjee Bomanjee, Esq. ... ... ... ... ... ... | 1 |
| Byramjee Manockjee, Esq. ... ... ... ... ... ... | 1 |
| Sorabjee Pirozsha, Esq. ... ... ... ... ... ... | 1 |
| Hormusjee Jewajee, Esq. ... ... ... ... ... ... | 1 |
| W. A. Russell, Esq., Principal of the Poona College ... ... | 2 |
| **SATTARA.** | |
| Dadabhoy Bezonjee, Esq. ... ... ... ... ... ... | 1 |
| **HYDERABAD.** | |
| Nawab Mookhtar-ool-moolk, Bahadoor (Salar Jung) ... ... | 10 |
| Dorabjee Dossabhoy, Esq. ... ... ... ... ... ... | 1 |
| Jevanjee Ruttonjee, Esq. ... ... ... ... ... ... | 1 |
| Jamsetjee Cursetjee, Esq. ... ... ... ... ... ... | 3 |
| Bapoojee Vincajee, Esq. ... ... ... ... ... ... | 1 |
| **MHOW.** | |
| Hormusjee Nusserwanjee, Esq. ... ... ... ... ... | 1 |
| **INDORE.** | |
| Muncherjee Pestonjee, Esq. ... ... ... ... ... ... ... | 1 |
| Jamaspjee Nowrozjee, Esq. ... ... ... ... ... ... | 1 |
| **JAULNA.** | |
| Dinshawjee Merwanjee, Esq... ... ... ... ... ... | 1 |
| Jamsetjee Manockjee, Esq. ... ... ... ... ... ... | 1 |